£4·50

IN SEARCH OF THE ENGLISH ECCENTRIC

Also by Henry Hemming

Misadventure in the Middle East:
Travels as a Tramp, Artist and Spy

IN SEARCH OF THE ENGLISH ECCENTRIC

HENRY HEMMING

JOHN MURRAY

First published in Great Britain in 2008 by John Murray (Publishers)
An Hachette Livre UK company

1

© Henry Hemming 2008

A CIP catalogue record for this title is available from the British Library

ISBN 978-0-7195-2212-3

Typeset in Bembo by Palimpsest Book Production
Limited, Grangemouth Stirlingshire

Printed and bound by Clays Ltd, St Ives plc

John Murray policy is to use papers that are natural, renewable and
recyclable products and made from wood grown in sustainable forests.
The logging and manufacturing processes are expected to conform to
the environmental regulations of the country of origin.

John Murray (Publishers)
338 Euston Road
London NW1 3BH

www.johnmurray.co.uk

For Mum

CONTENTS

Part Four: The Root of Change

Look at that eccentric wheel in that steam engine, what motion would you get out of it without that wheel's eccentricity – only rest. So in society you would get precious little driving force out of it, but for eccentrics having free and active motion. Let us encourage them, let us utilise them! – (Applause)

Extract from the opening speech by the first president of the Eccentric Club, 1781

I'm tired of eccentrics. There is something so smugly self-congratulatory about English eccentrics: quite possibly the fact they know they're trying to be eccentric. It's like those people from Liverpool who insist on telling you all the time how friendly and funny they are, rather than for instance just being friendly or funny: the I'm-mad-me English eccentric, with his loopy clubs and odd obsessions, is always, in fact, quite startlingly dull.

Euan Ferguson in the Observer, 9 May 2004

ACKNOWLEDGEMENTS

I've been dreading writing this part of the book, only because it would mean that the journey was truly over. The lights are up. Everyone must now go home.

Spending the last year travelling around England and getting to know it more intimately has been fun, and much of this stems from the hospitality of my interviewees. I am grateful to each of them for taking the time to talk to me.

For being given the chance to write this, I am indebted to my agent Jonathan Conway. He is a superb critic and a great negotiator. I don't think it is possible to have a better agent. Many thanks also to Roland Philipps and Rowan Yapp at John Murray for their shrewd editing and faith in the project, and to everyone at John Murray who has been involved in the production of this book, including the brilliant copy-editor Peter James. Rachel Cornwell and David Sim provided valuable advice and research assistance. I'm sad I wasn't able to use more of their findings. Ben Le Vay gave me some useful pointers early on. I am grateful also to various friends and family who have read the manuscript at different stages, including Al Braithwaite, Jack Kirkland, Dad, Bea, and lastly Helena, who was the first to read through most of this, and, as I found out, has an enviable knack of knowing instinctively when a passage is heading off in the wrong direction, or worse, becoming over-indulgent. Throughout the writing of this book she has been a source of support, silliness and inspiration, breathing love and life into the process from start to finish, and for this I am most grateful of all.

PART ONE
SETTING OUT

1

THE WHALE-SHAPED HEDGE

Though I had no idea at the time, it began with Krentoma. Usually the other tribesmen would talk about him with a grin. Or was it a smirk? Certainly whenever Krentoma's name came up a smile would form somewhere in the group and slowly spread, until I was surrounded by men smiling to themselves or at each other. Some would shake their heads. The leader of the tribe, Teseya, a stout man with a stomach that was solid and round like a basketball, had touched his head, rolled his eyes and chuckled silently, as if gagging. I was about to jump up and give him a motherly thump on the back when he stopped, turned to me and repeated the name as if it was a secret, or a curse of some sort.

'Kren-tom-ah,' I said to myself, trying to put the stress on 'tom' the way Teseya did, but not quite managing.

The next day I met him. To look at, he was unremarkable. His complexion was hale and worn, there was a tang of stale fruit on his breath and his eyes were small and dark. Nevertheless he was the spark. This was the man who, without meaning to, inspired my journey deep into the irreverent and inventive fringes of English society: a quest that would end a year after it began on a street in south London as I tried to find the remains of a whale-shaped hedge, yet by then I had already found the person I was looking for. The leader of the tribe. I won't say who it was as that might ruin it; and if you're one of those people that turns to the back of books to see how they end, don't. Please. It's not right at the back anyway. I've tried to hide it.

In the year leading up to that day in Brixton I would meet a cast of characters more outlandish, yet more gripping, than any I could invent: from reincarnated English monarch to gnome-collector and leopard-man via Ikea-loving dominatrix, dissident, crop-circler, hermit, sado-masochistic artist, celebrity aristocrat, Serpentine swimmer and superhero dressed as a baked bean, all the way through to the doyenne of English fashion, Dame Vivienne Westwood, and the jaded rock star known to the English tabloids as 'Potty Pete': Pete Doherty.

That was all ahead of me. For now it'll have to wait.

Once I had sat down, Krentoma asked if I'd like to see his house. Hadn't I seen it already, on the far side of the village? No, said Krentoma, turning to me. His gaze had the suffocating force of a limpet. That was not his house, that was merely where he slept. The house of Krentoma was different. He would not say why and instead looked away, his face full with the satisfaction of a man withholding an answer, heaved himself up and beckoned me to follow with a lazy swoop of his hand. He began to walk towards a wall of Amazonian rainforest. I started after him. The air was thick with an equatorial midday fug as we padded past the remainder of the village, no more than a handful of huts made from wood and straw arranged in a circle. Their doorways, uniform in design, faced away from the forest towards a communal centre, like wagons in the American Midwest parked for the night. I remembered being told the previous day that the exact position of each hut within the circle revealed the clan or social status of its occupants, that even the location or protean shape of the doorway was significant.

Krentoma remained two paces ahead of me. I began to wonder where we were going. The rainforest was unusually quiet for that time of day. Visually, though, it was as noisy as ever: a tapestry of green, vermilion, turquoise, cadmium yellow of different intensities, lime, jade, all dotted with peepholes that allowed glimpses of the scaffolding of trunks and branches that groaned with the weight of the canopy above.

Only a few yards into the rainforest we arrived at a clearing. Krentoma stopped. Before us lay two rectangular sections of concrete that looked like foundations for a house. Strewn about next to them, as if it was wreckage from a hurricane, I could make out a muddle of corrugated iron strips that had browned like rotting fruit in the warmth and damp. Krentoma stood with his hands on his hips and surveyed the scene, his eyes darting back and forth anxiously.

'My house,' he explained, in Portuguese.

I looked at him blankly.

'The beginning,' he said, correcting himself. His gaze returned to the discarded crusts of iron and concrete. 'I don't like these huts of wood and straw.' He waved over his shoulder at the village, screwing up his face. 'Too old, too old. This is the new house where I will live.' He beamed. 'Made from iron. In the forest. The house of Krentoma!'

He picked up a sheet of corrugated iron and waved it around. It rumbled like thunder in a school play. I nodded enthusiastically. He stared back at me and without breaking eye contact lifted the iron above his head and began to drum his fingers on the atrophied metal, making a sound just like rain. His hut would be waterproof, I decided, as I continued to stand with my hands behind my back, not knowing what to do, waiting for him to make the next move.

'It is good, yes?' Krentoma asked, smiling.

At this point I recognised him. Not in the sense of having met Krentoma in a former life, or remembering a friend who looked just like him – he was familiar simply as a type. An eccentric. He was the resident eccentric here in Nansepotiti, a village hidden in the heart of the Amazon rainforest. That was where I'd seen him before. Even the etymology of the word seemed to agree. Originally eccentric was written as 'excentric', meaning 'out of the centre' or 'away from the centre', which made Krentoma's decision to build his house so far apart from the rest of the village uncannily apt.

Krentoma was the villager who chose not to conform to all of the social mores, taboos and accepted truths that he had grown up around. Infuriating one moment, hilarious the next, he was both inventive and stubborn, a loner, a maverick, larger than life and at times Promethean, or at others childlike: an eccentric in every sense of the word.

Fine. He was an eccentric. But – in the words of the druid chieftain I would meet eight years later – so what?

Let me explain. What made him, or at least my understanding of him, different was that over the next two weeks in the village I got the impression that this particular eccentric had a *function* in the group he was a part of; it was as if his tribe, the Panará, actually needed someone like Krentoma in their midst.

Up until then I had thought of eccentrics as curiosities. Follies. Doilies rather than armchairs. Each one an oddity that their neighbours tolerate rather than champion. Yet just as every football team has its oddball goalie, and every court its jester, I began to sense that the Panará would be incomplete without Krentoma or someone like him. If he didn't exist, you'd have to make him up. The problem was, I had no idea why they needed him, nor did I know what it was that actually made someone eccentric. I certainly – perhaps fortunately – had no idea that Krentoma's role as resident eccentric had allowed him, and in some ways required him, to murder a fellow tribesman five years earlier. He had slit the man's throat in the middle of the night.

Instead I left the village and flew back to England toying with the idea that every group of human beings, from the heart of the Amazon to the outskirts of Aylesbury, had a deep-rooted need for a non-conformist, creative character in their midst: someone who teeters on the edge of social exclusion yet manages to remain on this side of the law, just, a figure who makes primordial connections that others in the group don't. A man or woman who does not care what other people think, and who symbolises the less inhibited and more instinctive and childlike approach to life that deep down most of us aspire to.

Just as it was fun to mull this over, I knew that this was exactly the kind of plane-philosophising I'm prone to when drifting in and out of sleep in a pressurised cabin after looking out of the window for too long. There was still very little I knew about eccentrics or eccentricity. I had met Krentoma, that was a start, but it wasn't enough. It seemed best to limit my theories on eccentrics to things I was sure of.

One of the only things I knew about eccentrics with absolute certainty was that England – home – was famous for them.

Eight years passed.

Tuesday 15 August 2006: it was about eight-thirty in the morning and I was slumped in front of a television, eating cereal, dribbling milk into my beard and watching BBC *London News*. One of the first items to appear was a report from Lambeth. Something to do with a hedge.

I focused on the screen and there, framed by the grubby white plastic of my antiquated Philips television, was Zac Monro, a friendly-looking architect in his mid-thirties. The voice-over announced that Mr Monro had once won the World Air Guitar Championships. He was now standing in front of a hedge wearing a ribbed black polo-neck with leather padded elbows that made him look like Captain Birdseye's First Mate.

Zac explained in an agitated, middle-class register that he had recently received a letter from the council complaining about the hedge in front of his terraced house. It wasn't that he had let the hedge run wild. No, the council had written to him because over the last few years he had carefully trimmed his hedge into the shape of a whale. It even had a blowhole with a blast of water shooting skywards that had been rendered with a white-flowering shrub that fanned out at its peak. In their letter the council claimed that Zac's topiary was obstructing the pavement and posed a threat to passing pedestrians. Blind people were being forced into the road, they argued.

Already I could feel some of Zac Monro's anger bubbling up inside me. You could see that this hedge was not forcing people out into the quiet, residential street. Yes, it bulged a little over the pavement, but you would have to be at least a yard wide to collide with it.

'None of the local residents mind the hedge,' Zac insisted, confidently. 'In fact they love it.' He was gathering momentum. 'The hedge gets compliments from passers-by the whole time. I mean some of them think it's a peacock but I've got used to that.' He paused. 'What I still don't understand is why the council even bothered to write to me in the first place. I was utterly astounded when I received the letter.' His eyebrows were knotted together now, begging the viewer to be astounded too. 'I mean have they really got nothing better to do?'

'Exactly!' I wanted to shout, though with no one else in the room there didn't seem much point.

The voice-over kicked in and a woman with a honeyed smoker's growl announced that Mr Monro would have to wait to find out what would become of his hedge. The next item on the news began but I couldn't concentrate. I was burning with a rare sense of indignation about Zac Monro and his whale-shaped hedge.

This man was an English eccentric. I was sure of it. A walking, talking, protesting, air-guitaring, hedge-trimming English eccentric, which, now that I thought about it, was one of the few facets of Englishness I imagined most English people could agree on. Some might even cherish it. The English eccentric was part of the 'England' global brand and deserved to be talked about in the same rarefied terms as cups of tea, bad teeth and the Sex Pistols. Although Zac Monro did not entirely look the part – he dressed conservatively and was perhaps too young to be a cardboard cut-out English eccentric – I was certain, in an instinctive way, that he was a modern-day incarnation of the English eccentric and he was being denied his eccentricity by Lambeth council.

His story seemed to confirm an otherwise vague hunch: the country I lived in was being wiped clean of its anomalies. It was being sanitised, its rough corners and illogical edges filed down, quietly, when nobody was looking, and it was only now, having witnessed via a television screen the plight of Zac Monro, that I realised what this meant: the English eccentric was about to become an endangered species.

Everywhere I looked this hunch appeared to be confirmed. On the radio, on television, in newspapers and magazines, thudding about like spent cannonballs, were expressions like 'the nanny state', 'clone towns', 'cultural globalisation', 'European standardisation', 'risk-averse parenting', 'risk-resistant planning', 'health-and-safety-ocracy', 'it's political correctness (gone mad)', all of which seemed to point to the same conclusion: English society's irregularities were being ironed out, one by one, and with this the eccentric was being fined, imprisoned or assimilated into the muddling median of everything I understood by the word 'normal'.

And yet, throughout the aleatory sprawl of English history there is a pantheon of men and women labelled outspoken, non-conformist or eccentric during their lifetime who have gone on to be seen by later generations as historically monumental pioneers endowed with originality and vision. From a distance, these opinionated misfits represented the crank-handle of English artistic and scientific advance.

The BBC's '100 Greatest Britons', compiled in 2002, is a cornucopia of individuals who have, at some point in their lives, been labelled eccentric or strange on account of their ideas before history devised a more magnanimous epitaph. As well as Sir Isaac Newton, you could say this of Isambard Kingdom Brunel, William Blake, Charles Darwin, Winston Churchill, Barnes Wallis, Alan Turing, Charles Babbage, David Bowie, John Peel, Queen Victoria, Lewis Carroll. And that's just from the top fifty.

There are also those like Henry Cavendish who have not become household names but whose reputations have undergone a similar eccentric-to-pioneer metamorphosis following their death. Cavendish loathed conversation and all forms of human company, spending the last thirty years of his life in isolation. He spoke only when strictly necessary, and was known as an eccentric recluse. He was also the first person to identify the elemental make-up of water and discover two key principles of electricity – Coulomb's Law and Ohm's Law – long before Charles Coulomb and Georg Ohm hit on them; he is now considered a brilliant scientist.

It was at this point that Krentoma crept back into my life, uninvited, as it turned out. Since leaving Krentoma's village deep in the Amazon, I had clung on to the idea that every tribe or group of human beings in some way needs a resident eccentric both to ground its other members and to inspire them. It seemed that human societies functioned better with an eccentric in their midst, just as the Panará appeared to operate more smoothly with Krentoma muddling about among them. But I had no way of proving this, so the idea had spent most of the previous eight years hidden away as a pet theory, one that was allowed out only on special occasions.

Having seen what was happening to Zac Monro with his hedge, this idea morphed into something more precise. England was being shorn of its eccentrics, yet the English *needed* their eccentrics and functioned much better as a group with them.

Just after eleven o'clock that morning the idea had turned into a plan. I was so excited that I had to go for a walk to calm down before putting it on paper to see if it made any sense. The plan was simple: I would go on a journey to track down England's last remaining eccentrics before they disappeared. I imagined them as a reclusive tribe facing extinction with me as the amateur anthropologist hoping to find them, catalogue them, document them, tag them if necessary, and then share their plight with the rest of the world. Before it was too late.

I felt a burning sense of purpose, as well as the thumping anticipation of a journey into the unknown.

The final part of the plan was that I would try and find the leader of this tribe, England's most eccentric man or woman. If no one else did, surely they would know how to save the tribe from extinction.

In 1859 John Stuart Mill wrote his defence of every human being's right to individual liberty, complete freedom of speech and, with a handful of exceptions, freedom of conduct. He called it *On Liberty*, and it became the founding text of twentieth-century Liberalism, with Mill installed as apostle saint. It also provided one of the earliest and most passionate defences of English eccentricity.

I studied it at school, though instead of reading *On Liberty* from start to finish, I picked at it reluctantly. For five weeks the print-out of this essay sat on my desk making me feel guilty every time I looked at it, like a thickset fruitcake given to me by an elderly relative. I had neither the heart to throw it away, nor the drive to finish it off.

Reading *On Liberty* in full I was struck by Mill's nervousness about the English character and what direction it might take over the coming years. Throughout, there is an undercurrent of looming, self-imposed catastrophe. Mill, the most influential English political writer of the nineteenth century, feared that English society was beginning to worship custom over innovation, and compared Victorian England to ancient China, whose culture stagnated when it became obsessed with custom and appeared to shun eccentricity.

It's easy to forget when reading *On Liberty* quite how much English society and 'Englishness' itself – still a fairly new concept – had changed during the century leading up to its publication. England in 1859 had come a long way from the licentiousness and relative debauchery of the late eighteenth century. That was a time before widespread industrialisation, a more bawdy and carnal era when neither men nor women took regular baths, there were no sewers, and in any major metropolis you could see bulls being baited, cocks being thrown, criminals being executed, or you could slip with unembarrassed ease into a demi-monde of courtesans and harlots more brazen than anything imaginable in the mid-Victorian period.

By 1859 English society had extricated itself from this. Prudish civility appeared to rank above instinct. That is the context of John Stuart Mill writing, as if on a sandwich board suspended from his shoulders: 'In this age, the mere example of nonconformity, the mere refusal to bend the knee to custom, is itself a service. Precisely because the tyranny of opinion is such as to make eccentricity a reproach, it is desirable, in order to break through that tyranny, that people should be eccentric.' Mill went on: 'That so few now dare to be eccentric marks the chief danger of our time.'

Our time. Though written 150 years ago that sentence felt timeless – it could have been written at the beginning of the twenty-first century, perhaps as part of a newspaper editorial or the concluding line to a television documentary. Perhaps the English permanently imagine their eccentrics to be endangered? I needed to find out.

Mill also prized original thought. 'It will not be denied by anybody,' he wrote, 'that originality is a valuable element in human affairs. There is always need of persons not only to discover new truths, and point out when what were once truths are true no longer, but also to commence new practices.'

He went on to admit that there aren't that many people capable of the kind of truly original thinking that changes the way we see the world, and described the few that can as 'the salt of the earth; without them, human life would become a stagnant pool'.

The idea of a 'stagnant pool' was interesting. It also gave me an idea for where to start my journey.

2

THE BOY WHO NEVER
GREW UP

'He dared you to do it?'

'Yep. My mate. Little fuck.'

'Wow. You'd do this for a dare?'

'Mmm-hmm.' He glanced over my shoulder at a line of buoys that marked the edge of the course. Nestled comfortably on each was a seagull that stared back at him.

'Well, good luck with it,' I said.

'What? Oh yeah. Cheers.'

'Not long to go.'

'Too right.'

'And do you think you'll win?'

'Never know. If everyone else has a seizure on hitting the water I might be in with a chance. Otherwise no, I don't think so.'

He tugged down on his shorts to reveal a pair of dark-green Speedos. His legs were iPod white, the flesh pimpled by the cold. As he struggled to pull on his fluorescent condom-like swimming hat I wished him luck once more and stepped away.

Elsewhere in London people were mostly warm and in bed. Some had woken at dawn, the unusual weight at the end of their beds demanding attention and precluding a lie-in; others would probably come to in the next half-hour, bleary-eyed after a night drifting into and out of dreams about bread sauce, mothers-in-law, giant birds and slightly smaller ovens.

I, on the other hand, was just cold.

It was 7.30 a.m. on Christmas Day and I was standing on the banks of the Serpentine in Hyde Park. On the lake in front of me lay an armada of swans, geese and ducks. The sky was leaden. Beyond the water a line of orange streetlights running the length of Park Lane pricked the gloom.

At first I had been pissed off about getting up so early on Christmas Day. It was a sacred day, I had told myself, not so much in the religious sense, but in my cultural understanding of the occasion: getting up in the dark first thing in the morning to stand in the cold seemed both gruelling and unfair, and from the moment I had stepped outside the only thing I could think about was the cold. It had got worse down at the lake, with the crisp morning air accented by a light wind. After ten minutes of writing notes in longhand my fingers lost all feeling in their tips and I began to mumble surreptitiously into a Dictaphone instead, looking and feeling like an amateur sleuth. Not long after, my nose gave up all attempts to stem the flow of snot streaming from it. Nevertheless, after an hour or so, I was starting to enjoy myself.

I was there to witness the annual race for the Peter Pan Cup, bequeathed to the Serpentine Swimming Club in 1904 by J. M. Barrie, the creator of Peter Pan, and himself a renowned eccentric. Each year this cup is awarded to the winner of a hundred-yard thrash through the Serpentine first thing on Christmas Day. From the moment I heard about the race, I knew it was the place to start my search. From what I understood the word to mean, this event reeked of eccentricity.

'And you know we swim *every* Christmas, no matter what the weather's doing,' boasted Jeff, a former traffic warden.

'So have you ever won the race?'

'Oh yeah,' he said, his face registering both modesty and wounded pride. 'Few years back.'

'And today, the temperature, is this normal? I mean how cold is the water?'

'Four degrees, I think.'

He was used to this kind of question and relished it, in a well-mannered way. I think he liked watching the effect of his answer. The problem was, the words 'four degrees' when put together like that don't mean much to me. I often have no idea whether I'm being told an exceptionally cold, exceptionally hot or merely lukewarm temperature. A few minutes earlier I had overheard a similar conversation about the temperature of the water and the answer had been 'forty'. The person asking had looked horrified. Encouraged, the person answering had added that it had been thirty-four several years before. The questioner had looked even more worried. From the way Jeff had said 'four degrees' I guessed this was impressively cold, so I looked aghast.

'No matter how cold it is, we always swim,' he went on, enjoying himself. 'Some years we have to break the ice before we get in.'

We were down at the water's edge so I knelt down and put my hand in the lake. At first I couldn't feel a thing. Then, suddenly, a coruscating chill shot through my body: a steely, teeth-clenching sensation that screamed like a sergeant-major at my hand to get itself out of whatever it was. Now! I jumped back. Jeff chuckled. He shifted his weight from one foot to the other.

'Not warm, is it?' he said.

'No,' I said, nursing my hand. 'Not at all. And tell me, because I'm sure you're asked this a lot, but why? Why do you do this? Why would anyone do this?'

Jeff repositioned himself.

'Well, for me, it's the nature. I've always swum outside. I didn't go to one of them schools with indoor pools or anything. I was at a school where we swam outside, you know, natural, and I think I just got used to that. You can't beat swimming outside, especially with all them fish and birds alongside you.'

'Don't you ever get attacked by the swans?'

'Oh no.' He liked this question. 'The only problem with the swans here,' he came close, his voice grim with conspiracy, 'is that some of them, they like to take part in the race. And they cheat. They'll see us swimming, and they'll start swimming alongside us to the finish line. Only they'll fly the last few yards so they cross the line first.'

At this point we were joined by Alan, who ran the Serpentine Swimming Club. He was tall and in his sixties with features that over the years had been knotted into a giant question mark. Two days earlier I'd emailed him about the possibility of meeting members of his club. I had told him I was planning to write an article about the Peter Pan Cup, which was true – sort of. I hadn't mentioned anything about trying to hunt down England's last remaining eccentrics because I was worried that might put him off. The semantics of my quest were still in flux.

'Journalist he is,' Alan told Jeff, dropping his shoulder in my direction. Jeff smiled.

'So,' I said, pointing my Dictaphone at Alan, 'tell me what kind of people join the club.'

'Oh you get all sorts,' Alan replied. 'We got sirs, lords, doctors, musicians. Got a famous cellist. Er. Conservative MPs. Look there's one over there, I saw him on the television once. Sir Anthony Cleaver he is. On a select committee. Surgeons, bankers. Who else? Jeff. We've got Jeff. That's variety for you.' Jeff spluttered. 'Ex-parking-meter attendant he is,' Alan continued. 'Got a Roller now, haven't you?' Alan grinned at Jeff. 'Yep, a real mixture here.'

What he didn't mention, for me the most interesting thing about the Serpentine Swimming Club, was that most of the swimmers were over fifty. You'd think swimming in icy water first thing in the morning would lend itself to younger, more punishable bodies.

'But the thing about this race,' Alan continued, 'what people really like about it, is it's a leveller. No matter who you are, once you're all in the water, everyone's in trouble. And because of the handicap system—'

'What's that?'

'Means we start the swimmers at different times. The weakest swimmers go first. Best go last. The youngest swimmer here is a thirteen-year-old girl, the oldest is, let me see, eighty-four. But the handicap system means they've both got a chance of winning.'

'More and more women here,' said Jeff, dubiously.

'Right,' said Alan, deadpan. 'Because of the net.' A vision appeared in my mind of an enormous woman-catching net that Jeff and Alan had set up somewhere in Hyde Park. 'Yes,' Alan continued. 'People look us up on the net. So more and more women join, and more people come to the Christmas race. We're a bit like pantomime now, I suppose.'

'Though no woman has ever won the Christmas Day race,' said Jeff, glancing over his shoulder at the crowd, who at that moment looked particularly cheery, in a wholesome Christmassy way.

Plate XVI b

H. Henning

Anon

A Serpentine Swimmer

'I'll see you chaps in a moment,' said Alan, remembering something. A man in a trilby and canary-yellow Hawaiian shorts ambled towards us.

'I forgot to tell you, Henry,' Alan shouted, nodding at the man in the trilby, 'we get some real eccentrics here!'

These were the words I'd been longing for. They sounded even better than I had imagined. Inside I was whooping and cheering and setting off fireworks because I hadn't mentioned to Alan my eccentric-seeking agenda.

The man in the trilby was called Duff. He was, at a guess, two or three years this side of forty and, less of a guess, spent a lot of time in the gym. Duff had a bionically powerful upper body that gave off a diluted hum of aftershave. His greying fair hair had been trimmed into a crewcut.

'So why do you do it?' I asked. Duff's face opened into a well-managed smile.

'The history,' he said in an anglicised American accent. 'I grew up with *Peter Pan* being read to me. You know, the original, Kensington Gardens J. M. Barrie book. It's all set round here. Peter Pan sailed on the thrushes over here, to that island and so on.' He pointed towards the bridge bisecting the lake. 'That and the fact that as a child I wasn't allowed to open my presents on Christmas morning until we'd all watched my dad swim in the race. And you know, you always want to do what your dad does.' His mind zoomed out. 'I mean, there are people who see us doing this each year, who think to themselves, "Oh look, it's the nutters who go swimming at Christmas." But really, I wouldn't swap this for anything in the world. There's no more beautiful place to be. There's also the therapeutic element. As my dad used to say, no matter what problems you have in life, if you come down to the Serpentine at six o'clock on a winter's morning, and there's ice out on the concrete, and you walk out on that board with no one else around and you dive in, those problems will disappear.'

Probably because you'd have more pressing things to worry about, I wanted to say, like when to get out, and how. Instead we gazed out in silence at the miniature archipelago that had inspired Peter Pan.

J. M. Barrie often referred to Jack, George, Peter, Michael and Nico Llewellyn-Davies as the other inspiration behind Peter Pan, writing: 'I always knew that I made Peter by rubbing the five of you violently together, as savages with two sticks produce a flame . . .'

This archetypal boy-who-never-grows-up has since worked his way into the collective Western imagination; there's even a psychological syndrome named after him. Yet there is something about the relationship between Barrie and the five boys who inspired his most famous creation that, at times, and to a certain sensibility, is unsettling. More so now than it might have been at the beginning of the twentieth century when *Peter and Wendy* was first published. Some of the passages in Barrie's diary when read out of context might suggest he harboured sexual feelings towards these boys, although there is no hint that any of this was consummated. His fascination with the Llewellyn-Davies brothers appears to be borne of something else, something entirely unsexual. As Andrew Birkin, an authority on all things Barrie, wrote, he was 'a lover of childhood, but was not in any sexual sense the paedophile that some claim him to have been'. Instead of hoping for sexual gratification, Barrie had a pathological craving for what he imagined to be the weightlessness of childhood. He longed to be Jimmy Barrie, prepubescent boy, adored by his mother and father – something he was not – and free from the pressures and tiptoed intricacies of adult life. He wanted to return to the ranks of, as he called them, the *unadulterated*, and to exist in a place where he did not have to worry about how other people might judge him.

As well as being dubbed a closet paedophile from time to time, J. M. Barrie was frequently referred to as an eccentric; and in many ways this race in his name was a paean to the perceived weightlessness of childhood in the eyes of an adult, and to the importance of remembering the sense of what it is to be childlike – something that would become a leitmotif of the journey that had just begun.

A crowd had gathered near the board from which the swimmers would dive in. On the railing were two signs saying, 'NO DIVING', ambassadors of an England bent on removing the possibility of eccentricity. I pointed them out to Jeff. He shrugged.

'Park authority, isn't it? Hasn't ever stopped us.'

Beyond the board was a grubby changing room that smelt of sweat, mud and instant coffee. A huddle of swimmers emerged wrapped in towels, chatting hurriedly to each other, eager and ready. Between their legs several dogs scampered back and forth, barking or sniffing at the hairy goalposts surrounding them. The aural back-drop to this, faint like distant fireworks, was a light-hearted kind of banter. It had no rugby-club smugness nor football-terrace barb, but was good-natured and friendly.

A little before nine-thirty everyone stood to attention as a great shriek erupted from the changing room. An Irishman in full piping regalia processed through the nearly naked swimmers with a bagpipe hooked beneath his arm. The drone of his pipes shattered the morning. A Jack Russell yapped at his feet. The man advanced towards the jetty followed by a cavalcade of swimmers. Press photographers took pictures, each one grinning to himself in the knowledge that today, the slowest of slow news-days, they could take a picture of a man picking his nose and it would be published as news.

Jeff filed past in Speedos and condom hat.

'Who do you think's going to win, Jeff?'

He shook his head. 'Tricky one. Quite a few favourites. Alan Nash? Er. Anthony Cleaver. *Sir* Anthony Cleaver, sorry. Kevin Murphy. No, he won last year. Don't know. Difficult on Christmas Day. Too many people . . .'

With that, Jeff was forced along the gangplank by the crowd of swimmers behind.

Because of the handicap system the Peter Pan Cup did not start with one almighty splosh, as I had hoped. Instead Alan called out different numbers from the sidelines and, in orderly twos and threes, the swimmers shot powerfully into the lake. One girl panicked and jumped rather than dived. Someone behind me made a limp joke about trying to walk on water. Spectators shouted encouragement. The one cry I could hear more than any other was 'Come on, Grandad!'

Once everyone was in the water I began to see how difficult this race was. There was such a log-jam of bodies pounding about in such a tiny area that it was hard for even the stronger swimmers to force their way through. Jeff had told me before about 'dreaming', when a swimmer puts his or her head down and thrashes away but because they're cold and flustered they go diagonally, or sideways. Sometimes backwards. This usually results in a crash.

As much as they were competing with each other, the swimmers were also competing with themselves. Our bodies are not designed to swim at speed through water this cold. Jeff's teenage son – hoodie-wearing, quiet, watchful – had talked about how sometimes, towards the end of a race, he would feel his fingers clench involuntarily into a fist as he struggled towards the finish line.

As Duff had put it: 'It's not natural what we're doing. So when you're out on that board, you have to say to yourself, let's get into this water, it's not going to kill me. It's going to be very cold and my body's going to react to it, it's going to seize up, it's going to be hard to do everything, but I just have to make sure I remain conscious, get some air in, do a good stroke, and I'll get through it all right.'

The swimmers were now halfway through the race. None of them had dropped out – yet – and a field of about fifteen or twenty had broken clear. The shouting became louder and more feverish.

Rather than accelerating to the finish, the race slowed as the cold took its toll. I could feel the tension and tried to imagine the pain, but couldn't.

Finally, there was a winner. A woman. In the club's 141-year history only men had won the Peter Pan Cup. She bobbed up and down in the water and punched the air repeatedly, the way athletes do when they win a race. The rest of the swimmers finished and climbed out of the water and before long I was surrounded by a herd of plump, reddened bodies. I could smell exertion and lake-water. Each face grinned as hard as its mouth would allow. Again I was reminded of how old most of the competitors were. The average age in a race dedicated to the boy who never grew up must have been at least fifty. It was an extraordinary sight, like something out of the film *Cocoon*, where three old men find a swimming pool full of rejuvenating water (and several alien-inhabited pods), and swim about until they become as fit and spry as teenagers.

No one in the history of the Peter Pan Cup has had a heart attack or seizure on jumping into the water. In fact, very few of the elderly members of the Serpentine Swimming Club get ill or catch colds, according to Jeff and Duff. Something about these people kept them healthier than others their age. Freakishly so.

As the swimmers hobbled past, wincing, their feet sensitive to the pinprick pebbles set within the concrete, I wondered whether this was a part of what it was to be eccentric: the desire and ability to suspend your adult self to reclaim momentarily something of your youth.

I decided not to wait for the cup to be presented as I wanted to be at home and near a Christmas tree. I had made a start, I told myself as I picked my way through the crowd. My hunt for England's last-remaining eccentrics was under way. But, annoyingly, the Peter Pan Cup had not given me many clues to where to go next. I had hoped it would. Nor did it provide a contender for England's leading eccentric. Instead it had forced me to adjust my focus: rather than trying to find a spot where eccentrics were likely to gather, as I had done that day, I needed to start tracking them down one by one and get beyond part-time eccentrics, that is people who might occasionally be involved in an unusual event like the Peter Pan Cup but otherwise lead lives that were well-lit displays of normality. That way I'd find full-time eccentrics.

Shortly before the race I had read about a woman who ran a gnome reserve in Devon, and as I continued along the banks of the Serpentine towards the carpark I realised that this was exactly the kind of person I should be meeting.

'Well done, Grandad,' I could hear behind me.

'Time to get the bird in.'

'Can we go now?'

'Well done, Dad.'

'Was it cold?'

'How do you feel?'

'Think you can do it faster next year?'

James Burnett, also known as Lord Monboddo, was at different times during his life dismissed as a crank, heretic and eccentric. His dates span the eighteenth century. Monboddo was one of the first people to suggest that man was descended from primates, and is now acknowledged as having anticipated the evolutionary principle of natural selection long before Darwin hit on it.

In his book *The Origin and Progress of Language* Monboddo explained this idea, as well as various others relating to his study of primitive languages. He once said, jokingly – or at least half-jokingly, it's hard to tell – in response to a jibe about the idea of man's descent from primates for which he'd become notorious, that some men were born with tails, and that these were chopped off at birth by discreet midwives. Cartoonists of the time subsequently drew him with a tail peeking out of his tailcoat. Dr Johnson concluded: 'It is a pity to see Lord Monboddo publish such notions as he has done: a man of sense, and of so much elegant learning. There would be little in a fool doing it; we should only laugh; but when a wise man does it we are sorry. Other people have strange notions, but they conceal them.' Monboddo was not deterred. He did not mind what men like Dr Johnson thought and trusted his view of the world over and above the orthodoxy of the age he lived in.

In a similar sense, John Stuart Mill was depicted wearing a dress by cartoonists after he wrote *The Subjection of Women*, and was made out to be a similarly eccentric figure on account of his novel belief in racial equality.

It reminded me of a story Jeff the ex-parking-meter attendant had told me before the race. 'And the sun was just coming up over there,' he had begun, away from the others. His diction had slowed to the more measured pace of a man telling a favourite story. 'Everything was white frost, there was a mist on the water, and the sun come up, and it lit the bridge up pink over there. And I was the only one out swimming. No one else there. And the old red helicopter took off from Kensington Gardens, and it came across the other side of the park. And they obviously spotted me, so they came across and they were hovering over me, you know, so I don't know who was in it, but, like, I was just swimming along—'

'When was that?'

'Probably about ten or so years ago. Something like that. Don't know whether it was Princess Di, or Charles, or one of those. They obviously spotted me as they were going somewhere. And they were probably saying to themselves, "Look at that idiot over there, all by himself.'" He chuckled. 'But, you know what, I didn't mind. Didn't bother me one bit what they thought.'

I liked the way he had said this. Rather than sounding stubborn or bloody-minded it suggested a learned indifference to embarrassment: an enviable kind of social toughness that seemed to be at the very core of the archetypal eccentric I was trying to find. Even if I hadn't found him or her, I was beginning to get an idea of what the English eccentric would sound like.

3

POSSESSION OBSESSION

Ann Atkin had an unusual walk. Everywhere she went she seemed to float, her feathery frame only just heavy enough to be troubled by gravity. Round her withered neck was a paper-thin turquoise scarf tied in a knot. Her face was lined and her nose arched, like a latterday Virginia Woolf. Her hair had been dyed chestnut brown several months before and now looked solid and purposeful, like clay tamped down on her scalp; at the roots you could see grey coming through in unruly bursts.

'I'm not sure if you should see them like this,' she said, gliding towards an oak copse. 'The gnomes don't like to have visitors when they're hibernating.'

'But I've come all this way,' I pleaded lightly.

'Well,' she said, uncertain. 'A quick look, no more. Then we can go inside.'

She turned back to the path.

It was a bright, wintry day in Devon and I was about to enter England's only gnome reserve. There are others in Denmark and Italy, but Ann's was the first and remains the world's largest. 'TELE-VISION HAVE VISITED 60+ TIMES!' read a sign near the entrance.

The idea came to her about thirty years ago. Her husband, Ron, is a self-taught cognitive therapist who takes people on journeys into their subconscious. They met as students at the Royal Academy; he paints oil portraits in brooding, earthen browns, she makes cosmic watercolours dotted with fairies and vegetal shapes. One day in 1978, Ron took Ann on a journey into her subconscious where she saw nothing but gnomes. They were everywhere, up to their tricks, mischievous, shy, each one wearing a fire-engine-red cap, playing, sneaking about or, as she put it, *gnoming*, and from that moment she knew she wanted to collect them. Slowly this collection grew. Some she bought, others she made, and from time to time gnomes came to her – visitors to the reserve regularly leave them anonymously as they know they'll be looked after properly by Ann – so now she has several thousand in her collection.

'Forgive me,' I began, 'because I should know, but what is a gnome?'

'Oh!' she cried. 'Do you really not know?'

I made a hopeless face. 'I mean, I know what they look like.'

'Each one is as old as the hills, and as young as a baby.'

'Like a grey-haired baby.'

'Exactly.'

'And how about pixies?'

'Dear oh dear.'

'I know . . .'

'Pixies are just playful. They're not as old as gnomes. Fairies are like pixies only they have wings. And all the gnomes have names.'

At this point the path entered the reserve. To the left was a gnome-sized road-sign marked '3 MPH', and beyond it several acres of woodland crisscrossed with paths and jammed full of gnomes. It was all I had hoped for (and perhaps a little more). Everywhere I looked there were clusters of the little creatures, their scarlet caps and blue or green coats lit occasionally by the dappled sunlight flitting in through leafless foliage. Some were massed together awaiting a winter clean, looking like Roman soldiers in formation, others were frozen in a series of dioramas: there was a gnome abseiling down a rock next to a miniature beach signposted as Putford-on-Sea; nearby, gnomes watched a Punch and Judy stall; others sunbathed or played in the water. There were gnomes fishing, playing chess, making music, smoking pipes, riding motorbikes, flying planes, fooling about – in fact just about everything you could imagine a gnome getting up to that could be shown before the 9 p.m. watershed.

'I would give you a gnome cap and a fishing rod to take round with you,' she said, her hands on her hips. 'Only it's winter and they're all locked up. In the first year we didn't hand out caps to visitors, and it didn't seem right.' Ann puffed out her cheeks. 'The gnomes didn't like it. Now we offer everyone red caps, and a fishing rod if they like. Ninety-nine per cent of them take the caps. It's lovely! The gnomes certainly prefer it that way.'

She stopped at a large gnome chiselled out of stone with lichen spreading like a disease over its base.

'Now this is the first gnome we had here. Siegfried. He's very ugly, I know, but he's the first. We've even made a monument to him. You see he got cross because he wasn't being acknowledged as the founder of the reserve.'

Ten yards away was a bust of Siegfried on a pedestal, his name inscribed in the stone below.

'He's still my favourite though,' she sighed, gazing at him lovingly. 'I think most collectors are like that. We always treasure our first.'

In most of my initial trawls through the internet looking for eccentrics I had found people described as 'eccentric collectors'. The words 'eccentric' and 'collector' seemed to be happy bedfellows, the latter rarely going anywhere without the former.

There were collectors of post boxes, or traffic cones, some who collected nothing but milk-bottles, or sickbags, lawnmowers, prams, mail carts, bassinets, discarded packaging, newspapers, as well as the more obvious collectors who hoarded stamps, dolls or works of art. I made a list of the different things English people collected obsessively, but gave up by the time it was several pages long, concluding that there were few, if any, non-perishable mass-produced objects that were not collected by someone somewhere in England.

As well as collectors who sought out physical objects, there were collectors of numbers. Plane-spotters, for example, were the Brahmins of the spotting caste-system. Beneath them in this curiously regi-mented and elitist hierarchy of spotting came train-spotters, and below them the spotter untouchables: bus-spotters. One of the best things that can happen to you as a bus-spotter is for your train to be cancelled – though why would you be on a train in the first place? – and for a replacement bus service to take you to your destin-ation. The buses used on these occasions are relatively vintage, meaning you get to note down a number few other spotters will have. There is also a man from Bristol who spots pylons.

Still, I did not understand the link between eccentricity and collecting. Why were so many collectors thought of as eccentric?

The various dictionary definitions of the word 'eccentric' were of little help. 'Eccentric' signifies 'being odd or capricious in behaviour or appearance', or any one of 'whimsical', 'peculiar', 'erratic', 'unusual', all of which seemed imprecise or a little vague. Already there was something I could add to this definition. Eccentricity was fundamentally benign. This was at the root of the link between collecting and eccentricity. Collecting inanimate objects is not harmful. It can come across as peculiar, at which point it enters the realm of eccentric, but it does not harm. The moment a collector begins to collect something more sinister, like the eponymous protagonist in John Fowles' *The Collector* who moves on from butterflies to nineteen-year-old girls, he is no longer eccentric; he becomes 'sick', 'twisted', 'mad'. Society cannot express meaningful disapproval using the word 'eccentric'.

I was getting somewhere now. In its most generalised sense, describing an individual as eccentric suggested they existed at the periphery of what is acceptable, but have not yet broken a major taboo and incurred the opprobrium of society.

And what of the urge to collect itself, described in 1897 by William Hazlitt, bibliomaniac, in *Confessions of a Collector*, as 'an inborn and indestructible human trait'? This was interesting too, mainly because there is no clear-cut psychological definition of why people become obsessed with their collections. Freud, not surprisingly, links the urge to collect with traumatic experiences from childhood. He felt there was a causal link between the need to collect and the experience of potty-training and the shock of watching your creations being flushed away by your parents. Still bitter about this thirty years later, Freud argued that collectors hoard in order to salve the pain of having their turds taken away from them at such an early age. Although I wasn't sure about the potty-training part of the theory, the link to childhood was significant. The way most of us are fanatical collectors at some stage during our childhood strengthened the link forming in my mind between eccentricity and the child that each of us used to be.

'So do you get a lot of children here?'

'Yes,' Ann replied, sounding and looking puzzled by the question.

'Yes, children love it here. But we're all children really.' Strangely, the way she said this made me feel like a child – one who had just got something wrong. 'The gnomes bring out the child in us,' she went on. 'Especially the grown-ups who've forgotten how to see like a child. That's very important, you know.'

We finished the tour of Ann's gnome-infested woods and went into her house. She made tea while her dog, Daisy, barked at me. Then we moved through to the room where Ann sculpted gnomes from clay.

At this point I should mention the third person there: Helena, my girlfriend, who works in radio. In fact one of the first times we met was when she interviewed me on a small London radio station. So it's Helena who's the professional interviewer in our relationship. She's the one with the BBC-issue microphone and mini-disc recorder. I'm not. All I had was a Dictaphone (which she had given me), and that meant I was on edge as I took my seat in the 'Pixie Kiln' and thought about what to ask Ann. Rows of unpainted gnomes glowered at me from around the room. Not only was I conducting an interview with an experienced interviewer in the background, but I was also trying hard to avoid the e-word.

As before, I was unsure about the effect of the word 'eccentric'. On the phone I had explained to Ann that I was trying to track down England's most extraordinary people. She had seemed to like that.

'The most important thing here', she began, unprompted, 'is to be a hundred per cent serious, and at the same time a hundred per cent fun.' She said the last bit again and did a little jig, with her hands up in the air and both palms facing me, as if to say don't shoot. I had never met a woman this old yet this lithe. There was something miraculous about her energy.

She told me more about her life, the reserve, the history of gnomes in England and Sir Charles Isham, who got it all going when he returned from a trip to Germany in 1847 with a collection of terra-cotta gnomes.

I asked the right questions. I think. Helena asked the ones that I didn't, and after half an hour came the moment that changed the conversation, and with it my entire journey.

Apropos of very little, Ann produced from the top drawer of the worn, paint-covered desk next to the window where she decorated her gnomes a hand-made A4-sized folder, bound along the spine with black plastic. On the cover, printed in what looked like size 24 Times New Roman font, bold, were the words 'Britain's No. 1 Female Eccentric'. Beneath it was a picture of her standing next to a familiar looking man in his eighties.

'Who's that?' I asked.

'Ah, that's, um . . . that's with Norman Wisdom.' She held the book nervously, half wanting to thrust it in my hands, half wanting me to take it from her. 'It's from a competition, a prize thing they did a while ago. An eccentrics competition.'

I tried to remain still. 'Register nothing!' I told the muscles in my face, especially the ones on either side of my mouth which I seem to have least control over.

'Tell me about the competition,' I said quietly, biting my cheeks and looking away.

'Well,' she began. 'I was invited up to London. They had a dinner for all of us. Ten of us.'

'And who were—'

'We were all eccentrics apparently, but I don't like that word much.'

'Ah. Why not?'

'Well, some people when they use it, you know, it's a bit . . .' She grimaced. 'Oooh, that person's eccentric.' She frowned, and looked thoughtful again. 'But I suppose it's about how you define eccentric. They say an eccentric is someone who does what they want, don't they? Someone who isn't worried about what other people think. So in that sense, yes,' she fixed her gaze on me, her pitch climbing in to a crescendo, 'I'm an eccentric. Britain's number-one female eccentric!'

Her arms went up in the air and she did a seated version of her exclamation-mark jig.

Brilliant, I thought to myself, feeling as though I had just won something. But there was more.

'Tell me about this prize, the best British eccentric prize.'

'Ah. It all took place in that building in, where was it, in London, somewhere like Hyde Park . . . The Orangery!' she cried as if we were in an Agatha Christie novel and she'd just worked out whodunit. 'It was a lot of fun. There was this man Weeks, and he's very important, you know, because he wrote a book about eccentrics, and the competition was because of this book. He's a, what's it called, a neuro— A neuroscientist. Or neuropsychologist. I'm not sure. But all I know is that it's the only book in the world just about eccentrics and what makes people eccentric. Can you imagine! No other scientist has written a book about it. What else . . . It was sponsored by Corn Flakes, of all things. Then there was a man from the *Daily Mail*, Ben Le Roy I think he's called. So they got together the ten most eccentric people in the country and I came seventh. I was the only woman there. Such a lovely day,' she sighed.

4

THE SCIENTIFIC STUDY

Ann was mostly right. About a month after two passenger planes crashed into what was the Twin Towers in New York the Best British Eccentric 2001 awards ceremony took place in London. The event was staged in the summery splendour of the Orangery in Holland Park; once a conservatory, now a restaurant. It had been dreamed up by a PR firm hired by Kellogg's Fruit 'n' Fibre who hoped the free press generated by an event like this would amount to more than a series of paid-for ads. It did not, and although there were photos of the event in several London papers and it featured in a smattering of 'and-finallys' in the local news, this was the first and last Best British Eccentric awards ceremony.

On the day, of course, no one knew, and the mood at the ceremony was bright. After a night at the Dorchester Hotel the nominees were driven to Holland Park where a meal was served, a glass clinked and the results of the competition announced.

The winner was an inventor from Marlow called Lyndon Yorke. In photos from the event he wears a grin so large he seems to hide behind it. His cheeks are flushed the colour of glacé cherries. As well as building a car entirely from wicker, Yorke created the world's first river-going Edwardian-style tricycle–catamaran. He wore a safari suit and pith helmet to receive his prize – a holiday abroad – and in his speech thanked his neighbours who had, he said, 'Put up with all the cacophony coming from my garden shed over the past years. None of them knew what I was doing . . . But now they will.'

It felt like the finale to a rom-com. I could imagine him punching the air as he delivered that last line. *But now they will!* He had shown them. He had triumphed against adversity, won the day, got the girl

– well, the award. He had also manoeuvred himself into pole position as possible leader of my eccentric tribe.

As well as Ann Atkin and Lyndon Yorke, the eccentrics that day included a champion toe-wrestler called Alan 'Nasty' Nash; Captain Beany from the Planet Beanus (a Welshman who liked to dress up as a baked bean); the world's black-pudding-throwing champion; an obsessive French knitter; and a man dressed as a pirate claiming to be the world's champion plank-walker. Each nominee was awarded a 'Dafta' statuette by Sir Norman Wisdom, their eighty-six-year old host.

It looked like a fantastic day. The smiles don't feel staged and you can imagine each of the contestants feeling proud or in some way vindicated by this celebration of them, their character and outlook. Some had never been to London before. Each felt like a celebrity. They also got on extremely well with each other, finding they had much in common.

The only person missing from the photographs of the event, and in some ways the most important figure there, was Dr Weeks.

Dr David Weeks is a respected neuropsychologist based in Edinburgh. He is responsible for the world's first and so far only scientific study of eccentricity. In *Eccentrics: The Scientific Study* Weeks compares contemporary understanding of eccentricity to 'a Black Hole in the domain of psychology', adding that 'psychology takes itself, its image, and its methods, far too seriously'. He puts this quite early on in the book, on page 3. You get the feeling he wants to position himself a little apart from orthodox psychology as middle-man between you, the reader, and the necessarily forbidding establishment of psychology. There was something enjoyably scruffy about this. It made me read on in anticipation of the next polite outburst.

Eccentricity, he continues, is parked in a scholarly blind-spot between psychology and psychiatry. Psychiatrists tend to be drawn to patients who suffer from a disease that they can diagnose and treat, while an eccentric is someone who does not suffer from a psychiatric condition. This was an important element of what made someone eccentric. In fact they are wary of seeing a doctor at all – Weeks estimated that on average an eccentric will see his or her doctor once every eight and a half years. Psychologists, at the other end of the spectrum, are generally more interested in people who represent the norm rather than an anomaly. So by definition the eccentric slips between the clutches of psychiatry and psychology. This is what made Weeks' investigation so rare.

Weeks and his fellow researcher began this survey back in 1984. In time it would become the most comprehensive survey of eccentricity anywhere in the world, involving the largest group of subjects ever sampled by psychologists. But to begin with, their experience was similar to mine: they couldn't work out where to start.

Realising he wasn't going to find his subjects in hospital waiting rooms or in asylums, nor on the expensively upholstered couches of Edinburgh's psychiatrists, Weeks decided to advertise. He left a series of cards in a demographically diverse range of locations: pubs, launderettes, libraries, supermarkets and university halls. Each one read: 'Eccentric? If you feel that you might be, contact Dr David Weeks at the Royal Edinburgh Hospital.'

A journalist saw one of these cards and wrote a piece about it in the local evening paper, which led to an article in the *Scotsman*. From there the story snowballed. Journalists from all over the country pounced on this search for eccentrics, and before long Weeks and his assistant were the subject of nationwide media coverage. They estimated that in the years 1984–7 their appeal reached the eyes and ears of roughly 30 million people in the United Kingdom. Yet herein lay one of his biggest problems. The people who came to him were often self-selecting – individuals who described themselves as eccentric, which placed undue emphasis on those who *wanted* to be known as eccentric. Often those who are genuinely eccentric will not want to be described as such.

The visionary film-maker Werner Herzog, a man who has often been called eccentric, once told an interviewer, 'When you look at my films you see there is absolutely nothing eccentric about them. When you sit three feet away from me do you see anything eccentric, do you?' 'No, Werner,' the interviewer replied, 'absolutely not.' 'I am dead centre,' he went on. 'In comparison to me the rest are eccentric.'

Whether or not his subjects were self-selecting, Weeks' survey produced a landslide of data. England in 1984, we are told, was home to around 6,000 eccentrics. One for every 10,000 non-eccentrics. So in 2008 there should be nearly 7,000 English eccentrics at large in the country. Almost enough to fill the stadium of a non-league Conference football team – though that would never happen. The eccentrics Weeks interviewed would squirm at the thought of being part of a homogeneous swarm cheering on the same team. They'd prefer to be the streaker running across the pitch, or perhaps the mascot.

Weeks' typical eccentric is someone who knows from a young age that society thinks they are unusual. Most of the time, like Herzog, they see themselves as ordinary and the world around them as eccentric, an idea that has an almost Confucian ring of possibility to it next to another of his findings: the average eccentric has an IQ of 115–20, compared to 100 for the typical non-eccentric. Week's eccentrics are also single-minded. Their eccentricity is rarely the result of ignoring logic, but of pursuing it to an obsessive extreme. They see their take on the world as authentic, and are happy to come across as outspoken or opinionated, to the point where they are unaware of the effect they have on the person they're talking to. Weeks noted that his subjects rarely identified signals of 'disbelief, confusion or boredom' in the body language or facial expression of the person interviewing them. I liked this bit. It allowed me to imagine Weeks interviewing his eccentrics with tears of boredom streaming down his face, pulling faces, begging them to stop, while the eccentric carried on regardless with a blow-by-blow account of their life.

Eccentrics also have an unusually high level of self-reference in the way they talk, much higher than you might find in clinical samples of patients suffering from mania or schizophrenia. Every topic of conversation is routinely brought back to themselves. The eccentric becomes the egocentric. The only other people to self-reference quite as much are children. Perhaps by dint of this, the eccentrics Weeks met were mostly unmarried or single with strange living arrangements or peculiar eating habits. In other words, they rarely craved the company of others.

What else? The eccentrics he interviewed were bad at spelling.

They were often the first-born of their siblings, would have a mischievous sense of humour and were generally happier than the rest of us, which segues neatly into one of the most intriguing results of the survey: eccentrics usually live longer than non-eccentrics. Part of the reason is that in old age they have multiple hobby-horses on the go, perhaps a collection, an invention, a book to write, and these lend structure to retirement. This longevity is also due to the degree of happiness they experience each day, something that owes a lot to not worrying so much about what other people think of them. This boosts their bodies' immune response systems, which in turn strengthens their endocrine and nervous systems, allowing them to survive a little longer. My journey acquired another dimension. If I wasn't off to find the secret to eternal youth I was at least trying to get an understanding of why eccentrics lived longer than the rest of us.

Not only do they delay death, eccentrics are also fascinated by the event of it. One described by Weeks kept a collection of coffins in his house for his guests to try out when they came to visit. He also kept his drinks cabinet in a coffin. Another bought her coffin several years before she died and would regularly clamber in before summoning her servants to ask if it was a good fit.

But where does all this begin – what *makes* someone become an eccentric?

Although he found no recurring patterns in the early childhood of his eccentrics, Weeks saw commonalities in their experience of school. This makes sense. For most children, going to school represents the first taste of a social setting designed to reward conformity, curb instinct and impose a particular version of morality using various systems of reward and punishment. The child is initiated into what Kafka called 'the Lie'. As he once put it, 'education is but two things: first, the parrying of the ignorant children's impetuous assault on the truth, and second, the gentle, imperceptible, step-by-step initiation of the humiliated children into the Lie'.

An eccentric, by Weeks' reckoning, is always going to react against this imposition of the Lie, and by resisting it will learn for the first time to live without the imprimatur of mainstream society.

Sport is one way of gaining approval at school, and few eccentrics find themselves drawn towards it. They simply don't feel the need to prove themselves competitively against their peers and are happy instead to work out their own indices of success and failure.

There's something uniquely English about this emphasis at school on sport, or what Jeremy Paxman calls 'the Game'. It's fairly recent too, becoming widespread only in the second half of the nineteenth century. In many ways this was the response of a morally ambitious middle class to what they saw as the indiscipline of the preceding Regency period. The Game, when played properly, would breed the ideal Victorian Englishman. According to Paxman this figure – the quintessential chap – was 'honourable, decent, stoical and brave'. He believed in fair play, knew when he was out, and was a team player. He was also as loyal as a gundog, which is handy when you have wars to fight and empires to maintain. However, this kind of person was unlikely to be truly eccentric or non-conformist, at least not to begin with. Young men brought up on the Game became part of 'the Breed': 'bold, unreflective and crashingly pragmatic, men you could trust'. George Orwell refers to them as 'blimps', whose 'chief asset was their stupidity', and describes the culture that worshipped their mediocrity as one where 'to be "clever" was to be suspect. If you had the kind of brain that could understand the poems of T. S. Eliot or the theories of Karl Marx, the higher-ups would see to it that you were kept out of any important job.' This was exactly what Mill feared when he wrote *On Liberty*.

Writing at a similar tine to Orwell, Vladimir Nabokov, who had recently swapped Soviet Russia for Cambridge University, was amazed by the way English undergraduates played football. He described them as being crippled by a 'national dread of showing off', compounded by a 'too grim preoccupation with solid teamwork', neither of which, he felt, from his position as goalkeeper, was 'conducive to the development of the goalie's eccentric art'.

Eccentrics rarely care for the rhizome of rules represented by the Game. The only sportsman who might warrant a place in a study of eccentricity is William Webb Ellis, the Rugby School pupil who famously or apocryphally, picked up the ball during a game of Association football and ran with it, inventing rugby in the process.

Typically, school will leave a lasting impression on an eccentric.

This is where it begins. Most of Weeks' subjects treasured like shrapnel from an explosion particular moments of ridicule or humiliation they had experienced during their schooldays, each one a memento of marginalisation, in the hope of one day meting out revenge on the pupil or teacher responsible. So did George Orwell, who once listed the four reasons why he, or indeed anyone, wrote. First on the list was: 'Desire to . . . get your own back on the grown-ups who snubbed you in childhood'.

As well as being their first encounter with a large yet tight-knit community that has both centre and margins, and is governed by rules, school represents the first occasion a child is either inclined or steered towards eccentricity. You can't really talk about someone being eccentric without a similar social structure in place.

So eccentricity is not hardwired into an individual from birth. It emerges only when that person joins a group. My understanding of the word lurched forward again.

Not long after reading Weeks' study of eccentrics I heard about a play called *English Eccentrics* being performed in Eastleigh. I rang the production company to ask for an interview with the lead, and was politely told to get lost. Still in a state of excitement I drove to the south coast with Helena to see it. We set off late so I had to drive fast, faster than I should have done. We got to Eastleigh just in time and took our seats as Prunella Scales and Edward Fox walked on stage. Both looked immensely bored. They were accompanied by a grinning pianist who hammered her instrument as if it was a church organ.

I'd been wrong to call it a play. *English Eccentrics* was in fact an hour-long train of two- or three-line anecdotes about eccentric personalities 'through the ages'. Each snippet was Victorian and smug in its morality, the kind of stories you could tell someone else's grandparents (and even they would doze off).

Worse, the actors had decided not to learn their lines. Instead they stood mostly still and read their parts from leather-bound scripts. They did this slowly and clearly. The audience was elderly and they smiled hard at each punchline. Sometimes they'd laugh and it would make a muffled snorting sound.

The whole thing felt dead. There had to be more to eccentricity than this. The mood in the theatre was unbearably polite and twee, and I felt sorry for each dead personage being momentarily resuscitated on stage. Their characters had been tamed by wilfully demure biographers and I left Eastleigh wanting to know what they were really like beyond their one or two amusing habits. I was also beginning to sense a fundamental division between the historical incarnation of the 'English Eccentric' and the contemporary, more three-dimensional eccentric that Dr Weeks described.

Weeks' book had transformed my understanding of English eccentricity. The play in Eastleigh had not, although it had given me an idea of what I was up against. *Eccentrics: The Scientific Study* had confirmed several hunches, shot down others and posed plenty of questions, particularly about the history of English eccentricity. How might this received stereotype affect someone's behaviour today? And was this English inclination towards eccentricity that I'd heard so much about timeless or did it have a starting point?

More important at this stage was knowing how to move forward. After reading about a panoptic array of different eccentrics I'd started to form a rough taxonomy. The word taxonomy sounds omniscient and rigorous. What I had scribbled down was neither. Nor was it exhaustive. Already I knew this journey would involve a personal selection in the sense that there would be many individuals, dead or alive, who fell into my field of inquiry but could not be included. I didn't have room. This was part of the reason why my taxonomy was so useful – it meant that each character that appeared would represent a different facet of the term.

Although there were several figures who belonged to multiple categories, for all its gaps and overlaps my system meant that I was no longer rushing headlong at eccentricity, trying to grab it all at once like a contestant on *The Crystal Maze* at the finale where they had to catch as many of the fluttering tickets as possible. With categories I had a sense of order. And calm.

So far on my journey I had met part-time eccentrics at the Serpentine, tick, and in Ann Atkin, a collector eccentric. Another tick. My idea for the next branch of English eccentricity came from one of Weeks' most interesting findings, up there with the idea that eccentrics lived longer, had higher IQs and were generally happier than the rest of us. At one point in his book Weeks had argued that the English eccentric was predominantly male and that there were roughly nine male eccentrics for every one female – exactly the gender breakdown at the Best British Eccentric 2001 Award.

In Ann Atkin I had found an exception that literally proved the rule, yet there was another kind of eccentric who in my mind was usually female. This was where I would take my journey next. Only it was hard to know where to find the person I had in mind.

5

TOO MUCH LOVE

An elderly woman sits in an armchair. She's wearing a cardigan and a blouse above the kind of Marks and Spencer skirt that wouldn't make it into one of their adverts with a nineteen-year-old dancing down a beach. It's a skirt you'd find hanging on a poorly lit rail towards the back of the store: a brown pleated affair that ends exactly where it shouldn't, about six inches below the knee. You can see where her socks finish. The elastic forms a pinched valley in her lower calf.

Around her feet is what seems to be an impractically deep shag-pile rug. You look harder and realise that the rug is moving in fits and starts, semi-coagulated and volcanic as if it is the surface of a stew. Then you notice a tail, a pair of eyes, another tail, until you register that you're looking at a swarm of thirty cats sashaying back and forth around the feet of an elderly film actress playing the part of a generic Cat Lady.

At least that was the idea.

I have a friend called George who, just as I was working out where to find a real English Cat Lady, was preparing to shoot a short film about a fictional cat lady. She was, according to the script, 'in her sixties . . . not necessarily poor: money and its usual manifest-ations in a home hold no interest for her. Her only focus is her pets. A widow, she lives alone; her cats are her companions and her obses-sion; she is dotty rather than senile. Cats themselves are everywhere . . .'

She's an eccentric lover of animals. This was to be my next cate-gory.

That the idea of this Cat Lady exists in this country and is thought to be at all lovable was symptomatic of the peculiarly English idea that anyone who loves animals can never be *that* bad. As a nation, we are preternaturally obsessed with pets. Only in England could a former Home Secretary file a weekly column in the country's most popular newspaper written from the point of view of his dog. In 'Sadie's Week', in the *Sun*, David Blunkett MP was referred to as 'the bearded one', while the nation was kept abreast of any new toys or chews Sadie had been given, as well as that week's interesting run-ins with squirrels on her way to parliament.

Ever since the Vicar of Morwenstow in the early nineteenth century was known to tour his parish on a donkey with a pet pig by his side, or William Purslow of Shropshire who died in 1809 and was famous for having tamed two hedgehogs so that 'they perambulated the streets with him in a degree of discipline that astonished beholders', the English have been remarkable for their soppiness towards animals.

The twist at the close of George's short film came when you realised that the Cat Lady was murdered not by the hoodie-wearing ne'er-do-well you're shown earlier on in the film, but by her cats. They have nibbled her to death.

It is an excellent twist, and a triple assault on a very English set of prejudices. Not only is the victim a lover of animals, and so does not deserve death-by-cat, but she is geriatric, and that's unusual for victims of fictional and exotic deaths. Best of all, this ending allows the cats to transform from anthropomorphised cuddly toys that we stroke and talk to as if they were one-year-old nephews into anonymous footsoldiers within a feral swarm.

Once or twice a year a story appears in the English press about an elderly animal-hoarder who has collected more animals than they can realistically look after. Just over 70 per cent of animal-hoarders convicted in the UK up to 2005 have lived alone and been female.

Rosalind Gregson of Silverdale, Lancashire, is an English animal-hoarder who strayed beyond the designation 'eccentric'. In 2005 she was charged with forty-nine counts of causing unnecessary suffering to an animal after the RSPCA found 271 malnourished animals caged in her rat-infested cottage, including 246 Maltese terriers, various cats, birds, a rabbit and a chinchilla. Nine of the animals had to be put down immediately. At her trial Gregson was described as being 'eccentrically dressed' and 'clutching a plastic bag', and as such conformed meticulously to her stereotype.

Obsessive animal-hoarders will rarely see what they have done as wrong and will argue that they are the only ones who can really look after the animals in their care. Sure enough, Rosalind Gregson denied any responsibility for causing cruelty towards her animals when questioned in court.

As many of the organisations dedicated to improving the lot of animals in England will point out, there is nothing lovably eccentric about the 'mad cat lady' when she goes this far. What's more contentious, and problematic, is defining where and how Rosalind Gregson fits into John Stuart Mill's exhortations to eccentricity and his notion that eccentricity should be encouraged wherever it is found. Clearly in the case of Rosalind Gregson, her eccentricity should not be encouraged – though I wanted to know how far you could go in your eccentric and largely tolerated love of animals before English society decides that you've broken a taboo. What happens when people become scared by the idea of you?

Some time ago I had read about a man who appeared to be the personification of this conundrum. Born in England, the 'Leopard Man of Skye' had spent the previous twenty-one years living a largely feral and hermit-like existence in the remote Scottish highlands. From what I could tell (going on a handful of articles in newspapers and a three-year-old video clip on the internet) he had spent this period without electricity or running water and did not wear clothes. Not only had he become animal-like in his lifestyle, but his body was tattooed from eyelid to little toe with leopard-spots – tens, if not hundreds of them that coated almost every square inch of his body. This was why he was known as the Leopard Man.

It took me a day and a half to get to the island where he lived. I drove north up the spine of the country past the Peak District and Lake District, into Glasgow, into the Gorbals – by mistake – out of the Gorbals – at speed – and along the banks of Loch Lomond before crossing a bridge to the Isle of Skye where I began to look for him.

The signs during the last four hours of the drive were in both Gaelic and English, and as people in Skye told me, repeatedly, there were now schools operating exclusively in Gaelic, as well as television channels, websites and radio stations, all proof of a burgeoning Scottish identity that made the country I had just entered feel foreign. It reminded me of a recent survey which showed that only 14 per cent of Scots would describe themselves as British. Seventy-nine per cent preferred to call themselves Scottish, while south of the border only 48 per cent of English people in 2006 thought of themselves as British, down from 63 per cent in 1992. As an identity, 'Britishness' was hollowing out. While it remained important in the Orange half of Northern Ireland, or perhaps in the branding of a fish-and-chip restaurant in Hong Kong, in England the word 'British' was slowly losing relevance. 'English' seemed to be taking its place, even if English nationalism remained obscure: a minority sport that only a handful of people went in for, a bit like archery or pot-holing.

Being surrounded by Scottishness in its self-confident Gaelic-speaking tartanness reminded me that there was something else driving me on in my journey, something I had not yet acknowledged. As well as trying to record the last gasps of what I imagined to be a dying tribe, the English eccentrics, in setting out on this journey I had hoped to get a better understanding of what it meant to be English. Personally, I did not know what it meant, to the point where this uncertainty seemed to be the 'Englishness' I was trying to locate – though in recent years this lack had become more acute. Perhaps it was part of growing old, growing up, or maybe I was just envious of all the non-English people I had met with a national identity they could at least describe even if they did not subscribe to it. By travelling through the English margins I imagined that I would get an understanding of what constituted the English mainstream, in the sense that the centre defines itself in relation to its periphery.

On Skye I found the village of Kyleakin, a neat fishing village set beneath broad hillside. The whitewashed houses beamed amid the greys and greens like the teeth of a news reader. I parked and began to ask around for the Leopard Man.

'Oh aye, the wee man?' a fisherman mused.

'Yes, Tom Leppard, isn't he?'

'Aye, he's over at the south shore of the Loch, past the castle. But you can't get there on foot. You'll need a boat. I'd go ask down at the pontoon.' He gestured at a jumble of masts and rigging glinting in the mid-distance. 'They might be able to run you over. And make sure to bring him something as a gift, a bottle of rum, he likes that. Dark rum, mind.'

Dark rum it was. With no off-licence in Kyleakin I drove back to the mainland, bought a bottle of Demerara rum and returned to the pontoon where a handful of fishing boats were moored. Each one was squat and tough-looking with leaves of paint peeling from its side. The rigging jingled in the breeze. Everyone there knew of Tom Leppard, which was encouraging, but none of them would take me over to meet him. Immediately I sensed they were protective of their resident eccentric. You see, as the woman in the post office explained, media people had come up in the past from wherever it was they came from, back in the early 1990s, and exploited him.

After three hours of pleading with the good people of Kyleakin for a ride to the Leopard Man's hideaway, accosting people in the street, going into every shop, asking in pubs, I met Ian. He was a softly spoken bus driver who in the past had run people over to see Mr Leppard, though he hadn't done this for a while, not since he unwittingly brought a German Satan-worshipper who later murdered someone with an axe, claiming Tom Leppard as her inspiration. Ian rang Dodo, and Dodo agreed to run me over there. He said he'd bring his mate Keith. A light breeze picked up as two men ambled towards us.

'All right, Dodo,' said Ian. 'All right, Keith,' before turning to me. 'You're in safe hands now,' he said, with what I later realised was sarcasm.

Dodo and Keith had lived in the village all their lives. They were best friends. Dodo was shorter and more plump, and was generally the fall guy. Keith was there to correct him. His face looked tired from the strain of having done this for the last forty years.

'Aye, my wife was saying just now,' Keith explained, 'if she ever wonders where I am, she knows I'll be round at Dodo's.'

'Aye, and my wife says the same,' Dodo added.

'What, round at yours?'

'Spot on.'

'What do you mean, you daft twat?' said Keith.

'You know.'

'No I don't.'

'You do.'

'I do?'

'Now you do.'

'I do then.'

'You see?'

'What are you talking about, Dodo?'

'Be quiet now, Keith,' he said stepping into the boat. 'Let's get this lad over to see the wee man.'

A few minutes later I was in a red rubber dinghy powered by an outboard motor the size of two shoeboxes stacked on top of each other, being driven out to sea by the Scottish equivalent of the Chuckle brothers. We pootled along for about fifteen minutes, three men in a boat, Dodo and Keith making fun of each other and telling tales, when the engine died.

'Ah,' said Dodo.

'Ah,' Keith nodded.

'It appears we have a problem.'

'And what you gonna do about it?' Keith inquired, deadpan.

'Well, hang on and let me look at the bugger,' said Dodo.

Dodo heaved the engine out of the water, removed the cover and began to poke about in the wiring. His face creased in confusion.

'You've knocked the lanark out,' Keith gasped.

'What d'you mean I've knocked it out?'

'You've knocked it out, pal. There it is, floating in the water.'

This did not sound good. I had no idea what the lanark was, but it sounded important. I wanted it right back where it belonged. Dodo leaned over the edge of the boat and fished about in the water before reappearing with a piece of plastic which he jammed into the engine.

'That's better,' said Dodo, standing up and banging his head on the only metal bar in the dinghy. The chances of him doing that were anorexically slim.

'Well done, Dodo,' Keith groaned.

'Christ alive.' Dodo rubbed his head gingerly. 'Okay. Let's have another go.'

He fired the engine and it purred.

'See?' He grinned. 'Not just a pretty face after all.'

'No one said you were.'

'No one said you were either.'

The engine cut out again. Keith sighed.

Dodo fiddled some more with the engine, swearing at it, muttering to himself as he tried to start it, yet every time it cut out.

'Right, lads,' said Keith, eyeing us up. 'Time to paddle.'

'Wait a second, pal,' Dodo spluttered. 'Rolling a fag over here.'

Keith and I watched for a few minutes as Dodo struggled to get a fist-sized clump of tobacco into his Rizla, before all three of us started to paddle towards the mainland. Our oars were the size of salad spoons. Five minutes later we paused. We hadn't got any closer. In fact, we were now further out to sea than when we had started. The sun went in behind a bank of cloud and the flank of Scottish coastline went from being bright to looking dour.

'Not really working, is it?' said Dodo. He tried the engine again but it just hissed at him. The dinghy continued to drift away from the shore as the wind picked up. All my excitement about meeting the Leopard Man had evaporated. Keith rang his wife and asked her to call a friend who could tow us back. She rang back to say he couldn't because he was over on the mainland at a funeral.

'Maybe he can come to ours tomorrow,' he grumbled.

Dodo told me to look towards the far shore. I strained my eyes until I could make out a dot bobbing in and out of the bushes near the water's edge.

'That's your Leopard Man,' said Dodo. 'Probably seen us and's wondering what we're up to.'

I thought about swimming the distance. Whoever he was, I reckoned I'd be safer with him than with these two.

Finally Keith got through to his friend Chris who said he'd come and tow us back to the village. The Leopard Man would have to wait. Half an hour later Chris arrived in his fishing boat, attached our dinghy to the stern and we chugged back to the village. Dodo's engine failing was one of the funniest things that had happened in Kyleakin for some time, and Chris ribbed the two of them all the way back.

Satisfied that I was not a sinister media-type out to exploit the Leopard Man and film him without paying, Chris agreed to take me over the following day.

'So I'll see you in about five hours?' I shout as Chris clunks the boat into reverse.

'No problem,' he replies, glancing round. 'See you then.'

'Right. Don't forget!' I add, in a weak half-joking voice before turning to face the man standing next to me.

The Leopard Man is wearing a woolly hat, a fleece with a flap that covers his groin, flip-flops and little else. His legs and head are bare and covered in a caparison of leopard markings. Though short he has the proportions of a lank man. His fingers are distended and his palms have long ago been dyed a bluish grey. When he blinks, his eyes flash an effete green that diffuses the apparent threat of his markings. Tattooed on to his eyelids are cats' eyes. The Fontana slash of each pupil is black and the iris surrounding it green.

'Well,' I start, following up on Chris's brief explanation of what I was doing. 'Really kind of you to talk to me.'

He looks at me and blinks. 'But you don't know what I'm going to do to you yet,' he says, slowly. The sound of the fishing boat grows soft. I can hear gulls cawing from the shore next to us. The faint smell of kelp billows up around us.

'You're right,' I mumble. 'I don't.'

It feels like the opening to a bad Hammer horror movie.

A really bad one.

'Right,' he says, and begins to head up from the shore before coming to a sudden halt.

'Hang on.' His blue hand shoots to his mouth and feels around inside. 'I forgot to put my teeth in. Haven't spoken to anyone in a while you see.' He has the delivery of a pensioner, each word coming out deliberately as if it needs a little push. 'I won't be a moment.' He smiles and goes off to find his dentures. For a man in his seventies his stride is irresistibly energetic, and feline.

Plate XIII b

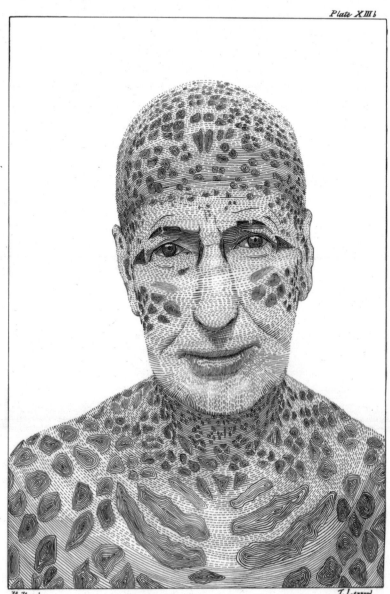

H. Henning   T. Leppard

The Leopard Man

Not long after he reappears and we settle down to talk.

'Can we talk about labels?' I ask. We are in a low-walled enclo-
sure open to the sky. The warmth of the sun seeps through me like
a dye. 'I mean, is there any label that you'd be happy to use to
describe yourself?'

He thinks about this for a long time, and when he answers, he
does so forcefully. 'Selfish. I'm selfish. I've got all this.' He nods over
my shoulder. 'And I want to keep it. I don't want to share it with
anybody.' There's nothing cocky about the way he says this. It's confes-
sional. I remember that he is a Catholic. He has a prayer book with
matins in Latin and English; though there is no priest out here.
Instead he has his birds. An overweight sparrow flutters down to
perch on the dais where Tom leaves food for the gulls. 'I can act on
the spur of the moment and do whatever I like, how I like, when
I like, and that', he smiled, 'is paradise.'

'What's been your happiest moment here?'

'I don't think I have one,' he says in his polite, home-counties
accent. It is incongruous to his markings, his lifestyle, the setting,
everything really. Tom Leppard is not the Diogenes-like wildman I
had half expected.

'Oh,' I say, beginning to feel sorry for him.

'Oh no.' He senses the condolence in my voice. 'For me, to be
extremely happy or extremely sad I need to be around people. If
you're alone, I think you can only be content. You don't get real
highs and lows. But being alone gives you much greater inner joy.
I'm very content here.' He beams without thinking about it; there's
no sense of him trying to convince me of this, he just *is* contented.
He smiles almost as much as Ann Atkin. 'Whenever I get miserable, it's because a human is involved,' he goes on. 'There's nothing
here that could make me miserable. I know everything that nature
can do to me, so nothing comes as a shock.' He flutters his green-
lidded eyes at the breeze and sets his protuberant hands on his
knees.

'So you've never wanted to live here with anyone else?'

'No.' He shakes his head. 'Absolutely not. My whole life before I
came here was living with other people, from school to the Navy
to the Army.'

49

And that's what his life has been, more or less. School. Navy. Army. Leopard.

Evacuated from London during the war, Tom was raised by nuns in Devon, though they didn't like to be called nuns. They preferred to be addressed as Sister. Tom remembers being beaten by Sister Augusta, who always kept a cane hidden in her habit.

Aged fifteen he joined the Royal Navy and over the next twenty-eight years served in the British Army, the Merchant Navy, the Rhodesian Light Infantry and finally in the SAS, and although he rose to the rank of colour sergeant, this was only at the very end of his career. You see, Tom has an unusual relationship with authority. While his time in army-like institutions helped hammer his brain into an order-receiving shape, he never got over his dislike of marching – 'foot-stamping' as he called it – or the idea of being part of a homogeneous unit. Whenever he felt this happening he'd want to break away and would disobey orders, or 'be a bit naughty', as he put it, sounding like a schoolboy who had pinched a Jammie Dodger at break-time. This would get him kicked out of wherever he was. His happiest moments as a soldier or sailor came when he was allowed to work apart from the group in a cocoon of relative autonomy, thus achieving a state of ex-centricity.

Life in the armed forces for Tom was an exact replica of his time at school in the way his days were governed, and from his account of it I realised that he had been an outsider at school. When he left to join the armed forces this marginality was exaggerated into eccentricity.

This had an important bearing on eccentricity as a whole. It rammed home the idea that reasonably strict, school-like institutions are the social settings most likely to breed eccentric characters. This helps explain why over the years there have been so many eccentric judges, army officers and academics. This is not to say that the people who serve in these professions are all eccentric, far from it, but these institutions by their nature and the security of their structure are not threatened by having a marginal character in their midst: someone who generally abides by the rules, yet at the same time represents a shot of rebellion and benign non-conformity. They are usually cherished or tolerated in these places rather than expelled. A less secure structure cannot cope.

Tom retired in his late forties and moved to London. It was the early 1980s and he hated everything about the place. He was a misfit. While most people would just move away from a city they disliked so much, Tom decided to project this sense of apartness on to his flesh. He chose to become visually freakish, and over the next three years had the world's largest and only head-to-toe tattoo inked into his skin until he looked like a man who had become a leopard, or vice versa. He also changed his surname to Leppard so that any notoriety that followed would not reflect perniciously on his family, especially his nephews and nieces who were at school at the time.

It took three different tattooists to do it. The first decorated his back and messed it up, partly because it was his back and Tom couldn't really see what was going on; the second repaired the damage done by the first, and before long he was sleeping on this tattooist's floor. He didn't go out, didn't get into the tattooing scene, the parties or the people. Nothing about London interested him apart from getting the tattoos done and visiting his mother, the only member of his family with whom he kept in touch. The second tattooist covered his entire body apart from his head and his hands, something he refused to do in case Tom later came to regret it. Tom eventually found a third, more maverick tattooist who finished it off, and by 1986 it was complete. His skin was 99.2 per cent covered in tattoos and Tom entered the *Guinness Book of Records* as the World's Most Tattooed Man. But there was more.

Just months after he was awarded this title Tom was jailed on account of the £5,000 worth of damage he wreaked on a solicitor's office in Tooting.

Shortly before the last tattoos were finished Tom had been paid £600 by a Turkish friend to marry his cousin. He was short of cash and agreed to do it — it was a sham marriage and everything went according to plan until two weeks after the wedding when, as agreed, the Turkish girl filed for divorce. To do this she had to invent a reason why the marriage was coming to an end. What she wrote sent Tom into a rage. He wouldn't tell me what she had insinuated, but whatever it was caused him to destroy her solicitor's office. He spent four months in Wandsworth Prison. He liked it very much in there. He told me he found the sense of routine particularly pleasing. No marching either. On his release he bid farewell to civilisation and moved to the ruined remains of a croft on the shore of the Isle of Skye where he would live in obdurate isolation for the next twenty-one years of his life.

'Have you ever been in love?' I ask.

'No.' He smiles a little knowingly. 'Are you leading up to this German girl?'

'Which German girl?'

'The one that was mixed up in black magic, Satan-worship or whatever they call it, and is meant to have killed someone because of me.' In the way he speaks, even about this, something he should feel angry about, he is as courteous as a butler.

'I had no idea,' I say. This isn't true, but I decided earlier not to ask him about it in case it upset him. Tom tells me what happened.

In 2001 a young German Satanist called Manuela Ruda murdered her friend Frank Haagen. In court she argued that she was acting on the instructions of the devil who had told her to 'kill, sacrifice, bring souls'. She thought Frank would be ideal because he was funny and would make a great jester in Satan's court. In the years leading up to his murder she had travelled to Skye and visited Tom four times over the course of a month, yet in statements to the police she suggested that she had lived with him, implying that Tom had steered her towards Satanism.

'Which was rubbish,' he says. 'All that happened when she came over is I'd get on with my chores.' Tom has a lot of chores. Each day is a bullet-point list of chores that just won't do themselves. Most involve washing. 'And she would just stand there, gazing at me. I'd be wearing next to nothing, though I kept my privates covered. Out of respect for her. I didn't mind her coming over. There was nothing remarkable about her. Perhaps she was trying to convert me to devil-worship, I'm not sure. Later she wrote to me from Germany, when she was in jail. She started to talk about us becoming married, and the letters became crude, so I stopped replying.' He looks up, suddenly sounding interested. 'What's your time?'

'Twelve.'

'You don't mind if I feed them?' he says.

'The birds?'

'Yes.'

'Of course.'

He pads over to the bird table and places diced cubes of processed cheese on the wooden surface. He then ushers me back to a respectful distance as the birds flutter down to the table he has set up in their favourite bush, spear a chunk of cheese and move to a branch to eat in private. He smiles.

His companions in paradise are five seagulls as well as this over-grown, dysfunctional family of finches, blue tits, robins and sparrows. For the gulls he dices corned beef and leaves it out in his open-air hut. For the smaller birds he feeds them cheese and a mixture of peanuts and seeds that he buys on the mainland using his pension. He paddles over every two weeks to collect it, making him living proof that you can be an eccentric on a modest budget. If he ever leaves home for more than five hours he will make special provi-sion for the birds. His birds.

Between the huts are neat gravel paths made from pebbles he has carried up from the beach over the years. At times, they make his enclave look municipal. Two of the former sheep-pens are open to the rain while the third is covered and dark like a Stygian cave with a roof made from tarpaulin. It casts a surgical bluish light into a narrow galley where he eats his food or prepares the birds' meals. The doorway is tiny and once inside I have to stoop. Around me is a tapestry of shelves and wires with tools, cutlery, clothes or bottles of rum stowed with care. It is as if we are on board a ship and a storm is on its way. A hurricane couldn't move this lot. The skeleton of what I can see has been built with scraps Tom has combed from nearby beaches over the years. Outside are two sea kayaks, each black with bitumen, that he uses to tow flotsam and scrap back to his base. The space is spot-less and smells of talcum, with every surface below waist height dusted with a film of this white powder that he uses to dry himself after dips in the stream outside. It's a trick he learned in the Navy.

Hidden beyond the kitchen is his bedroom. It's immensely dark, and snug like a womb. He turns his mattress every day. I ask him

why and for the first time he looks cross. 'Because you *do*,' he replies.
I don't question it.

At the entrance to his bedroom there is a shelf of books, each
one wrapped in plastic; I can see *The Iliad*, *The History of Europe* and
several fat airport thrillers by Ayn Rand, Tom's favourite author.

We talk for several hours, sipping rum mixed with lemon concentrate.

Outside the sun is shining and the stream where he washes is
petulant and noisy as it debouches from the bank of forest above. It
is abundant, green and tangled while the view out to sea is the opposite, the kind of thing someone like me who has spent most of his
life in a city impulsively says 'wow' to every time he catches sight
of it. The grass and bushes framing the view have been clipped.
Everywhere I look I see traces of Tom. His interventions are precise
and functional, yet never aesthetic. His home is a pocket of extreme
utilitarian order amid a wilderness and I'm startled by it, I can't place
it. Just as I'm startled by him.

Tom doesn't know how much longer he'll stay here. He's seventy-
two now, and although his limbs do not creak when he kayaks to
the mainland, the journey of just over a mile takes longer than it
used to. His eyesight is getting worse, his body slows, sores that won't
heal have appeared amid the tattooed splendour of his being and
he's started to forget things. He will set out from his kitchen with
a job to do but thirty seconds later it will have vanished. He'll pad
back to his cave smiling at himself and tutting. While he worries
about this, it does not dim the lustre he somehow exudes.

I ask if I can take a photo. He nods, pops into his bedroom and
reappears naked but for a tiny black thong made of a rubbery semi-
opaque material. I take a picture and we walk to the stream. He tells
me that getting the tattoos done didn't hurt too much, apart from
the one in his right buttock – that really hurt. Funnily enough the
ones that hurt the least were the ones he feared most, those on his
eyelids. Getting his penis tattooed didn't hurt either. He shaves all
of his body hair, his eyebrows, underarms and scrotum.

Once naked and in the water he spins his body round several
times. The water is about as cold as the Serpentine on Christmas
morning, perhaps two howls less icy. Tom is hardy and doesn't mind

too much. I stand a little awkwardly next to the stream, not knowing where to look. He is oblivious, wrapped as he is in that lovely gossamer skein of contentedness.

The boat that will take me back to the village appears in the distance.

'Do you miss anything about England?' I ask as he puts his clothes on out of respect for Chris the fisherman.

'No,' he smiles. 'I don't miss it at all. You see, England for me was London and I hated London because I was lonely there.' The boat is moored now. 'I never get lonely here.'

I say goodbye and he comes to shake my hand. It is an unexpectedly firm handshake. I climb into the boat and Chris takes me back to the village, back towards the England that Tom has deserted. I am in a daze. There is something bewildering and bewitching about this man's joy, his contentedness as he put it. I wonder if I will ever meet anyone like that again, or if I have just found England's chief eccentric.

If Tom Leppard personified an extreme of the English obsession with animals, Charles Waterton represents the root. He was the original English animal-lover, as well as being one of the most interesting, outspoken and in some ways archetypal English eccentrics this country has produced. He is the patron saint of our obsession with animals as well as being the man responsible for the world's first nature reserve. He completed it in 1826 at his home near Wakefield in West Yorkshire at a cost of £9,000: a considerable sum now, a much larger one then. Waterton said he was able to afford it by giving up alcohol. Most of the money was spent on a 3-mile wall around his property. Within this walled garden, this paradise in the original Persian sense of the word, Waterton banned the use of guns. This was at a time when any non-domesticated animal that so much as moved in the English countryside was liable to be shot, which explains why Waterton's contemporaries found what he was doing so peculiar. They were genuinely baffled by stories of him building nests for his birds, or climbing trees in order to watch his beloved kingfishers dive into the lake. Why not just shoot them instead?

As well as being the first to build a bird-watching hide, Waterton was fond of drinking his own blood and was a great believer in bloodletting. He also had a fascination with mutant taxidermy, and would spend hours first preserving with mercuric chloride and then lovingly sewing together different sections of animals such as a porcupine with a tortoiseshell on its back and the face of a monkey.

Occasionally Waterton's love of animals got in the way of his social life. When guests came round to dinner he would hide in the hall; having rung the doorbell and received no reply they would enter, cautiously, at which point Waterton would leap out from wherever he was hiding and bounce up to them on hands and knees, once sinking his teeth into someone's leg until he drew blood.

Bloodletting and mutant taxidermy aside, 'Squire Waterton', as he was known, was most famous for his bestselling travelogue *Wanderings in South America*, published in 1825. His love of animals infects every page. One of its highlights is Waterton's description of jumping on to the back of a black cayman and riding it, which was, he wrote, 'the first and last time I was ever on a cayman's back. Should it be asked, how I managed to keep my seat, I would answer, – I hunted some years with Lord Darlington's fox hounds.'

The passages in the book where he describes the Amazon are the first anywhere in the English language to eulogise the natural beauty of a tropical rainforest. Up until then the rainforest had been a thing of danger to be encountered with trepidation. Not for Waterton. He saw things differently. In an age dedicated to wearing your hair in a foppish mop he wore a crewcut. He shunned soft beds and pillows as well as the strangulating cravats so fashionable at the time. He felt, quite simply, that they were not necessary and wasn't bothered about how others might interpret this indifference. He also tried on several occasions to fly, and built a large pair of wings with which he tried to take off from a sheep-pen on his estate. According to Edith Sitwell, a biographer of English eccentrics, he was also an extremely happy man: 'Few of us are so full of life, love, curiosity and plain joy.'

Towards the end of his life, in 1848, to confirm Waterton's status as an eccentric Englishman decades ahead of his time, he became England's first eco-campaigner when he fought a successful legal action against a soap-manufacturing company whose toxic emissions were damaging his trees.

At his funeral, following his careful instructions, Waterton's coffin was placed in a coal boat and towed the length of the lake in front of his house by a barge with a cross set in its prow. Legend has it that a flock of birds flew alongside the funerary cortège, and that when the coffin was placed in the ground and the mourners began to intone a Benedictus, a single linnet bird sang in harmony with them.

Charles Darwin was a friend of Waterton's and referred to him once as 'an amusing strange fellow' after dinner at Waterton's house, where the party 'consisted of two Catholic priests and two Mulatresses!' which, judging by the exclamation mark, was unusual. It was Darwin – and specifically Dr David Weeks' interpretation of one of his findings – that gave me the idea for my next category of eccentricity.

Mill's *On Liberty* came out just six years before Waterton died. Eighteen–fifty-nine, when Big Ben first rang, was also the year Joshua Norton, an English bankruptee living in San Francisco, declared himself to be Emperor of the United States (he reigned from 1859 until his death in 1880 and was looked after by the citizens of San Francisco who fed and housed him). More importantly, 1859 was the year that Charles Darwin's *On the Origin of Species by Means of Natural Selection* was published.

As most children in the non-devout Western world are taught, Darwin's principle of evolution by natural selection is based on the idea of the survival of the fittest. While he certainly acknowledged the need for the greatest possible diversity in this, and at one point suggested that 'a high degree of variability is obviously favourable', for Dr Weeks Darwin did not go far enough. By the time he had finished his ten-year study of eccentricity Weeks was convinced of the pivotal role eccentrics had played in the evolution of English society. In *Eccentrics*, he argued that had Darwin based his observations on human behaviour he would have found evolution to be based not on the survival of the fittest but on 'the survival of the most creative, or the survival of the rule-breakers rather than the rule-enforcers, even the survival of the outrageous'.

This was manna. Manna from Weeks. It exorcised completely the memory of watching the corpse of English eccentricity being dusted down in Eastleigh, and allowed me to imagine that eccentricity meant something more than that. Perhaps society really did become static, stratified, averse to change and in thrall to custom without a dose of eccentricity in its margins, as Mill and Weeks seemed to suggest.

When you think of the eccentric in these more abstract terms he or she begins to resemble a trickster figure. Within the mythology of just about every pre-industrial culture there exists an imaginary trickster whose role is to subvert and test society's understanding of what is or is not permissible. Trickster is the taboo-breaker and taboo-tester, the one who suggests the possibility of change by paradoxically both flouting and upholding society's conventions. He operates from the fringe too. 'Every group has its edge, its sense of in and out, and Trickster is always there, at the gates of the city, and the gates of life . . .' as Lewis Hyde explains in his excellent *Trickster Makes This World*.

Whether he is the Greek Hermes, Nordic Loki, American Indian Coyote, West African Eshu or Legba, Chinese Monkey King or African-American Signifying Monkey, trickster is the wise fool, the creative idiot, the one who speaks in a silence and says the unsayable. He is the well-mannered ruffian with a knack for sniffing out the inconsistency in his surroundings and exploiting it or making fun of it. Trickster forges connections that others either will not or cannot, and because of this he is prized and books are written about him. Trickster was also uncannily similar to Weeks' more lofty version of the eccentric, a character 'positively associated with the ability to conceive startlingly original artistic and technological breakthroughs'.

This was heady stuff, and sufficiently light yet sweeping for me to get carried away with its implications. It also revealed a limitation in my journey so far. I hadn't really expanded the boundaries of eccentricity to include this trickster figure. For my next category I needed to find someone who not only inhabited the tolerated margins of English society, but was in the business of producing startlingly original artistic breakthroughs. A character whose actions fundamentally challenged or changed the way people imagined the world around them yet without posing a threat, in the way that a tattooed leopard man or a woman with a collection of gnomes might not. With part-time eccentric, collector eccentric and animal-loving eccentric accounted for, I went to find a more trickster-like version of the English eccentric.

6

THE MAN WHO FAKES FAKES

I'm crouching in the tramline of a wheat field. Above me a silvery tendril that looks like the path of a tracer bullet stretches towards the horizon and to the left I can see the moon. It is full, and the sky clear, but my eye keeps being drawn back to the line above that flickers and shimmers as the night breeze swoons sleepily over us.

Behind me a man is standing in the middle of the crop. The space around him is an inverted pedestal. He holds two surveyor tapes and is leaning back a little to keep them taut. It makes him look like a waterskiing scarecrow. The figures around me, each one no more than a darkened blob with the moon casting them in silhouette, are quiet and on edge.

A few minutes ago someone spotted the beam of a torch zigzagging back and forth across the wooded valley that abuts the field. It began to move towards us at speed. Perhaps it was a farmer who had heard us? We had walked away, hurriedly, feet stumbling into divots and potholes cloaked by night. A man near the front began to run and so did I. No one knew what to do. We got to the gate at the far end of the field and squatted in the shadows. The beam disappeared − perhaps he was continuing towards us with his torch turned off? A pleasant flood of adrenaline worked down my body like a chill, starting in my shoulders yet petering out by the base of my spine. Apparently the beam of the torchlight was not strong enough to be a farmer lamping for rabbits or foxes, and besides it was moving too shakily. Whoever it was, they'd see us lit up like seven Christmas trees if we went out into the field. Perhaps we should call it off, one man said. A question mark appeared above our heads in a collective thought bubble.

The moon that night was like a floodlight. Its strength and

melancholy hue abstracted the landscape around us, bleaching its craters and indentations of gradient out of sight. It was as if the fields had been covered with baize and were now a giant tabletop, with the trees on the horizon as overgrown avocados, and the hillside opposite a curtain, its tapestry of thickets, burrows and scrub reduced to a series of undulating folds and curves.

There was a whispered discussion about what to do. Nobody knew. Then J, the man whose house we had gathered at before, spoke up. His voice, though reedy, had the kind of conviction that you could follow. He said we should just get on with it and strode purposefully into the field. The rest of us filed meekly after him. The tractor tramline curved, taking us into the middle of the field, and soon the centre was laid.

There followed six hours of maths and grunt-work. Lines were marked, segments measured and remeasured, margins of error assessed and recalculated before we split into two teams and got out the stompers. A stomper is a plank of wood with a single length of rope attached to either end. To use it you place your foot in the middle of the plank and pull tight on the rope, as if setting the string on a crossbow. With the plank in mid-air, one foot in the middle of it and your arms keeping the rope taut, you line up the section of crop to be flattened before coming down on to the board with all your weight. The wheat flattens as one, like a body of Muslims prostrating themselves in prayer. You lean back, edge forward and crash down once more, flattening the next section. The sound is like chopped tomatoes being thrown into a hot frying pan. You repeat the procedure. You do it again. And again. And again, until you have worked up a sweat and your shirt sticks to the uppermost part of your back. All around you other men are stomping sections of corn. The field is silent but for this rhythmic crunching. In unison it sounds like a family of spaced-out cicadas, 'Crrrr–unch, step, pause, crrrr–unch, step, pause, crrrr–unch, step, pause.'

Silhouetted, and lit only by the moon, they look ethereal: six wraith-like reaper men scything a sacred crop. An owl sails noiselessly past and the moon, the egg-timer on proceedings, is now two-thirds of the way through its arc. It has just begun its descent towards the horizon. When we started it had been low and yellow, fizzing in the sky like an orange-flavoured vitamin tablet dissolving in water. Now it is tired and there is no longer any colour in its face.

At last it is done. We collapse in a circle at the centre, seven Pucks satisfied with the night's trickery. Cigarettes are lit and the group anticipates how the crop-circling community will respond when the circle gets spotted, *if* it gets spotted. They crack jokes about getting caught, about the farmer who is just round the corner or the crop-circling enthusiast out on patrol hoping to catch aliens making a formation. Dew coats the heads of corn and night, Shakespeare's 'vast sin-concealing chaos', our day, draws to a close.

Final checks are made to ensure that nothing is left behind, no watch, jumper or scrap of paper, because if everything goes to plan there will soon be hawk-eyed researchers inspecting what we have made and any trace of our humanity would ruin the effect. Satisfied that we have removed ourselves entirely from the process of creation, that the author is not only dead, but buried and has had his grave-stone kicked in, we leave.

I have just made my first crop-circle.

You'll find the earliest and least ambiguous reference to an English crop-circle in *The Mowing Devil* – not a periodical for die-hard lawn-mower enthusiasts but a four-page pamphlet published in 1678 describing two mysterious oval shapes that appeared overnight in a Hertfordshire oatfield. These, the pamphlet explains, were cut by 'the Devil himself'. It goes on to suggest that when faced by such a phenomenon, one that exists squarely beyond sensory comprehen-sion, you should 'reasonably gather that there are certainly such things as DEVILS'.

Fast-forward 300 years to the late 1970s and little had changed. Unexplained crop-circles began to appear in fields across Wiltshire and Somerset, only this time they were thought to be the work not of curly-tailed DEVILS, but of flying saucers, aliens or ancient Celtic spirits. Perhaps all three in cahoots.

This crop-circle phenomenon accelerated throughout the 1980s, the designs becoming geometrically more sophisticated while a cottage industry of self-styled experts speculating about the meaning of these formations grew up in tandem. In 1990 English crop-circling reached its statistical zenith. More than 700 circles were recorded that summer.

Then, in 1991, the whole thing looked set to cave in on itself. The now defunct *Today* newspaper ran a confession by two men from Southampton who revealed it was not aliens that had been making most of these formations over the last ten years, but them. The whole thing was a hoax! The headline that day was, 'THE MEN WHO CONNED THE WORLD'. Rather than trying to decipher the thoughts of reclusive paranormal pen-pals, the crop-circling experts, who called themselves 'cereologists', or croppies as they were known in the press, had spent the last ten years poring over the flattened doodlings of two men in their fifties called Doug and Dave. Their tools? A few wooden planks, a measuring tape and two baseball caps with picture wire fastened to the crown.

It was the kind of revelation you'd think would force the entire crop-circle mythology to collapse, like a Jenga tower with all three pegs removed from its lowest layer. But it did not. There were people who lost interest, yes, but a hard core of cereologist devotees remained, and in some ways Doug and Dave's admission only strengthened their conviction. It required them to develop a new set of answers to accommodate this revelation. In time this would make their arguments even less assailable to common sense.

By 2007 the crop-circling mythology was alive and well. Thanks to its repositioning as part of the thriving New Age movement, and the emergence of the internet, cereology was enjoying a wider and more international following than ever before. Also keeping it alive was the fact that these circles continued to appear.

But who was making them?

Since Doug and Dave's confession in the early 1990s there is one man largely responsible for keeping the whole thing ticking over. He is England's leading crop-circler, and with England as global epicentre of the circling phenomenon, that makes him the world's leading crop-circler. Allegedly. You see, John Lundberg never claims responsibility for any circle that he makes illegally. He works anonymously and under cover of darkness – though if crop-circling were an Olympic sport, Lundberg would be champion with at least three consecutive gold medals lining his mantelpiece, and would be on course for a knighthood and subsequent career as minor sporting celebrity launching government initiatives to get inner-city kids into sport.

In terms of the scale of his audience he was unlike anyone else I had met on my journey. What he got up to at night fundamentally challenged and often altered the phenomenological landscape of not tens or hundreds of people, but thousands, if not millions.

His very existence is denied by extremist factions within the crop-circle fraternity. The more militant ones – the Hezbollah element, as John likes to call them – have thrown bricks at him, shoved potatoes up his exhaust and regularly send him hate mail. They call him a fraud, a charlatan, a perpetrator of a heretical hoax, or they'll claim he's a covert member of the British secret service employed by the government to spin a web of disinformation.

'They're the sort of people who would quite happily see me killed,' Lundberg once said. 'Honestly. They would never say that to a journalist, but privately I'm sure they would.'

Undeterred, John Lundberg and a handful of other circle-makers have been flattening designs in fields in south-west England over the months leading up to harvest for more than a decade. Their formations are so brilliantly executed and geometrically complex that thousands of medically sane enthusiasts who inspect them are convinced that they have been made by 'beings of superior intelligence'. The word 'enthusiast' is important here. It underlines that you can often find in an image what you *want* to.

While the views of these crop-circling enthusiasts are certainly obscure, as well as non-conformist and perhaps eccentric, I didn't feel the lives of these cereologists represented, as Mill put it, experiments in lifestyle. They were followers of an obscure belief-system equivalent in some ways to a cult. They were members of a team, a gang, a tight-knit with-us-or-against-us unit designed to include and exclude. I was more interested in the guy running around behind the scenes allowing this belief-system to continue, the kind of person who skives off school while everyone else is trying to get into the 1st XI, someone who didn't want to be part of a tribe. For this reason I wasn't drawn to non-conformist groups with their own jargon like the crop-circling enthusiasts, or Goths, skateboarders,

Punks, the Bright Young Things before them, nor any other slightly rebellious 'herd of independent minds', in Harold Rosenberg's phrase. These groups were mostly anathema to eccentricity. In his study of social stigma, Erving Goffman refers to them as 'deviant communities', a member of which should not be confused with the one-off mascot figure Goffman calls an 'in-group deviant', who was in many ways identical to an eccentric.

Once I had decided it was John Lundberg rather than any of the crop-circling enthusiasts that I wanted to meet, I emailed him. He wrote back to say we should have lunch.

In the way he holds himself, his patter, dress, demeanour, John Lundberg does not look like an eccentric. English, yes, but not eccentric. His hair is specked grey and cut short so it sticks up in tufts from his forehead. He's in his thirties with a square jaw and a stoop, and there's an intensity to the way he talks or listens. In both you sense an obvious intelligence and perspicacity. I got the impression he says nothing that he does not mean. At the same time he is affable and quick to see a joke. He's a nice guy, is what I'm trying to say. I liked him.

Although he would fail most of Dr Weeks' criteria for characteristic eccentricity, his status as England's leading crop-circler – or circle-maker as he put it – seemed to fit my understanding of eccentricity.

'I think as circle-makers we certainly inhabit the chaotic fringe,' he said in a light south London accent. 'And yes, I think that's where innovation stems from.'

We were in a Mexican restaurant near the British Library. There was only one other table occupied and with no music the room had a slight echo. Outside it was drizzling.

'Great weather for circling,' he whispered. 'No dog walkers out.' He settled into his chair a little more.

'So you do it in the rain, or whatever the weather?'

'Quite often we'll do it in the rain, yes – we've been known to come back caked in mud.'

'But why?' I said. It came out as a bit of a whine. 'I mean what makes you want to do it on a cold night?'

Plate XX a

H. Hemming

T. Lundberg

The Crop Circler

His voice became more expressive, as if he really wanted me to understand this. 'I guess to begin with it was about wanting to make something that you could pass off as an original. That was it. Although by making a crop-circle you're not exactly copying an original, are you? You're faking a fake.'

Our food arrived.

'And how did it start?'

'Well, bit embarrassing to admit,' he said, tucking into his meal with gusto. 'But when I first became aware of circles, which was probably during the mid- to late '80s, I was willing to believe that there was something very odd going on, you know, maybe something alien.' He looked sheepish and his otherwise tough delivery went limp for a second. 'This was when I was at art school. You see, I'd been interested in the paranormal from a very young age, but I'd never been able to combine my interest in the paranormal with my art. Then I had what you could call an epiphany. Suddenly I realised that making crop-circles presented unbelievably fertile ground in which to be making art. Don't forget that at the time whenever you turned on the TV or radio you'd hear about these mysterious crop-circles.' He said the word 'mysterious' as if telling a ghost-story. 'So I went out and made a crop-circle. I just wanted to see what would happen, and over the last ten years I've really begun to understand the effect of what I'm doing, and it's incredible. I mean it. I really think it beats the hell out of Richard Long or any other land artists.'

'Why's that?'

'Because of the conceptual side of what we're doing. We're manipulating belief. They're just making sculptures.'

'And are there many others making circles?'

'Very few. We're the main group, me and about eight or nine others who come out with me from time to time.'

'And have you ever been caught, or been close to getting caught?'

'No, although in the mid-'90s the Hampshire Farmers' Union did put up a £2,000 reward for information leading to our arrest.'

'But nothing came of it?'

'Right. You see, to get to the stage where you can actually prosecute, you have to physically catch us in the act, in the field, making the circle. Everything beyond that is circumstantial and would not necessarily stand up in court. That said, one of the guys who worked with us, unfortunately, got done. He gave the wrong person some information which ended up with the police. Which ended up with him getting convicted. He was charged £75 damages I think it was.' Our plates were cleared. 'One of my collaborators, a guy called Rob Irving, a few years back wrote a piece for the *Independent* about crop-circles and a policeman came round to his house the following day. He said he wanted the names of the people who had been making crop-circles with him. Rob said he couldn't provide that, that it was privileged information. The policeman got a bit cross, and said he was only interested in the man-made circles.' He grinned. 'And Rob says, "But they're all man-made." And the police officer says, "Look. I don't want to get into a philosophical discussion here. But they can't *all* be man-made."'

Once the novelty has worn off and the adrenaline you feel as you stride out into the field no longer gets to the hairs on the back of your neck, I was confused about what made the idea of standing in a field on a rainy night more appealing than sleep, a warm bed or a body to curl up next to. For John it was the conceptual underpinning of what he does, which at first might sound like bullshit. He comes from a contemporary-art back-ground, and the idea that an artist could dedicate their life to making anonymous patterns in fields because of his interest in an intellectual concept feels in many ways unEnglish. We're meant to prefer utilitarianism to ideas. It's also suspiciously uncontem-porary – art. This, after all, is an industry that can drown in its obsession with irony, half-measures, self-glorification and trope. For John Lundberg the manipulation of belief that his circles allow is enough of a reason to go out at night and risk catching a cold, getting a fine or having a circling enthusiast throw a brick at you. His heroes are Emile d'Hory, Clifford Irving and Orson Welles, all masters of the ersatz. He has never been paid for making one of these illegal circles. Instead the possibility of exploring our innate desire to explain unusual phenomena as otherworldly, while pushing the limits of what it is generally thought a group of humans can do with a rope and a few planks of wood in one night, is enough. Or, in his words, 'It beats the crap out of pushing paint round a canvas.'

John was bad at school. 'A complete shit,' as he put it. In his teens he got into trouble for something so bad he wouldn't tell me what it was. 'I did a very bad thing, Henry,' was all he would say. At that point in his life he saw art and art school as the way out, and is certain that had he not found art he would have ended up in prison.

When he got to art school he realised that making art was not about the freedom to do whatever you wanted, but product recognition. He became disillusioned. He found crop-circling. It offered salvation. He took it.

More than a decade later his hobby had become his profession and he made a good living creating legal crop-circles for cereal companies or bands pulling PR stunts, in between making his non-commercial 'real' circles for the benefit of the crop-circling fraternity. It was a strange and utterly unique existence.

Charles Saatchi once approached him and asked him to make a crop-circle in his gallery, but he declined, realising that a fake of a fake of a fake was a fake too far.

There is at least one other English household name who is, or was, fascinated by crop-circles, though he arrives at it from a very different perspective to Saatchi.

'Talk about a surreal experience,' John began. 'So Professor Michael Glickman, one of the leading crop-circle evangelists, was giving a lecture, and there's about twenty people in this room, most of them plastic-bag-rustlers if you know what I mean.' I didn't, but guessed that this meant train-spotter types. 'And at the back of the room I saw a guy who was an absolute dead ringer for Mike Leigh, you know, Oscar-nominated director famous for the gritty realism of his films. And I'm thinking, "This can't be Mike Leigh. What the hell would Mike Leigh be doing here?" So at the interval I go up to him and say, "You look just like Mike Leigh." He said, "I am Mike Leigh." I couldn't believe it! I assumed he was there researching a film. So I tell him what I do, that I make them and so on. But it turns out he's best friends with the guy giving the talk, Glickman, one of the most hardened cereologists, and is an absolute believer in the reality of crop-circles. He's even written the foreword to a crop-circling book.'

It is called *Vital Signs: A Complete Guide to the CROP CIRCLE Mystery and Why It Is NOT a Hoax* (capitals NOT mine).

'And how did the conversation go from there?'

'Er. Badly.'

'I bet.'

'He went to go and get some shortbread biscuits.'

John leaned back in his chair.

'What's that feeling like, of meeting someone who believes fully in crop-circles when you're the one making them? It must be very weird.'

'You go through different stages. Initially your impulse is to want to scream from the top of the nearest high building, "I MADE THAT." Especially when you see one of your circles on CNN. But ultimately you realise that that short-circuits the process. Being a circle-maker is an extremely masochistic pursuit.' He shook his head ruefully. 'You're an artist who can't claim his work, which puts you in a kind of weird situation. It's . . . You should find out for yourself. Really.'

We arrived at different times. It was important that no one saw me enter with John as some of the people there might have recognised him. Above the door were the words 'Coronation Hall' in an elongated, 1950s font. The building was long and low, its fittings a creamy Eton blue. That evening it was bursting at the seams like a Bigg Market super-pub at closing time on Saturday. All of the crop-circling beau monde were in attendance. They were congregating by the doorways, chatting in the carpark, holding seats for friends who had not yet arrived and doing that thing of craning your neck over your shoulder and looking around anxiously for your friend who is twenty seconds late. The room twittered with anticipation.

I had just walked into the 2007 Crop Circle Connector Convention in Alton Barnes, a small Wiltshire village that has been the global epicentre of crop-circling activity for the last thirty years. I was also trying my best not to look guilty. For the people in this room the idea, let alone the reality, of what I had done by making a crop-circle with England's leading crop-circler was repulsive.

The hall smelt of tea and the summery sweat of about 200 men and women, though all sensory input went mute as I heard several enthusiasts describing the circle I had helped to make. The conversation was just a few yards away. Making sure to look in the opposite direction I shuffled backwards towards it.

'It's phenomenal,' said one, breathlessly.

'A sure sign,' said another.

'Yet more proof.'

This felt fantastic. I thought I'd have to leave the room to shout or just go and grin at the evening sky. It wasn't the idea of spinning an elaborately constructed peccadillo that I found so thrilling, nor the sensation of helping to keep alive a mythology – though that was good – it was the thumping yet evanescent pleasure of watching someone be moved by something you have made. I'm not sure what it says about my paintings and sculptures but I couldn't think of the last time anyone had reacted like that to something I had made. This was different. Silent memories of the night flooded back, one by one, and like individual waves of tiredness each froze my mind momentarily.

I can't reveal exactly how many weeks had elapsed since that night in the fields, as that would give away the identity of our circle, which would render it impotent. It would become a dud, its magic confiscated; and you see we created a lot of magic that night. I'm not sure how to measure magic, which units to use, though you could start by counting the number of pages of internet discussion dedicated to our circle. There were plenty. Over the course of the summer, tens of pages appeared as computer-bound code-breakers tried to decipher the astronomical, religious or numerical significance of our circle. The field itself was visited by enthusiasts from all over the world and calculations were made about the repetition of the various motifs within the design, what the angles added up to, which ancient cultural traditions were implicated, the relevance of the date, the location and the staggering precision of the finish.

To puncture any of this would be like telling a four-year-old that Father Christmas didn't exist (though I imagine most croppies when told this by their parents wouldn't believe them; they'd accuse them of being MI5 agents working for Father Christmas.

The main attraction at the circling convention was Dr Horace Drew, a jowly, red-faced Australian with mean-looking hair who whispered that he was operating under a pseudonym. He wouldn't reveal why. Perhaps he'd forgotten his name. I didn't really care, but 'Horace Drew' wanted me to know that this was not his real name and that there was an intriguingly unknowable reason as to why he kept his identity hidden.

'Horace' began his talk by saying, 'I am a very well-respected scientist.' He then told the audience that as well as having a perfect understanding of 'Darwin theory' he was 'one of the first scientists to make a DNA'. Back in 1961, apparently. From here he plummeted into a great sea of half-truths, lies and pseudo-academic speculation about the meaning of crop-circles in a rant loaded with expressions like, 'This is absolutely scientific fact,' or 'Scientifically hundred per cent true.' Images of crop-circles superimposed with arcane mathematical diagrams flashed up behind him as he urged us to see that these formations were 'Proof that the ancients are trying to communicate with us. Anyone who says otherwise is just talking bullshit.'

'Horace' had the delivery of an evangelist, and the crowd – well, that was the strangest thing, the crowd loved it. They murmured encouragement throughout. All around me were gasps of 'It's so true!'

'Now it all makes sense.'

'But of *course!*'

'Ahhhh.'

After the talk I interviewed members of the audience, who were consistent in their beliefs: each acknowledged that, while some of the circles were man-made, most were not. They were far too complex to have been made by human beings. They'd say this in a very English, don't-be-ridiculous tone of voice. They prided themselves on being able to spot a 'fake', while others described the extraordinary healing power to be found at the centre of these circles. One man told me about strange lights he had recently seen near a circle.

In the background I could see John hovering at the back of the room. The magician in disguise. Though few recognised him the enthusiasts here loathed him, or at least the idea of him. He didn't seem to mind. While he was someone they disliked, he was also a man they depended on absolutely. Most of the circles described by 'Horace' had been made by John.

Allegedly.

Before leaving I asked him what it had been like to attend the convention.

'It was unexpectedly emotional,' he said, his voice low, eyes darting around to make sure no one was listening. 'It reminded me why I do it.'

This extraordinary dedication to his hobby and the reasons why he did it confirmed him as the trickster-like eccentric Englishman I was after – though I was not yet sure how his anonymity affected his standing in my search for the leader of the tribe.

If John Lundberg was in one respect a secretive rural graffiti artist, he wasn't the first. Once described as 'the genuine article, a double-stitched-and-riveted English eccentric', William Mounsey is the godfather of English rural graffiti.

Born at the beginning of the nineteenth century Mounsey was a solicitor from Carlisle who served as an army officer in the Middle East where he became fascinated with Jewish culture. On his return to England he took to wearing the sacred robes and full-face beard of a Jewish elder, and was soon known as 'the Jew of Carlisle'.

Mounsey was passionate about getting himself out into the country-side with a sharp metal implement in his pocket. He would make his mark in cliff walls or in the slippery flesh of rocks that lined the water's edge. Along the banks of the River Eden in Cumbria you can follow a trail of beautifully carved Stars of David, Mounsey's initials, or snatches of poetry inscribed into cliff walls and rocks by the riverbank, all written in Latin, Greek, Arabic or Welsh, and often with letters or entire words carved backwards so that they present a kind of code for enthusiasts to decipher.

What about urban graffiti artists – do they warrant a place in an exploration of English eccentricity?

Within the inward-looking world of English urban graffiti Robin Banks is a pioneer. Rather than ape American graffiti artists of the 1970s and 1980s in font, coloration and content by spraying his name repeatedly in a derivative and generic way, Banks, a.k.a. Banksy, has developed his own instantly recognisable style. It is full of anger, wit and satire. It is subversive, but not threatening. What's more it's easy to get: each work is a visual one-liner. Yet as one of the best-known English artists of the early twenty-first century, in an age beset with celebrity, Banksy is anonymous. He subscribes to no man's tribe, is radically individual, an artistic pioneer, marginal, illegal without being immoral, and is both tolerated and celebrated. In many ways he's a modern-day eccentric.

Yet the most interesting part of Banksy's story has less to do with him and more to do with the way he has been received by the English public. Similar to a series of other English inventors, rock stars and artists, Banksy's output was, initially, positioned at the very edge of acceptability and legality until widespread recognition pulled it into the centre and claimed it for the English cultural mainstream. By 2007 his art was going at auction for hundreds of thousands of pounds, his books selling tens of thousands of copies while his earliest public daubings in Bristol were being preserved by the local council as if made by prehistoric man.

Throughout, he maintains his anonymity. He is an enigma. He appears to be simultaneously centric and eccentric. Lionised as part of the mainstream, yet marginal. Was such a thing possible? I was not sure, but the possibility was as fascinating as it was confusing.

At one point John Lundberg was going to work with Banksy, until he decided that there was no point as his work was about *not* claiming authorship – that's what gives it its power, unlike Banksy's where there's no real ambiguity about who made it. At this point in the conversation John had told me about the principle of ostension which, he added, was at the heart of why he made crop-circles.

'In a nutshell, ostension is about the enactment of mythology.' He had placed his elbows on the table. 'So let's pretend there's a rumour about a ghost at the end of your road. A young girl who appears from time to time, and maybe she runs out in front of cars. A very specific piece of mythology, right?' I remember thinking at this point what a great teacher John Lundberg would make. His delivery was both snappy and direct in a way that made it almost impossible for your mind to wander. 'What ostension would be is if you or I decide to dress up as a ghost and actually go to that place, pretend to be that little girl, and someone sees this. So in their minds they would witness the embodiment of a mythology, and in this sense that mythology becomes real. That's a key part of what we do as circle-makers.'

'You flesh out pre-existing beliefs?'

'Sure. What I'm working up to is probably best explained with the story of a guy at the end of the eighteenth century, James Tilly Matthews. He was an inmate of Bedlam, and was convinced he was having his mind controlled by a machine. Essentially, he thought there was a mind-control machine buried somewhere near parliament being operated by French spies. Now because his doctor published an account of Matthews' treatment, the concept of a machine that could control minds entered our collective imagination. This was the first cultural reference to a mind-control machine anywhere in the world. And if we spin forward to the present day, there's a detailed culture of conspiracy dedicated to the supposed existence of mind-control machines. That's ostension. It starts with some guy in Bedlam saying he's being controlled by machines. It's written down and disseminated, and a hundred and fifty years later, bingo, you've got people adamant that the CIA is trying to control their minds. So you plant a seed in society, and once that begins to propagate, and for me it's inevitable that it will, at some point, the idea attains a certain reality. It's exactly the same with what we're doing. We're just making flat discs in a field. But the mythology surrounding them allows them to be interpreted as something else and lets people believe they're made by hedgehogs, or aliens, or whatever they say.'

Crop-circles, mind-control machines, the ghost who appears at the end of the road – perhaps in an identical sense there was a mythology of the English eccentric driven by ostension.

When in 2005 a struggling comedian called Tim Fitzhigham with a show coming up in the Edinburgh Festival rowed across the English Channel in an antique bathtub designed by Sir Thomas Crapper he was described as an eccentric. Sir Ranulph Fiennes told a journalist that Fitzhigham was 'keeping the art of British eccentricity well and truly alive'.

This seemed to be an exact analogy with the ghost at the end of the road. The fact that people who read about this man and his bathtub could interpret it as proof that eccentricity was 'well and truly alive' suggested that English eccentricity was a pre-existing mythology that was there to be confirmed. To be dubbed eccentric all you had to do was to dress up as one while doing something amiably harmless or funny. You didn't have to *be* an eccentric, you could just look like one.

This meant that at some point in our history the idea of the English eccentric had put down roots, and they were deep roots, because this idea was now much easier to confirm than dispel. It reminded me that I needed to find the point at which it all began.

Besides everything John explained about ostension the three most important words he uttered during our various conversations were: James Tilly Matthews. The story of this man's encounter with Bedlam gave me a way into late-eighteenth and early-nineteenth-century attitudes towards madness in England, and this revealed the point at which eccentricity became detached from madness. Matthews' story also brought into focus the madness of King George III, which would turn out to be pivotal in the history of English eccentricity.

In 1797, as John had suggested, James Tilly Matthews' life was turned upside down with a single word. From up on high in the gallery of the House of Commons he shouted 'Treason!' at a Home Office minister, the future Lord Liverpool, and was consequently detained in Bethlehem Royal Hospital for lunatics, also known as Bedlam, for most of what remained of his life (the last few years were spent in a private madhouse).

At the time, Bedlam was 'schizophrenia set in stone', according to the historian Mike Jay. To look at, it was monumental, with a façade modelled on the Tuileries Palace in Paris. Inside lay a cancerous inversion of this, a place where inmates were bled and given emetics so they'd vomit. Otherwise they were prescribed opium to keep them quiet, though unlike some of their predecessors they were not on show to the public. Earlier in the century members of the public would pay 2d to visit Bedlam and hire sticks to prod the inmates if they felt they weren't getting their money's worth.

Following Matthews' death in 1815 a House of Commons Select Committee adjured that Dr John Haslam, the apothecary at Bedlam and the man responsible for Matthews' treatment who had also written an account of it, should be dismissed. There followed wholesale reform of Bedlam, though this was not only in response to Matthews' mistreatment. It was part of a broader pattern of psychiatric reform largely set in motion twenty-seven years earlier by the madness of Matthews' sovereign, King George III.

From the summer of 1788 until the spring of the following year the King of England suffered what was believed to be his first bout of insanity (he is now thought to have suffered from porphyria). Rather than being shipped off to Bedlam he was treated by a team of medics led by the pugnacious yet talented Rev. Dr Francis Willis. There was widespread public sympathy for the ailing monarch, often expressed in hostility towards the doctors treating him. When he recovered in 1789 the nation rejoiced. A Prayer of Thanksgiving was distributed to every church in the country, there were balls, parades and fêtes, 756 popular petitions of thanks came in from around the country, there was a thanksgiving procession, to which the City of London contributed £1,020, and a triumphant and lavish service was staged in St Paul's Cathedral. There were even medals emblazoned with rays of sunshine cast to commemorate the event.

One of the many effects of King George's illness was it encouraged English understanding of madness to mature. Insanity lost some of its stigma. If the monarch could be struck down by madness, then so could anyone. It was no longer equated with ignorance, superstition or sin. Equally, once the techniques of coercion and restraint used on the King became known, a new-found public sympathy for the insane emerged.

Following the publication of a report that showed similar levels of admissions to lunatic asylums in mainland Europe as there were in England, the English also began to grow out of the idea that madness, so often referred to as the 'English Malady', was something from which only they suffered. At the same time insanity came to be seen as curable thanks to the well-publicised example of Dr Willis and his royal patient, despite the King's later relapses.

This gradual realignment of English attitudes towards madness during the Georgian era, sometimes referred to as the first psychiatric revolution, changed the way eccentricity was understood. It allowed clear water to appear between 'eccentric' and its unruly side-kick 'insane'. You can see this in an article published in the January 1807 edition of *Athenaeum*, where the author argued that while in England 'nothing is more common . . . to meet with persons who have got what is called a twist, that is, some wrong-headedness or eccentricity of practice', and that this may well expose them to mild ridicule, eccentricity 'within certain limits is tolerated, and accounted no subject for legal interference'. So being eccentric disqualified you from the madhouse. This was at a time when an increasing number of people were being incarcerated against their will in privately run madhouses. You can also spot this distinction in a number of legal rulings, for example in the case of *Anderson* v. *Burrows* in 1830, where Anderson successfully sued Burrows after he tried to have him thrown into a madhouse. Anderson argued he was not mad, but merely a gentleman of 'parsimonious and eccentric habits'.

By then the distinction between madness and eccentricity had taken root, allowing the latter to take flight – though this in itself still does not reveal when the term first came into use.

～

On 19 August 2006 in a property column in the Weekend section of the Guardian *there was a description of an island on the Thames. The columnist added as an aside: 'I like islands. They attract nutters.'*

The paper later received a complaint from a reader who felt the columnist was wrong to use the word 'nutter' because it made the piece uncomfortable to read. Instead, he suggested, the writer should have put: 'I like islands. They attract eccentrics.'

During the weeks leading up to his suicide in 2003, according to the Hutton Inquiry into the circumstances surrounding his death, Dr David Kelly was belittled by ministers and government officials who referred to him as a 'Walter Mitty' character, a 'rogue element', a 'show-off', 'a bit weird' and 'rather eccentric'.

The *Yorkshire Post, in a piece written not long after the Hutton Inquiry, argued that 'branding Dr Kelly a "show-off" and "eccentric" was wide of the mark'.*

I need to take stock of where I am. At last there is a trail opening up before me faster than I can run but I have to make sure I'm not haring down the wrong path. I need to put the journey, time and the people that inhabit both on hold.

It is eleven months since I saw Zac Monro and his whale-shaped hedge. What has changed? Or, put more carefully, what did I not do before setting out that I should have done? I did not think hard enough about what it means to be called eccentric, that's what. I did not try to work out why in contemporary journalism 'eccentric' could be a term of endearment much less hostile than 'nutter' in one context, while in another it is a term of belittlement and significantly worse than being called 'a bit weird' or a 'rogue element'.

To describe most of the subjects in his study Dr Weeks used aliases. This, he explained, was because of 'the ambiguous connotations, and the wholly unwarranted social stigma perhaps still attaching in some people's minds to the designation "eccentric"'.

'Maybe someone will say you're eccentric doing this,' Ann Atkin had said towards the end of our interview. It had felt unusual. I couldn't think of the last time I had been called eccentric and it was this more than anything else which made me see that like a paw with hidden claws this word contained a latent barb.

Charles Waterton described the sensation of being called eccentric as 'like an undeserved pinch'.

Ever since the eighteenth century there have been times when this word has been used to puncture the impact of a person or an idea – look no further than Lord Monboddo and his 'eccentric' idea that man was descended from primates. Labelling an individual eccentric does not turn them into an outcast, however. Instead it draws them in and renders them less oppositional or less of a threat. While 'eccentric' can be a term of endearment and often feels like a compliment in the sense that it is a virtue to be strong-minded, playful and inventive as well as relatively unconcerned about how others perceive you, it also envelops, like the corpulent arms of an overbearing matron, and this, strangely, is where its power lies. It can be used to extinguish the explosive potential of a marginal person or idea by holding them close.

I had also failed to predict that most of the time you can't use this word as a self-referent. Just as Yossarian, in Joseph Heller's *Catch-22*, would, by calling himself crazy, rule himself out of any such craziness, or the man who describes himself as charming is anything but, the term 'eccentric' can generally be applied only by another. This changes what I am doing. It means that if I tell an interviewee that I think they are eccentric and they say, 'Yes, I am an eccentric,' either they are an exhibitionist who thrives on being called eccentric and it's something they crave, a look-at-me-I'm-mad kind of person who may just be in need of attention rather than truly eccentric, or, more rare, they know that society thinks they are eccentric but are no longer fazed by this.

None of the people I had met so far fell into either category, and to limit my journey to attention-grabbing exhibitionists or those with skin so thick they don't mind what they are called might make the journey short and a bit repetitive. Precisely because this term is generally not a self-referent and works better when it is applied by another I *should* be seeking out people who don't refer to themselves as eccentric, as well as those who do. I decided that from here on I would begin by telling potential interviewees that I was searching for creative non-conformist individualists: marginal yet tolerated Englishmen or women who made original connections and saw the world differently to the rest of society. I would try to avoid the e-word. If they answered that call, then I wanted to meet them.

Though I needn't have worried about any of this before approaching Beany. He was happy to be called just about anything. He was also significantly less concerned with anonymity than John Lundberg.

7

LOOK AT ME

'Hello, Henry. Captain Beany here,' he began in his sing-song Welsh accent.

'Hello, Captain Beany.'

'Hello,' he said, sounding more relaxed. 'I was wondering how far you'd got?'

'Well, I've just crossed into Wales, so I should be with you in about an hour.'

'Brilliant. You see I was wondering if, you know, if you'd like me to bean up?'

'Eh?'

'You know, I was just thinking like—'

'I see what you mean.'

'It only takes a few minutes, you know, just a bit of make-up and body paint.'

'Perhaps we could start without? Then you could put it on later if you liked.'

'Okay,' he said.

I couldn't tell if he sounded relieved or a little peeved.

'That's a plan,' he went on. 'As it's only us. I don't mind. Anyway I'll see you in an hour!' His voice went up at the end of the sentence, like a slogan at the end of an advert.

'Absolutely.'

'Beantastic!'

'See you in a bit then.'

'Right you are, H.'

He hung up.

It was the first time I had heard the voice of the man who had changed his name by deed poll in 1991 to Captain Beany. Once a computer technician, Beany was now an amateur inventor, struggling entrepreneur, sometime painter, leader of the New Millennium Bean Party, Director of the Baked Bean Museum of Excellence and superhero from the Planet Beanus who came fourth in the 2001 Best British Eccentric Award. Over the last two decades he has run for political office at every level, from local council by-election to European parliament. His website. lists as accomplishments his appearances on *GMTV*, *This Morning*, *Lorraine Kelly*, *Ready Steady Cook!* and *It's a Wonderful Life* (South Korea). He has been insured against abduction by aliens and has made a record called 'Rapping with the Captain'. He was an eccentric exhibitionist. That was why I wanted to meet him. My collection was looking a little bare without one.

You don't need to venture far into the English cultural landscape to find yourself an exhibitionist. They are everywhere, doing everything they can to get your attention. From Speakers' Corner via the hopefuls who queue up to audition for the *X Factor* – 150,000 wannabe starlets applied in 2007 – to the dandified peacock you might see strutting the streets of Soho, or performers at the Edinburgh Festival, this country has a healthy distribution of self-publicising extroverts, people who crave an audience like a cushion needs a cover. Often they will design an *alter ego* who embodies this flamboyant and generally more loud part of themselves. This invented character allows a kind of protection. 'Man is least himself when he talks in his own person. Give him a mask and he will tell the truth,' as Oscar Wilde once wrote.

From a distance Captain Beany's life represented something more than the one-dimensional urge to don a mask and get the attention of a passer-by. Beany seemed to have taken the possibility of the performing exhibitionist to its extreme, which is why I wanted to meet him.

Yet I had no idea what he'd be like in person, and as the road drew me closer to him I became nervous. The idea of being the entire audience for a man who longed to perform made me anxious. Always when I meet someone like that I feel small, as if I have lost my voice.

I could still turn back, I thought, as the motorway slalomed past Cardiff. My back-up in the exhibitionist eccentric category was John

Westwood, a forty-two-year-old dealer of rare and antiquarian books who, when Saturday comes, or whichever day it is that Portsmouth FC are playing, becomes the larger than life 'Pompey Bugler', described by the *Sun* as 'one of football's maddest fans'. He watches his team half naked, his chest emblazoned with the tattoo 'I'M PORTSMOUTH TILL I DIE', wearing a curly blue wig, clown boots, waistcoat and elongated top hat as well as a drum that he'll thump from time to time. But it was Captain Beany I was off to see. If nothing else, he was one of the few people who didn't seem to mind being called an eccentric.

I parked beneath a crumbling block of council flats and climbed a communal stairwell. The smell was an acrid mixture of piss and disinfectant. I reached the second floor and knocked on a door. It was opened by Captain Beany, out of costume.

'Here I am,' he said, grinning broadly. 'Sorry to be in human form, but like you said, thought it might be easier that way.'

Beany was bald and had a shiny head. He was also shorter than I imagined and, at fifty-two, older as well. His skin came in tight over his face and his eyes were bright. They beamed like a child's as he led me through his small and impeccably clean council flat. It smelt of recently applied furniture polish. In his sitting room were several studded leather couches like one you might find in a Harley Street waiting room. With a squeak I took a seat while Beany went through to the kitchen to put the kettle on. Arranged over the walls and set within a custom-built set of shelves was an expansive collection of photos, cuttings and certificates documenting the life of Captain Beany. It was a shrine to Z-list celebrity. In the centre was Beany's Dafta statuette from the Best British Eccentric Award of 2001 that he had spray-painted gold.

'It was bronze coloured originally, you see,' Beany remarked on his return. 'So as not to contravene the Oscar regulations.' I couldn't tell if he was being ironic. He gazed wistfully at it before setting down two mugs of tea on coasters. 'Ah, I remember when I found out about those eccentrics awards. It was brilliant. I got an email from the people running the competition to say I was a regional finalist, and I thought, "Blimey! This is just what I need to spur me on."'

'And how was it? The awards ceremony?'

'Oh it was fantastic. I felt like a movie star. Afterwards when the press called up about the awards I would say . . .' – he put on a grand English accent – '"Yes, you are speaking to the number-one eccentric in the UK. I mean Wales, sorry."'

That reminded me: Captain Beany was Welsh. I was worried this might rule him out of English eccentricity.

'Oh don't worry too much about that,' he said. 'I'm not really from Wales anyway. From Planet Beanus, aren't I? So yes, where was I? Ah, the eccentric awards. Following the ceremony they did a feature on me in the local press, and also in the nationals. It was brilliant!' I soon realised that saying 'brilliant' was an important part of being Beany. 'And the funny thing is,' his voice became a whisper, 'that awards ceremony made me see I've been eccentric as long as I can remember. That's me. But it's brilliant. I can't fault the media, and people like yourself, and the internet. I've got loads of projects to do,' he said a little unconvincingly. 'I'm setting up my own business now. Oh. That reminds me, I've got a couple of things to give you.'

He handed me a worn plastic bag. Inside was a Captain Beany doll with a toothy grin and exaggerated chin as well as several flyers from his recent election campaigns, a certificate to say that I owned the Beany doll, stickers, business cards and a fridge magnet with a picture of Beany holding a BEANUS flag. On it was the slogan 'If the planet is worth saving – then let's save the planet!' The environment was in, he told me, and if it meant more coverage for him he was right behind it. He had signed everything in the bag, dedicating it to me.

How had this happened? How had Barry Kirk arrived at this point, alone, a middle-aged superhero living in a council flat? I asked him about his life up until Captain Beany.

'From the beginning?'

I nodded.

It starts at school. He remembers being the one always looking out, not in. The joker. He would turn up to class wearing a false nose and glasses and the kids would laugh. So would the teachers. He was always 'acting a gong', as his mother said. Or as the teachers would say, 'Barry's just being Barry.' When he finished school he got a job in a computing firm where again he became class jester.

Plate X XVₐ

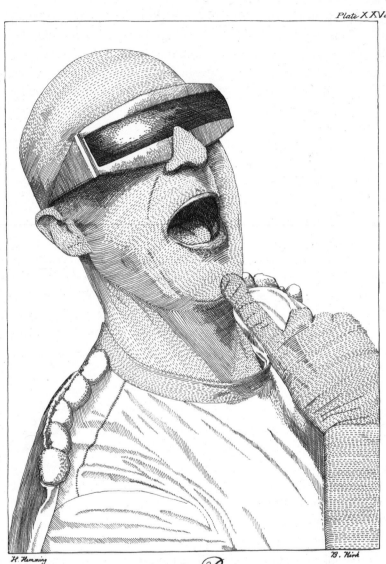

H. Hemming   B. Kirk

Captain Beany

'I would entertain the boys,' he said, eyes alight. 'Do impressions, wackiness. Take me on the razzle and get a couple of drinks in me and I would just go off my head! And everyone would say, "God, that Barry, he's a hell of a boy. He makes me laugh so much, he makes me weak in the head." Things like that. And sometimes I would get into embarrassing situations, like one time when there was a male stripper, and I thought, "Why don't I take my clothes off, do a bit of strippin' like?" So I did.' He mimed removing his clothes, and started up in the voice of someone else, '"Did you see that boy Barry? Ahh. What an arsehole."'

There was a softness to his voice as he said this, the words shooting out excitedly in his lilting Welsh accent. He was self-aware, and more fissile than I had anticipated.

'So, between you and me, I was wild then. Still holding down the job. But also I was letting myself go. I was putting on weight, the belly was getting fatter. And I decided I had to change my lifestyle, so I thought I'd train for the local marathon and get fit. Thought I'd get sponsored for it, so I said I'd get dressed up.' He pointed to a photograph. 'That was back in 1983.' I thought of Tom Leppard – this was the year he began to get tattooed. 'And it was fantastic! With this marathon running I could assert my imagination, dress up, get fit, and it was all for charity. So, hand on glove, if it wasn't for charity I'd probably be in a mental home by now!'

He said things like 'hand on glove' a lot.

This charity run was the first time Barry appeared in the papers. He got a huge kick out of seeing himself in print, and still does, regardless of what's been written about him. Framed on a shelf beside him was the front page of the *Sunday Sport* with a picture of him in Beany costume next to the headline 'BAKED BEAN FREAK'S BUM EXPLODES'.

'Um. Why did they write that?'

He looked nonplussed, as if watching television and he'd just noticed that his lottery numbers hadn't come up.

'Oh I don't know, it's a notion they got, that I ate so many baked beans my bum would explode.'

He moved on.

By now hooked on dressing up in public and getting noticed, photographed or written about, Beany went on more runs and designed weirder outfits. He pushed a shopping trolley from Cardiff to Port Talbot dressed as an angel. He went on a Flashathon flashing all the women in Port Talbot, his modesty preserved only by a box of Flash washing-up powder. Come Easter he'd have eggs cracked on his head for charity, which hurts a lot more than you'd think, he said, wincing at the memory. Back in the days of Eddie the Eagle he dressed up as Barry the Budgie – anything to get in the papers. But all this was merely the overture. Beany's life-changing moment came in 1986.

One afternoon he was in his flat rifling through his record collection when he came across the Who's third album, *The Who Sell Out*. It featured Roger Daltrey on the cover sitting in a bath of baked beans.

'And I thought to myself, "What a great idea".' He was breathless at the thought of it. 'So I called my local charity and said I was going to lie in a bath of beans.' He put his hand to his ear like a telephone. 'They said, "How long for?" I said, "Er. A hundred hours?" They couldn't believe it! Nor could I. When I worked out that meant four days and four nights I was a bit worried, but I couldn't get out of it by then. So I did it. We went to a local hotel, a supermarket donated a year's supply of beans, 360 tins it was, and I sat in them.'

'Did it get cold?' I said, trying to picture it.

'Ohhh, I'd never realised how cold it was, Henry.' He shook his head, still smiling, voice bright. 'I only had small pants on. Really hard to get to sleep as well. I was hallucinating baked beans I was so tired, didn't know what to do with myself. Raised £1,500 for charity though. Then when it was over, and I was shaking . . .' He grabbed his arms and shuddered. 'I said, "No more baked beans for me. That's it." Then the story went all over the world, I was interviewed on *Newsround* and everything. It was brilliant! So I had my five minutes of fame. "That's it," I thought. "Back to normal. Back to work." But then I got bored again and someone said I should be called Captain Bean, because before everyone was calling me Captain Kirk. You know, Barry Kirk. So I went to a solicitor and said I fancied a change. That was 1991. I had all my documents changed, including my passport, to Captain Beany. Even got my photo for the passport with me fully beaned up.'

The year before, in 1990, with crop-circling at its acme, Ann's gnome reserve flourishing and Tom Leppard settled in paradise, Beany began his career as a politician by beating the Liberal Democrat candidate for Aberavon into last place by nine votes.

'Another bean in the cap,' he grinned.

In 2001 he formed his own party, the New Millennium Bean Party, and has contested consecutive general elections in Aberavon and Cardiff Central. The last one, in 2005, didn't go so well, though his manifesto made it into the local papers which of course from Beany's point of view made the whole thing worth while. The press had picked up on some of his more obscure policies, including: children to choose their parents; Prince William to be given a bachelor pad in Cardiff so he can date Charlotte Church; a new royal yacht to be built so the Queen can get away from Camilla; BBC Wales to get a sense of humour; and all tattoos to be bilingual in both English and Welsh.

Though it was not exactly a coherent and intellectually acute critique of British society, there were a surprising number of interesting ideas in Beany's manifesto.

Having a joker, oddball or exhibitionist like Beany stand for election isn't that unusual in English politics. I was fascinated by how the English electorate responded to these eccentric candidates. The language used to describe them in newspapers, for example, is usually sympathetic or lightly amused. Rarely damning.

Also standing for parliament in 2005 was 'Lord Biro', a man who campaigned in an Elvis jumpsuit and won 116 votes in Wollaton West for the Church of the Militant Elvis Party. Then there was the Death, Dungeons and Taxes Party whose policies included lowering the school-leaving age to nine and the immediate annexation of France. They received 93 votes in York. Another candidate who caught my eye was a man claiming to be the reincarnation of King Arthur. He ran for Winchester but, like so many others, failed to recoup his £500 deposit. I made a note of his name, thinking little of it at the time.

From the way these colourful mascot figures are described you get the sense that as a group the English don't mind having them present at an otherwise sombre occasion. They restore some kind of levity, even if it's virtually unheard of for one of them to be handed political power. The only time an eccentric in this mould might get his or her hands on a slice of political power would be in a more decorative position like mayor, which is part of the reason why the eccentric and apparently gaffe-prone Boris Johnson could be taken at all seriously as a potential Mayor of London, and why the monkey mascot of Hartlepool FC, H'Angus the Monkey, was elected Mayor of Hartlepool in 2002 (before being re-elected in 2005).

Soon after Beany's first electoral mini-success in 1990 he was asked by 'Screaming Lord' Sutch to join the Monster Raving Loony Party. Beany declined, saying he didn't want to be part of another man's tribe, even if Sutch was someone he admired a great deal and I think wanted to emulate.

In a political career lasting more than thirty-five years David 'Screaming Lord' Sutch, '3rd Earl of Harrow', fought a total of forty-one elections, more than anyone else in British history. On several occasions, like Beany, he embarrassed the candidate from a major party into last place, and it was after he contested Margaret Thatcher's seat of Finchley in 1983 that the deposit required to stand for parliament was raised from £150 to £500, which you could count as an achievement. Just. Otherwise Sutch did not pose any kind of threat to the politicians he opposed. At one point the bookmakers William Hill estimated that there was a better chance of Elvis Presley crashing a UFO into the Loch Ness Monster than Lord Sutch becoming Prime Minister. But he continued to stand, and most of the British public continued to enjoy reading about him or seeing him on television. Something would not have felt right without him there.

When not running for parliament Sutch was the lead singer of a band, though he was the first to admit he had no vocal ability whatsoever. His live act included being wheeled on stage in a coffin dressed as Jack the Ripper while throwing worms at the audience. When out of costume he liked nothing more than to be at home feeding birds, a bit like Tom Leppard, or drinking tea with his mother, on whom he doted. Shortly after she died, he committed suicide.

What's so interesting about the eccentric Lord Sutch is that several of his 'loony' policies – including pet passports, patients to be sent to hospitals abroad, and the elimination of world poverty – don't sound so outlandish in a contemporary context. John Major once described Screaming Lord Sutch as 'by far my most intelligent opponent'.

The equally eccentric Lieutenant Commander Bill Boaks stood for election forty times, one less than the record-holder his friend Lord Sutch. Boaks was the first to suggest that the Royal Navy shouldn't scrap HMS *Belfast* and should instead use it as a floating naval museum. At first he was ridiculed. Campaigning on an armoured tricycle, he dedicated much of his life to getting people out of cars and improving road safety. He is also largely responsible for the pedestrianisation of Carnaby Street. Boaks was entirely fearless, and in protest at the speed cars drove would often set up his deckchair in the fast lane of the A40 and sit there reading the *Daily Telegraph* while traffic thundered past, horns blaring. Boaks died at the age of eighty-one. In a road accident.

Once he'd changed his name Captain Beany left his job to go and look after his mother, whom he adored. She died in 1991. On his biceps he had two tattoos, one of her, the other of Princess Diana.

'I liked Diana a lot,' said Beany, fingering the inked flesh on his arm. 'She was the odd one out from that royal family. The nonconformist, if you like.'

Following the death of his mother, Beany attempted to return to normality. He began to sign on every two weeks – though whenever a job came up that he was qualified for he'd never get an interview because of his name. The people at the employment centre told him to change it, insisting that he had no future as Captain Beany. This got to him.

'So I said, "Right, I'm going to prove you buggers wrong. I'm going to start my own business."' His voice became stern. 'So this,

Henry, is where we come to the crutch of the matter. I had a lump of money, but what was I going to do? Pursue the bean dream? Or go into the depths of insanity, go downhill and drink myself to death. So I said, "I'm going to form my own company, Captain Beany Enterprises." It was formed on April Fool's of last year!'

He was rocking back and forth at the memory of it.

He employed a local manufacturer to make Captain Beany dolls including the one in my party bag, which by the way was a great doll, and had I been the right age I would have happily spent a few hours swooshing him through the air.

'And I want charities to bean–ifit from it,' he said, his bean puns by now so engrained they were no longer flagged by a change of tone, just a slight pause preceding each. 'So these toys are selling in Woolworths, selling like hot cakes they are.'

'Fantastic!' I was completely on his side by now. 'They've been taken on by Woolworths?'

'Well, not exactly. They won't stock the dolls, but they give me a berth around Christmas time where I can sell them. They know the kids come in to see me.'

Beany is resilient. He has written letters to, 'Hamleys, Gamleys, Marks and Spencer, whatever, asking them to stock my doll. But it's hard. You see, round here,' he gestured at the room, every surface loaded with Beany memorabilia, and at Port Talbot beyond, 'I'm a big fish in a small pond. Elsewhere it's a bit different.'

London suddenly felt a long way away.

'You see, I have a feeling things are going to come my way soon.' He turned to me, smiling hard, his face worn with optimism. 'I really do.'

'Do you ever get depressed?'

'Oh yes,' he said, his voice once again softening. 'I get my lows, like anybody else. Because I know I've got something here.' He clenched his teeth. 'It's so frustrating. I should be out there travel-ling the world!' His voice went deep, to superhero setting. 'Captain Beany!' Then back again. 'But there are times when I don't want to be Beany, when I just want to go into my shell and be a normal person.'

He felt more vulnerable than I could describe.

'Have you ever been married?'

'No, no . . .' He looked at the Dictaphone and began to shout. 'Oh, hello. Never been married! Looking for somebody! Tin of beans. Someone wild, wacky and weird like me!' He lowered his voice and turned back to me a little sulkily. 'You see, I've had a couple of relationships, but usually they get to the point where either they have to adapt to me, or they try and change me. But they can't change me.'

'And do you ever get a negative reaction to what you are, to being Captain Beany?'

The thought twitched in his mind like paper drying in the sun.

'Yes,' he said. 'There are the ones who look at me and wish they could do something like me.' I could hear his mother speaking. 'But they don't have the guts. They're jealous of me, you see.' She was soothing him after someone had bullied him at school, stroking his head. 'It's a double-edged coin. There's people who love you,' he went on. 'But others who tell you to go and get a job and have a mortgage round your neck and conform.'

Often he wonders if he's made a mistake in becoming Beany. He's gone to see a psychiatrist to 'work out what he is', and was told he had nothing to worry about. Lord Sutch also went to see a psychiatrist to work out what he was, and returned triumphantly from a Harley Street clinic to give an interview to *Today* magazine that ran with the headline 'I MAY BE MAD BUT I'M NOT INSANE AND I'VE GOT A CERTIFICATE TO PROVE IT'.

Still, there have been times when Beany has lost his confidence, especially after one of his brothers died. But he's got it back now, he assured me.

'Full of beans!' He grinned hard like a teenage beauty queen five minutes into her routine. 'But when I think about my life, you know, whether I've been a success with fame and fortune, I think, "I've had a bit of fame. Not so much luck with the fortune." But at least I've made a contribution to society. I've raised over £100,000 for charity. But money is nothing. It's not the end but the means. Or the beans . . .'

He looked down at the floor.

'Do you think eccentricity in this country is on the wane?'

'Well, there's a very important psychologist, he's called Dr David Weeks. Have you heard of him?' I nodded. 'And he said that, as a nation, Britain has more eccentrics than the whole entire America, because we're an island. We're stand-alone people. We don't like to conform. But I don't think it's on the wane, I just think people are generally more reserved now. Perhaps there aren't as many people like me who want to dress up as lunatics. I don't know what I'd do if I didn't dress up.' He sighed, open and fragile, as he had been throughout our conversation.

Beany showed me round the Baked Bean Museum of Excellence, which was no more than the room next door that he'd stuffed full of baked-bean merchandise bought on eBay. I decided it was time to go, but before leaving I took a picture of him out of costume, something Beany would allow as long as I promised not to use the image anywhere. It was as if I'd stolen a part of his soul by photographing him without his mask.

On the way back I thought more about costume. Not only did it seem to be at the heart of eccentric exhibitionism, and a code for escape and the chance to be seen, but it was a part of what made an eccentric *look* eccentric. Being dressed in a way that's unusual for your age, era or gender is an important ingredient in being labelled eccentric, in the way that the comedian in his bathtub *looked* eccentric. Yet Beany seemed to be something else, something more than a look-at-me-I'm-mad exhibitionist. His need to inhabit a costume had become so deep-rooted that his entire life was now dedicated to it. Costume was a crutch that had supported him since the day he turned up to school in those funny glasses and through the big black frames could see nothing but laughter and sheer unabated joy directed only at him. You could say that the rest of his life has been spent trying to recreate that moment.

Costume of Screaming Lord Sutch (1940–1999)

Top hat with rosette in centre that reads 'VOTE LORD SUTCH'

Imitation-leopardskin jacket with more rosettes, badges and a
    plastic flower
Shirt with leopard-print pattern, purple cuffs and collar
Brass loudhailer with rosettes and badges attached to the side
Boots with leopardskin spats

Costume of Captain Beany (1955–)

All-in-one lycra orange bodystocking
Aqua-colour orange face-paint
Gold cape with 'BEANUS' emblazoned on circular background
    shape
Gold pants (worn over the bodystocking)
Three-quarter-length gold gloves
Gold visor with a horizontal mirrored slit
Flag with the logo 'BEANUS'
Gold boots laced up to the shin with gold laces
Gold buckled belt
Pouch on belt (bean bag) to keep keys, passport and credit
    cards
Laser Bean gun to thwart alien life-force

Costume of Henry Cope, 'The Green Man of Brighton' (early nineteenth century)

Green pantaloons
Green cravat
Green frock coat
Portmanteau, coloured green
A waistcoat decorated with green stripes
A green silk handkerchief worn around the neck
Green watch-string
Green seals fastened to the buttons of his waistcoat
Beard dyed green
Green garters

Green gloves and whip
Green brain (according to an anonymous poem written about
    him in 1806)

Costume of Beau Brummell (1778–1840)

Dark-blue tailcoat cut without a waist seam, giving the cutaway
    around the hip a gentle curve, gold buttons and unusually
    long sleeves set high in the shoulder, little in the way of
    shoulder pads
Plain shirt made of fine linen, washed and dried in the coun-
    tryside, and lightly starched
Neckcloth made from a triangle of Irish muslin, plainly seamed
    and folded over twice at its widest point before being
    wrapped around the neck
Tight cream pantaloons
Trouser stirrups
Pale and unadorned waistcoat
Braces (hidden beneath the waistcoat)
Black Hessian boots with tassle at the front

~

Beany's obsession with costume had permeated his being to its core,
and as I began to look beyond him to find other Englishmen who
had a similar love of dressing up, I kept reading about dandies.

The dandy is an entirely English invention, yet rather than being
a label this word represents more of a cult, in the sense that there
is an original dandy and there are those who follow in his footsteps. Beau Brummell was the original and most refined of
Dandiacal Bodies. Since the early nineteenth century successive
generations of poseurs from Lord Byron to Algernon Swinburne,
Oscar Wilde, Noël Coward, Stephen Tennant, Quentin Crisp and
George Melly through to the artist Sebastian Horsley or comedian Russell Brand have in some way followed his lead. Yet the
further removed from Brummell you go, historically, the more

cartoonish each dandy becomes, until you begin to lose sight of what the original looked like.

In an age of perfume, make-up on men, frills and feathers, froth and flummery, Beau Brummell was someone who took regular baths and wore clothes of a restrained palette. His outfits were famous for their simple, well-cut lines designed to show off a muscular physique, all of which feels removed from what the modern-day dandy has become, a shift begun by the flamboyantly unBrummellian Comte d'Orsay.

I began to wonder whether the idea of the English eccentric had undergone a similar process of gradual distortion as a result of successive reinvention over the years. Before meeting any other potential eccentrics I needed to learn more about how the idea of the eccentric had been handed down through successive generations, and what changes had taken place during the transmission. This would also give me a better understanding of exactly when this figure emerged.

It turns out that the vehicle, if you can call it that, largely responsible for bringing into the present the idea of the English eccentric is a tradition of books called 'eccentric biographies'. They have not only championed the idea of the eccentric Englishman but have helped to thread it into the fabric of our national identity.

Similar in form, most of these eccentric biographies consist of a series of 'historiettes', or potted biographies of eccentric characters. The tone is antiquarian, anecdotal, instructive, so they read as a series of cautionary tales with the moralising taste disguised by a pinch of humour.

From the *Bradt Guide to British Eccentrics* and Brewer's *Eccentrics, Rogues and Villains*, published or republished in the twenty-first century, you can trace the genealogy of these eccentric biographies back via *Timpson's English Eccentrics* (1991), *A Book of English Eccentrics* (1984), *The Man Who Ate Bluebottles and Other Great British Eccentrics* (1981), *The British Eccentric* (1975) and many more until you arrive at one of the best known (though least readable) works in the genre: Sitwell's *The English Eccentrics*, now in its umpteenth edition. Dame Edith Sitwell, a social and intellectual snob capable of put-downs such as 'A great many people now reading and writing would be better employed keeping rabbits,' or the more sweeping 'The man of genius and the aristocrat are frequently regarded as eccentrics because [both] are entirely unafraid of and uninfluenced by the opinions and vagaries of the crowd,' published her compilation in 1933 when the popularity of the genre was flagging. The book sold well, suggesting that the English had not lost their appetite for eccentric biographies, because it is only when you continue back past Sitwell into the Victorian era that you find the cult of the English eccentric at its apogee.

The Victorians fawned over eccentricity like no other version of English society, and it is largely thanks to their fascination with the subject that the idea of the English eccentric exists at all today.

Most of the Victorian eccentric biographies produced to feed this hunger were nationwide in scope, books like Wilson and Caulfield's *The Book of Wonderful Characters* (1869), Cochrane's *In the Days of Dandies* (1890), or *English Eccentrics and Eccentricities*, written by the printer, antiquarian, druggist, sub-editor of the *Illustrated London News* and servant to the radical Sir Richard Phillips, John Timbs. First published in 1866, it was reprinted at least four times during the next three decades. Many of the characters in Sitwell's book, particularly her ornamental hermits, were pinched from Timbs' work. You can also see the Victorian fascination for eccentrics writ large in the novels of Dickens, where just about every character other than the hero or heroine could be called eccentric.

As well as these compendiums, there were biographies of individual eccentrics like J. R. and H. H. Robinson's *The Life of Robert Coates* (1891), or C. J. Apperley's *The Life of John Mytton* (1870); and, often overlooked in any survey of the Victorian literature of eccentricity, the works that focus on a particular region, like *Yorkshire Oddities* (1877), or *Sunderland Notables* (1894).

James Gregory, the only historian to have studied this subject in real depth, describes the pride with which Victorians from, say, Newcastle would talk about their city's unusual characters and eccentrics. They helped bolster regional identity. The authors of ballads, engravings and written collections such as *Lore and Legend* would dab at the eye and sigh nostalgically over eccentric Geordies who once made the place 'Canny Newcastle'. With the rapid urbanisation of the north-east, the memory of these characters had suddenly become precious like toys from childhood that are about to be thrown away.

Just as they were important in constructing both local and national identity, the memory of these eccentrics also kept a large number of artists, balladeers and publishers in business. An advert for *Wonderful Magazine*, a monthly periodical devoted to eccentric characters, urged the public to go and buy the magazine to provide the publisher and his hacks with 'Ready Rhino' – thieving slang for cash. As well as eccentric biographies there were music-hall performances commemorating well-known eccentrics of yesteryear, mugs, tobacco-stoppers and even walking-stick handles with the faces of famous eccentrics carved into them.

For the first time in its fairly brief existence, the idea of the English eccentric was being commodified. The fact that they were dead allowed these eccentric characters to become equivalent to curios or artefacts that you could, in a sense, collect and feel ownership over. So the Victorian mania for tales of English eccentrics fed into the contemporaneous interest in the *Wunderkammer*, a cabinet of curiosities, as well as the universal urge to dream up taxonomies and impose them on the world around you, just as I was doing with my categories of eccentricity. That I talked about 'my' eccentrics confirmed this unthinking sense of ownership that stems from collecting. Ownership also implies some kind of benevolent superiority, which reinforces the idea that at all times the eccentrics in these Victorian biographies were positioned *beneath* the reader.

What else drove this Victorian interest in eccentric characters? Perhaps more than anything else it was nostalgia for an age before mass industrialisation and straitlaced conformity. Eccentrics embodied this bygone era. They were more *natural* than their successors. There was nothing manufactured, mechanical or customary about them. You could also point to the Victorian fascination with the grotesque. With their emphasis on the weird and wonderful, eccentric biographies were in many ways literary freak-shows.

For other Victorians this love of eccentrics was born of something else: their growing concern that 'character' in English society was being eroded. John Stuart Mill, Herbert Spencer and Charles Dickens shared this fear. In various articles, essays and novels they wrote ominously about society's increased emphasis on conformity, authority and order, worrying that one day it would stifle creativity.

Continuing back from the Victorian heyday of eccentric literature towards the Regency there are fewer eccentric biographies and they are generally more expensive. Yet the genre remains healthy. At least sixty books describing eccentric characters were published during the first half of the nineteenth century. It's only when you reach the late eighteenth century that the trail goes cold, abruptly.

Eccentricity is not a timeless English trait that continues back past the Dark Ages to Roman times. It doesn't even make it as far as the Tudors. Oliver Cromwell would have given you a blank look if you'd buttonholed him about the state of eccentricity in England. As would Shakespeare, or Sir Isaac Newton, though he might have thought you were talking about a planet with an eccentric orbit.

One of the earliest eccentric biographies ever published appeared in 1788. The only one to precede this was the Rev. Nathaniel Wanley's *Wonders of the Little World*, published in 1678. Both Robert Browning and Charles Darwin read it as children. Although it doesn't specifically mention English eccentrics, and 'eccentricity' doesn't appear in Wanley's index of characteristics – if it had, it would have appeared between 'Eaters great' and 'Effeminate men' – this book has a similar form to the eccentric biographies that follow. For any hunter of eccentricity, it is the holiest relic. A fully preserved Brontosaurus skeleton, El Dorado and Year 0 somehow rolled into one.

According to the Rev. Wanley, a vicar from Coventry, *Wonders* examined 'what man hath been from the first ages of the world to these times'. To make his venture sound more noble he quotes the revered philosopher Francis Bacon on the advisability of creating a 'collection . . . of the extraordinaries and wonders of human nature', which is roughly equivalent to *Heat* magazine mentioning Proust in its editorial. The only other book that in any way pre-empts Wanley's *Wonders* in the sense that it compiles lists of odd behaviour and presages, subtly, the notion of English eccentricity is Robert Burton's *The Anatomy of Melancholy*, first published in 1621. Similarly, if it had been published when he wrote it, John Aubrey's *Brief Lives* would have been a harbinger of the Victorian eccentric biography. But it isn't, because it wasn't. Instead it remained largely in manuscript form until 1898, two centuries after the author's death.

Not only do you find the first reference to eccentricity as a characteristically English trait in the late eighteenth century (in a periodical), but this is the moment when eccentric biographies began to take off. This correlates perfectly with the first legal references to the term as well as the moment when insanity began to be better understood following the apparent madness of King George.

I had my starting point.

All that remained was to work out why this cult of the English eccentric began, what purpose it might have served, and what permutations the eccentric character has undergone from his first appearance in the English cultural landscape through to the present, when a computer technician called Captain Beany could be crowned Britain's fourth most eccentric personality in an awards ceremony sponsored by a cereal company. I also wanted to understand why every time I explained to someone what I was writing about they started to grin the moment I said the e-word.

8

IT'S FUNNY BECAUSE IT'S TRUE

There can be few things less enjoyable than dissecting what makes something funny. Having a wisdom tooth removed without enough anaesthetic and not being able to tell the dentist because your jaw is clamped open, that's less enjoyable. Realising you've fallen out of love, filling out a tax return, reading a book on post-modern art theory, getting a parking ticket, your pet dying, being shot at – in fact, there are plenty of things worse than analysing what makes something funny, but that doesn't excuse it. The reason it needs to happen here, briefly, is that being with Captain Beany had suggested a link between eccentricity and comedy and I wanted to understand it. Perhaps it might inform what remained of the journey.

At its most pared down, humour is based on an unexpected connection, be it a collision of words, people or ideas. It's funny partly because you don't expect this combination, also because it's not *meant* to happen, so there is a sense of a norm or a (minor) taboo being transgressed. Often there is a slight thrill attached to this because somewhere in the back of your mind you imagine yourself to be the one breaking the taboo so you transgress vicariously. You are able to laugh freely because you don't feel threatened by this mishap.

When the fluffy white rabbit that guards the Cave of Caerbannog in *Monty Python and the Holy Grail* turns out to be an efficient and energetic killing machine you laugh because it's a film, you're not there, so you don't feel threatened by it, on top of which when you first saw the rabbit nibbling at the grass without a care in the world, you didn't expect it to be capable of decapitating anyone. At least I didn't.

By the same token for many people there may be something funny, in the lightest sense of the word, about running a gnome reserve, dressing as a baked-bean superhero, or covering your body with leopard markings and living as a hermit in Scotland. They are unusual, and because they are not threatening you can smile, laugh, or feel some kind of joy inside you rather than fear.

Bound up in this was the one part of what I was doing that I had begun to find unsettling. You see, in gathering together a series of people who led unusual lives that posed no threat to society, by the definition of what makes something at all funny I was setting them up to be laughed at. While there are different levels of laughing at – you can laugh *with*, be lightly amused, titter, wet yourself in a fit of hysteria – it was hard to escape Umberto Eco's idea that 'Comic is always racist: only the others, the Barbarians, are supposed to pay.' Or, in less epic terms, when you laugh, you do so at someone's expense.

Eco's line was probably designed to apply to comedy in its most generalised and macro form. It may not have been written to apply to the English and the way they use humour because this would have changed the dimensions of what he was trying to say. In England humour has a different shape.

Trying to make a joke, no matter how badly judged or poorly timed, and being able to take a joke, is hugely important to English people. Humour permeates every aspect of our lives. As Kate Fox once wrote, 'Virtually all English conversations and social interactions involve at least some degree of banter, teasing, irony, wit, mockery, wordplay, satire, understatement, humorous self-deprecation, sarcasm, pomposity-pricking or just silliness.' We are especially fond of irony. 'Irony is inescapable. We're conceived in irony. We float in it from the womb. It's the amniotic fluid,' as Hilary explained in Alan Bennett's *The Old Country*. Too many humourless social exchanges in a row and we start to feel something is amiss.

Like so much of the English contemporary character, it was not always this way. Only in the eighteenth century did writers begin to pick up on an English brand of humour dedicated to irony, sarcasm, buffoonery and the unmasking of pretensions. This was in contrast to the more coy witticisms you'd hear across the Channel.

European visitors to England were also amazed by the number of satirical political pamphlets in circulation, and by their ferocity.

As well as laughing at different things, and being able to cope with being laughed at, the English also seemed to laugh *more* than their European counterparts. Friedrich Wendeborn, a German pastor working in London, wrote towards the end of the eighteenth century that the English had 'grown more gay' over the last century, adding that what should have been the most serious chamber in the country, the House of Commons, was often lost in laughter. A Russian visitor to London, Nikolai Karamzin, noted in 1790 that the natives of this unusual island would 'take pride in the fact that they can make fools of themselves to their heart's content without accounting to anyone for their caprices'. Laughing at a fellow countryman or being laughed at yourself was usual. This is crucial when trying to understand why the English eccentric, at heart a figure of light amusement, emerged when he did.

Foreign writers also picked up on the emphasis on 'character' in English humour, something that would come to be seen as an English obsession and, in turn, become one of the other key foundations on which the idea of the English eccentric was based. For another, we must turn to the Church.

The original English comedian, the local wiseguy, joker, jester, or 'artificial fool' as he was known in medieval times, was despised by the Church and frequently dubbed 'evil'.

In the centuries before Richard Tarlton, jester to Queen Elizabeth I, the man who could 'force a sad soul to laughter' and whose epitaph read, 'all clownes since have been his apes', or Will Somers, Henry VIII's fool who could joke the king out of his darkest moods, the Church would excommunicate men they thought were pretending to be 'natural fools'. The opening lines of Psalms 14 and 53 – 'The fool saith in his heart there is no God' – were interpreted as further proof that artificial foolery was the work of the Devil.

This was part of the unique relationship between the Church and 'genuine fools' or 'natural fools': individuals who were thought to be in some way mentally disabled or impaired.

In St Paul's first letter to the Corinthians the apostle calls Christians 'fools' in the eyes of non-Christian society: 'For we are made a spectacle to the world . . . We are all fools for Christ's sake.' He urges Christians to develop strong character as well as the ability to withstand being laughed at, as if natural fools – both leitmotifs of the trial and torture of Jesus, as explored in Mystery Plays of the thirteenth and fourteenth centuries. In one such play performed in York, King Herod imagines Jesus to be the local jester who has come to entertain him. Herod has heard about this man who's famous for his magic tricks (water into wine, raising the dead, healing the sick and a few others) and who has a penchant for king-games (Herod has also heard the one about him being called the 'King of the Jews'). Clearly, this man was an artificial fool: a jester or joker who made a living getting a laugh. Jesus is led into Herod's court. Herod offers him a seat on his throne. Jesus does nothing. Herod goads him into performing but Jesus refuses to play along because to do so would imply complicity in this game-playing, and that would confirm him as an artificial fool. Even if it's ironic that a tale condemning artificial foolery should be presented by actors, themselves artificial fools, the moral instruction is clear. Jesus was not a jester. It also engenders compassion for the natural fool who exists at the edge of society through no fault of his own. He is made out to be pure and noble by his lack of artificiality.

This confirmed the role of the Church as protector of the natural fool in an era preceding asylums and psychiatry. Clerics would provide these people with physical protection in the form of food and a place to sleep, as well as moral shelter. The King looked after natural fools too, as set in stone by the Statute de Prerogativa Regis of 1339 which ensured that should any Englishman 'fail of his wit' the King would protect his estate and guard its profits. Already both Church and King, the central pillars of English society, were shaped in such a way that they protected individuals who found themselves on the fringes of society, and were genuine rather than artificial.

This complements the thrust of all Christian teaching which is, after all, based on the idea of following an outspoken loner who endures ridicule, is unconcerned by how society perceives him, sees the world differently to those around him and is not afraid to share his unique vision – a man who inhabits the margins of society and is revered upon his death.

It sounded strangely familiar.

In the words of a devout Christian police officer whom I met several months later: 'You could certainly say that Jesus was the original eccentric.'

In terms of my understanding of eccentricity this was important; it revealed two things: part of our affinity for eccentric characters stems from the fact that our morality is rooted in the Church of England tradition; also that in England there has been a consistent moral dichotomy between artificial and natural characters – the Tom o'Bedlam in *King Lear* who is in fact Edgar in disguise, next to the genuine Bedlamite for whom you are conditioned to feel sympathy – with the latter routinely lionised and the former vilified.

Yet both natural and artificial fools share one thing. They are known for saying the unsayable and in the process revealing a hidden truth. *It's funny because it's true.*

Eccentrics too are individuals who will say what they see, as they see it. They share a childlike tendency to speak honestly when others find it too embarrassing, or at times when the rest of the group simply hadn't seen it like that.

In his army days Beau Brummell was known as the regiment jester, the man who'd keep 'his brother officers in roars of laughter' with his ability to invert the world around him. 'For many years I had made a habit of turning jests upside down to look for the truth in them. For it is the concealed truth that makes the jest,' said the eccentric military inventor Geoffrey Pyke in 1931. William Scott, or 'Cull Billy' (cull meaning half-witted), an eccentric Novocastrian from the early nineteenth century famous for marching behind soldiers or preaching in the street, would astonish his listeners 'by his shrewd answers to questions when put to him'. As well as being someone whose name alone would make people laugh, Krentoma the Amazonian Indian was described by an anthropologist who studied his tribe as being the figure who was expected to subvert the world around him, and so reveal a hidden truth.

In many ways the eccentric, the natural fool and the local wiseguy perform the role that Goffman described as 'in-group deviant'. He, and very rarely she, is generally more colourful and clownish than others in the community and easier to approach. The normal rules of social distance don't quite apply. As well as being marginal, this in-group deviant will also become a kind of mascot figure that the group will defend when he is under attack.

Importantly, this character comes to be seen as someone who can and will say the unsayable, unmask pretensions, invert or subvert the norm and in the process reveal hidden truths. What he does is bound to be funny because it's unusual and it involves some kind of minor transgression. A group without at least one of these characters becomes stagnant. Too many and it is lopsided.

Beany was certainly an in-group deviant, with his life a procession from classroom wag to office joker and finally town clown. What distinguished him from a stand-up comedian was that you didn't pay to see him perform. This was significant. In many ways when you go to see a professional comedian you're paying for the opportunity to laugh without feeling guilt. If you were to laugh at Beany when you saw him out in the street you might feel a shiver of remorse later.

A Victorian housewife reading about an eighteenth-century English eccentric would find it easier to laugh, however lightly, not only because this person was dead, but because they were caged within the horizontal bars of a text. It was equivalent to laughing at a comedy sketch on television – which helps explain the popularity of these books about eccentrics.

The Funniest Joke in the World

Opening scene: A suburban house in a boring looking street. Zoom into upstairs window. Serious documentary music. Interior of small room. A bent figure (Michael Palin) huddles over a table, writing. He is surrounded by bits of paper. The camera faces the man as he writes with immense concentration on his face.

Voice-over: This man is Ernest Scribbler . . . writer of jokes. In a few moments, he will have written the funniest joke in the world . . . and, as a consequence, he will die . . . laughing.

Ernest stops writing, pauses to look at what he has written. A smile slowly spreads across his face, turning very, very slowly to uncontrolled hysterical laughter. He staggers to his feet and reels across the room helpless with laughter before collapsing on the floor and dying.

Voice-over: It was obvious that this joke was lethal . . . no one could read it and live.

Ernest's mother enters. She sees him dead, gives a little cry of horror and bends over his body, weeping. She notices the piece of paper in his hand, picks it up and reads it. Immediately she breaks out into hysterical laughter, leaps in the air and falls down dead. Cut to news-type shot of commentator standing in front of the house.

Commentator: This morning, shortly after eleven o'clock, comedy struck this little house in Dibley Road. Sudden . . . violent . . . comedy. Police have sealed off the area, and Scotland Yard's crack inspector is with me now.

Inspector: I shall enter the house and attempt to remove the joke.

An upstairs window in the house is flung open and a doctor appears at the window, hysterical with laughter, and dies hanging over the window sill. The commentator and the inspector look up and then continue as if they are used to such sights.

Inspector: I shall be aided by the sound of sombre music, played on gramophone records, and also by the chanting of laments by the men of Q Division. [Points to a group of dour-looking policemen standing near by.] The atmosphere thus created should protect me in the eventuality of me reading the joke. [He gives a signal.]

The group of policemen start moaning and chanting Biblical laments. The Dead March is heard. The inspector walks into the house.

Commentator: There goes a brave man. Whether he comes out alive or not, this will surely be remembered as one of the most courageous and gallant acts in police history.

The inspector appears at the door, helpless with laughter, holding the joke aloft. He collapses and dies . . .

From the first episode of Monty Python's Flying Circus *aired late in 1969*

The influence of *Monty Python* on comedy is similar to that of the Beatles on music. In many dictionaries 'Pythonesque' is a word (meaning 'a style of humour: bizarre and surreal'). Unwanted email is called spam because of a *Monty Python* sketch. The Pythons and their eccentric brand of comedy are also quintessentially English. Jeremy Paxman ranks them in between 'Christopher Wren' and 'easygoing Church of England vicars' in his list of Englishness. You could also argue that their worldwide popularity helped export the idea of the English eccentric around the world (when Michael Palin, one of the *Monty Python* troupe, went to meet the Dalai Lama for a travel documentary His Holiness recognised him immediately from a *Monty Python* sketch).

In the 1960s Vivian Stanshall performed alongside members of *Monty Python's Flying Circus* on the TV comedy programme *Do Not Adjust Your Set*. Stanshall was lead singer of the Bonzo Dog Doo Dah Band, as well as being a painter, poet, raconteur, alcoholic and comedian who lived on a houseboat. He was often referred to as a 'great British eccentric' by people who didn't know him, a label he loathed. In his eyes it suggested he was putting on an act. Stanshall maintained that he was not, which of course suggests he might have been a genuine eccentric. 'The mark of a true eccentric is that the dividing line between the act and the person has been long lost, or left behind. A true eccentric is never acting,' as Dr Weeks put it. Or as the same idea was explained by Edith Sitwell, 'If one is a greyhound, why try to look like a Pekingese?'

It was for this reason that Tom Leppard did not like to be called an eccentric, and perhaps why Ann Atkin wasn't so keen on it either. Over the last century this label had acquired an undertone of fakery, artificiality or acting.

This dichotomy between artificial and natural, work of the devil versus life of Jesus, or Elvis impersonator next to Elvis, was the key to understanding what the English eccentric had become. The people I wanted to meet were those who seemed to be eccentric with a small e – the in-group deviants, non-actors, real-deal eccentrics, the Krentomas of this world – while there were also those you could call Eccentrics with a capital E who were dimly aware of a Victorian stereotype and wanted to mimic it.

Towards the end of 2005 the internet search engine Yahoo! launched its 'National Treasures' campaign. This was 'a celebration of English eccentricity and normality', which, as subtitles go, is either very profound, suggesting the possibility of *centric* eccentricity, or equivalent to mounting an exhibition of urban and rural culture in being so unbelievably vague as to lack any real meaning.

The idea was for the British e-public to send in their wackiest and zaniest photos. There was a competition and a prize. The website contained banners that read: 'New wave of eccentric behaviour sweeps Britain', or 'The Eccentric Revolution!' There was a quiz that told you how eccentric you were, and the whole thing was narrated by a comic-looking actor wearing a three-piece tweed suit, four-day stubble and an ill-fitting army officer's peaked cap: an impersonator of an impersonator. There were statistics about the number of people in Britain who bought red socks or felt hats, both of which were on the up, apparently, facts intended to prove that the country was becoming more eccentric. They didn't. All they showed was that whichever Yahoo! minion was in charge of research that day clearly had other things on their mind. The most extraordinary part of this campaign was the scientific expert they had talked into endorsing it. Respected neuropsychologist Dr David Weeks gushed: 'This campaign really celebrates what British individuality is all about . . . the Yahoo! Mail campaign is a great opportunity for individuals to seek the eccentric within and capture it in a digital photograph and send it in.'

I stared open-mouthed at the computer screen. Surely this was exactly what British individualism was *not* about. The foundations of my eccentric-studying world wobbled. Unless I'd been reading his book upside down I was pretty sure Weeks' scientific study of eccentricity asserted unambiguously that an individual either was or was not eccentric. Eccentricity was not something you could work on, like going to the gym to build up your quads.

Weeks had also put his name to statistics such as 'We show our eccentric sides most often within photos and funny emails.' Apparently this emerged from his ten-year study of the subject – conducted between the mid-1980s and mid-1990s when for most of us the word 'email' was a typo rather than an interactive tool you could use to express your inner eccentric. What's more, the internet seemed to represent the opposite of eccentric solipsism; it was a place to share ideas, form groups and become more normal.

I felt let down. Up until then Weeks had been my book-bound guru to eccentricity. I had imagined meeting him one day in Edinburgh. We could have shared our thoughts on eccentricity and swapped theories about the pivotal role of the eccentric in English society since the late eighteenth century. He might have gone on to say fatherly things to me. I would have left feeling a diluted oedipal charge of affirmation and competition. Who knows, perhaps later on we could have had a fight with light-sabres. But no, it was not to be. I was on my own now.

The only useful thing to emerge from this car-crash of an e-campaign came towards the end of the main page. A bullet-point read: 'According to 1 in 5, The Marquess of Bath (1st) is the most eccentric Brit.'

My next category awaited.

9

THE ARISTOCRATIC ECCENTRIC

On the brown road-sign was an icon for a country house – three floors, slanting roof, pediment and pillars. It was a great icon. The pared-down geometric lumps made you think immediately of an English country house, one of the 'comfortable padded lunatic asylums' that Virginia Woolf described dotting the English countryside. For many, the man I was about to meet was in a similar sense an icon of English aristocracy.

Beyond a Maginot line of huts and bumps the drive wound through rolling parkland given over to a safari park, and down a slope towards Longleat, perhaps the best-preserved example of High Elizabethan architecture anywhere in England, where the family of Alexander Thynn, Viscount Weymouth, Baron Thynne of Wermister, the Marquess of Bath, Lord Bath, LB or just 'Bath' has lived, slept, dined and worn interesting outfits over the last 450 years.

After a series of conversations with men and women holding walkie-talkies I was led into a drawing room and told to wait. Blinds had been pulled down against the day and the room felt overcast. The smell brought back first dust, then dog, and finally a little damp.

'Just to warn you. He doesn't like being photographed on his left-hand side,' his secretary informed me, pacing up and down. 'Now where is he . . . Ah. I can hear a dog. Yes. That usually means he's on his way.'

Seconds later the man voted 'Most Eccentric Brit' in the recent Yahoo! survey lolloped into the room. He was tall, about 6 foot 3, broad and heavy, as I would find out later when I helped him up from a low-slung sofa and felt my back give as he heaved on my arm. His hair was arranged in a tousled, greying mane which made him look like an ageing musketeer. His beard was patchy while his eyes bulged wilfully from their sockets, giving him an incredulous air.

Plate X a

H. Hemming   A. Thynn

The Marquess of Bath

Boudicca, his almond-coloured Labrador, scampered in after him. We both fussed over her, cooing and wooing as she performed several high-speed circuits of the room, shooting under tables, over chairs and between legs before collapsing on the floor exhausted.

While Lord Bath settled on his favoured day-bed I took in his get-up for that day. It included a tartan cloth cap fixed to his head like a skullcap, red velvet pantaloons, cotton slippers and a multi-coloured quilted kaftan that looked like a tattered version of a certain Technicolor dreamcoat. I explained why I had come to see him. He said nothing. 'He's quite hard of hearing,' I remembered his secretary telling me.

'So,' I said, turning up the volume, 'DO YOU THINK THE ENGLISH ECCENTRIC IS IN DECLINE?'

He laughed. 'No. No, I don't think so.' His vowels were refined. 'I think it's as important a part now in the formation of what we are and how we behave as it ever was.' He said all of this quietly, to make it clear that there was no need for me to shout. 'It's a defence against the, let me see, the forces of uniformity, which are certainly in existence. It's about being entitled to do one's own thing.' His voice was reassuring. 'That strain has, I think, always been very strong in English culture.'

'I saw an online survey of eccentrics. In which you came first.'

'Really?' He looked happy about this. 'Yes, I think I heard about that. On the next list I was omitted though. I do find it very difficult to think of myself as outrageously eccentric.'

'Does it bother you when people call you that?'

He smiled. 'I don't think it's something to fret about. I think if it's part of someone's language that they want to regard me as an eccentric that's fine.' He began to titter. 'I don't make any special claims that' – putting on a mock-serious voice – 'I should be higher up the list of eccentrics.'

At this point it's worth running through why anyone might consider him eccentric.

The Marquess of Bath is perhaps best known for coining the term 'wifelets' which he uses to refer to his various lovers and mistresses. At the last count there were seventy-four. As well as the wifelets there is his slightly haphazard dress sense, his immensely long autobiography

– about which I'd learn more later – a belief in pantheism; the several occasions he has stood for parliament advocating an independent state of Wessex; his proposed Thynn Henge (like Stonehenge, only in Longleat); the acres of murals made from paint mixed with sawdust that he has smeared over the walls of Longleat's West Wing, including the notoriously raunchy Kama Sutra Room. There is also his persona: the way he holds himself and the irresistible mild-mannered lovability of this man. All of these, combined with regular appearances on daytime national television alongside cuddly animals, have turned him into an icon of aristocratic eccentricity.

I asked him about the time he stood for parliament as a candidate for the Wessex Regional Party.

'Ah yes,' he began, seeming to like the question. 'I first proposed the idea of independence for Wessex at a tourism conference in Taunton, but nobody was terribly interested. They told me to sit down and suggested I kept quiet. So in 1974 I ran for parliament the first time. The second was in 1979. Quite an ordeal!' he said, sounding pooped.

'How so?'

'Well, when you're standing at street corners telling people, "Vote Wessex Regionalists!" and people are asking, "What's Wessex?" it's quite hard to know at what point to start the communication.' He smiled wistfully.

Bath received 521 votes.

'Quite a flattering number I think,' he added.

In Bath's proposed order of things Wessex would be a constituency within a united Europe. 'It could be that Wessex finds itself fighting battles alongside, what shall we say, Normandy?' he explained. 'Against the Ruhr area perhaps. We would find new allies, and our identity might at those times be very much closer to those allies, in our interest in art or literature or something.'

'And you went canvassing door to door?'

'Oh yes. The only trouble was when the husbands came home from work to find me in the house with their wife. Though that wasn't much of a problem. No, only irate remarks. No physical violence.'

I imagine he has a considerable aversion to physical violence. As a child he was beaten regularly by his father, the man dubbed 'The Mad Marquess' by the media after opening Longleat to the public. He once thrashed him with a riding crop after he spilt some water. A mutual enmity between father and son was at the root of the defining moment in Lord Bath's life. This came about when he was in his early twenties and at Oxford.

'I wanted to work out why I was so determined not to conform to the lines that were handed to me on a plate,' he began, with an urgency in his voice. 'I wanted to know why I felt such discord and apartness from my own family. So I worked it all out: my religion, my politics, my morality. It all came under the heading of my particular individualism.' He pronounced his words with a degree of precision, as if they were slippery and might get away from him unless he took care.

'Right. Like a kind of creed?'

'Yes, you could say that,' he answered. 'There were two things that became important to me. Learning about the totality of the universe, how one inevitably must be a part of it and sink fully into it, yet also it was important to have one's reasons for keeping some bits aside. This also helped to explain why I was getting on so badly with my father. I began to see it in terms of frictional individuality.'

'And were you ever close to your father?'

'No, I'm afraid not,' he said, sounding like a doctor when asked by a terminally ill patient if he has long to live.

With his theory of being in place and National Service out of the way, Bath realised there was little or no role for him at Longleat. His philosophy had turned him into a black sheep and he felt, as Edith Sitwell once did, 'like an unpopular electric eel in a pond full of flatfish'. Instead he went to Paris and trained as an artist on the Left Bank. He travelled, he fell in love, and as relations between him and his family deteriorated further he became increasingly introverted, penning the first of many unpublished novels: 'Angry Young Men' (His first published novel would be the fourth he wrote, a 'psycho-drama on the subject of baby-battering', written while looking after his newborn daughter in the south of France.)

At about the same time, in his late twenties, he began to keep ever more precise accounts of his life in a series of journals, and by his late twenties Bath had completed a retrospective week-by-week account of his entire existence. He had become a compulsive hoarder of his past.

This lifestyle, in case it's at all unclear, was underwritten by extreme wealth. As Henry James Byron suggested in the mid-nineteenth century: 'Poverty and eccentricity are very bad bedfellows' (though they get on occasionally). Like many landed English aristocrats before him Bath's financial security provided a platform for his eccentricity while his inherited social standing allowed him to exist slightly apart from what society imagined to be normal, marginal or immoral. As Mill saw it, individuals were often required 'to possess a title, or some other badge of rank, or of the consideration of people of rank, to be able to indulge somewhat in the luxury of doing as they like without detriment to their estimation'.

Lord Bath's obsessive diary-keeping is at the core of what he considers to be his greatest achievement, his autobiography 'Strictly Private'. It is more than seven million words long. To give you an idea of quite how enormous that is, imagine seventy copies of the book you are reading now lovingly glued together and piled on top of each other. Having tried a mock-up of this in my bedroom involving similarly sized books I think 'Strictly Private' would be about 6½ feet tall, depending on the thickness of the paper and the font-size. There is no known autobiography in the English language that comes close to Bath's behemoth. I asked what drove him to do it.

'Well,' he began, sounding defensive, as though he hadn't really considered this, 'it's the idea that there's a task to do, and, methodically, I do it.'

'Do you think writing all of your life down is a way of preparing for death?' I asked, immediately wishing I hadn't as I watch the question settle on his face.

'Er. If you regard the life's work as something in the head that needs to be done, the completion of that can be compared to preparing oneself for death, certainly. But I don't want to dwell on it too much!' His face lit up again. 'I just feel it's something to be done, and death will be somewhere. Much of "Strictly Private" will remain unpublished until after I die.'

His wife has objected to the publication of the parts in which she appears.

'It's hugely disappointing, the first time I asked her at least. But I have it all down, out of my mind, and the publication can be for the next generation.' In his smile there is a sadness dovetailed by the satisfaction of completion.

Some of 'Strictly Private' is not so private, and can be viewed online. As you'd expect it is minutely detailed, yet parts of it are written with a surprising candour. Bath is quite happy, for example, to recount the time as a teenager when his dog had a litter of puppies and he decided to give 'these puppies the tip of my penis to suck. I don't suppose that I did it very often, or even for very long, but it was a pleasure which I still recall. And I suppose that within any statistical inquiry, I should now be listed among those who have indulged in bestial sex. I just mention this – to keep the record straight.'

In case you thought he'd been up to anything unusual.

From the drawing room we went on a tour of his murals, all painted in a naive and childlike style using Bath's signature paint-and-sawdust mixture that made the walls bulge towards you, with the encaustic several inches thick in places.

'Very hard as well,' he added, making to punch the wall.

Near the drawing room was his Paranoia sequence, the most terrifying of the Longleat murals, where tornadoes of red and yellow twist, gather and batter into different parts of the wall like invective, each passage poisonous and loaded with intent. Among these swirling shapes you could make out catatonic figures.

'So we start here with the dragon,' Bath announced with the delivery of an auctioneer. 'And the unborn foetus that emerges from the womb and out into the persecutions of my upbringing.'

'It looks quite drug-induced,' I said.

'What's that?'

'Like being on a trip.'

'Well, of course I've had acid,' he agreed. 'But I didn't paint these under acid. I think when people paint under acid they tend to be more colourful.' I couldn't think how it was possible to make it more colourful. As he moved off down the hall I asked him about a section involving an enormous policeman with a girl whispering in his ear.

'Ah, yes. The policeman.' He stopped and turned to me. 'He represents society, conformity. And my father. The girl there, that's my elder sister. Yes. That kind of thing. The two of them working together as a team.'

'How about this one?' I asked, pointing at a terrified-looking boy in the corner with a dog next to him.

'Now, that's the frightened little schoolboy,' he intoned. I turned to look at him. 'Yes. I think that's roughly my identity,' he said, his voice stout, yet immensely vulnerable. I wanted to stop the interview right there. I felt as though I should do something. I couldn't really give him a hug as he was twice my size and it would have ended up with him hugging me. But everything about this painting and how he had just described it made me feel sorry for Lord Bath. I'm not sure how this is possible as I had always imagined that to feel sorry for someone you need to feel superior in some way. I did not. I felt sorry for him because at that moment in our conversation he seemed to be a man marooned by the event of himself.

He was at the end of the hall now.

'And down here at the end,' he carried on, 'because I couldn't really leave them out, I decided one has to include one's parents.'

Amid the maelstrom of colour were framed portraits of his father and mother in sober creams. The coloration and line had a 1920s Art Deco feel to it. Just above the portrait of his mother was a grotesque demon with a huge cock that he brandished at the woman below. Because of the way it had been painted, combined with the position of the picture, the phallus looked like a feather bower continuing up from the portrait of his mother.

'Yes, my mother said once that she wasn't so sure about the headgear I'd given her!' he chuckled, before gazing down at Boudy who was keen to move on. She was trying to paw open the next door. Bath pushed it open for her and she scampered ahead, her claws on the floor sounding like dice in a shaker as we advanced through to a spiral staircase. Here were portraits of Bath's wifelets. Bluebeard's Collection, as he called it. Beneath each painting was a numbered brass plate, 1 through to 74. Bath was seventy-five years old.

'And these are all the wifelets you've ever had?'

'Yes. It goes almost all the way up to the top.' His voice went up in pitch. 'But I'm not finished yet!'

I gawped respectfully at the paintings. Bath's son Ceawlin once said of this staircase, 'It must be tremendously difficult for my mother to walk down.'

Soon we were in the Kama Sutra Room, which the prurient thirteen-year-old in me had been looking forward to. The figures here were more life-like, as if painted by a different hand and, as you'd expect from a Kama Sutra Room, they were all hard at it in imaginative positions. Each twosome or threesome was set within a circular apple shape.

'And are these all from *Kama Sutra*?' I asked a little pompously.

'No,' he said, staring intently at a man holding a woman upside down by the thighs with his head between her legs. 'No they're not. They're just me trying to be inventive. Trying to see what you can do with two bodies.' He turned to a picture of a woman being spit-roasted. 'You see, before I made this room, there wasn't any attention being paid to my work, so for me this was a good step forward for everything else I was doing.'

'Right. And do you sell much of your work?'

'Oh no.' He turned to me, eyes bulging. 'I've only ever sold three paintings in my life.'

At this point a number of things clicked into place. In the way he described them, Bath's greatest achievements were undoubtedly the Longleat murals and his almighty autobiography. The string of novels rejected by publishers were each included as chapters in 'Strictly Private', and in an identical gesture the paintings he had made as a young man that had failed to catch the eye of the dealers or collectors of the day had been taken off their stretchers and interpolated within the Longleat murals. Just as it is difficult to ignore a manuscript that is seven million words long, you can't really tidy away into the attic two-inch-thick murals that cover three floors of one wing of a large country house. In choosing to make both 'Strictly Private' and his murals so shockingly prolix Lord Bath had ensured that they could not be overlooked, because, I realised then, having his artistic output ignored over the years has hurt. He was not oblivious to what society thought of him. As an icon of eccentric English aristocracy, Lord Bath had found an identity that involved neither rejection nor scorn, but affection. It took me back to the Amazon for a moment. When Krentoma realised he was a terrible huntsman – I was told he couldn't hit a peccary if it had had its feet tied together and was placed in front of him – he sought an alternative identity in the tribe, and by becoming village shaman he granted himself status within the group. Similarly, having been the black sheep of the family, Bath relished his new role as the nation's pet aristocratic eccentric. It gave him a lovable identity. This was something he has struggled without for much of his life.

Our tour finished in his lair at the very top of the house, a suite of rooms quite unlike anything else in Longleat. Everywhere you looked were gadgets, lazy-boy chairs, half-eaten sandwiches, an enormous television, pot-plants, slowly flashing LED lights, yet none of his paintings. It looked like well-off student digs, a Peter Pan crow's-nest rather than the bedroom of a wealthy marquess. It took me back to the Serpentine, J. M. Barrie, and the eccentrics who never grew up.

Boudy came to lick me goodbye. I took the lift to the ground floor, manoeuvred past various gift shops and wandered out into the mid-afternoon sun fairly certain that I had not just met England's leading eccentric.

'A book about English eccentrics? Okay.' The brain ticks, a smile forms, but it's a cautious smile. I'm used to them by now. 'So I guess you're meeting lots of eccentric lords in country houses?' they say in a slightly higher pitch, to show they mean it light-heartedly. This has become a stock response to the one-line explanation of what I'm doing. I try and tell them that no, that's not quite what I'm up to. I'm trying to take a slightly different approach. It's not that I want them to think I'm writing a DPhil about the effect of eccentricity within post-critical existentialism, but at the same time I don't want them to think that I'm simply putting together a parade of aristocratic eccentrics. By then they're telling me about their great-uncle whom I must meet; he's a *classic* eccentric, and says the funniest things.

For many people the English eccentric will always be an elderly aristocratic or upper-class male living in a time-warp somewhere in the English countryside. Even the regularly outspoken Christopher Hitchens, in a piece about British eccentrics for *Vanity Fair*, focused almost exclusively on 'the upper classes'. This stereotype wears unusual clothes and is quintessentially lovable, harmless and old fashioned. That is why Lord Bath regularly tops polls on eccentricity.

Twentieth-century compilations of eccentric biographies have played a part in this. By generally omitting other kinds of eccentric personalities they have exaggerated this emphasis on the eccentric toff. Originally an eccentric was anyone who deviated excessively from the norm, so the term could include physical abnormality. Strongmen like Thomas 'Samson of England' Topham or Seth 'Suffolk Giant' Blowers were famous nineteenth-century eccentrics, as was the bad-natured dwarf of Durham, Count Boruwlaski. Having a misshapen nose and an unusual character might also, once, have rendered you eccentric, as would being a mathematical genius. Deviations from the social norm might qualify you for eccentricity as well, so Thomas Britton, a nineteenth-century Novocastrian was dubbed eccentric on account of being a bibliophile, chemist, antiquarian and classical-music aficionado while making a living as a coal-seller.

By the early twentieth century those who compiled and read eccentric biographies winced at the idea of including paupers or those with physical deformities. It was no longer socially acceptable to be amused at their expense. Toffs remained fair game.

In the history of the eccentric English toff two broad categories emerge. On the one hand there is the Regency rake, who is generally randy, flash and extravagant, while on the other there is a more well-meaning Edwardian gentleman: a Bertie Wooster figure who would have ummed and aahed and looked flustered had he found himself sitting next to an archetypal eighteenth-century eccentric swell.

This more recent incarnation of the toff as harmless and quaint, a category Lord Bath has made his own, is also fleshed out by men like Lord Berners, a twentieth-century composer famous for letting his horse Moti roam around his tall-ceilinged country pile as he fed her buttered scones, or painting his doves pastel shades of pink. Then there's Brinsley Le Poer Trench, Earl of Clancarty and an avid follower of UFOs who believed in the hollowness of the earth, claimed descent from aliens and founded the all-party House of Lords UFO Study Group. The list could go on, but it won't. At least not here.

The earlier stereotype is personified by men like Sir Francis Dashwood, founder of the Medmenham Monks, sometimes known as the Hellfire Club, who were rumoured to have held ritualistic orgies at Medmenham Abbey and the West Wycombe Caves. Or the less devilish but equally eccentric Robert 'Romeo' Coates, a sugar planter's son, famous for being Georgian England's worst actor.

Extravagantly rich, Coates would pay to appear in plays and wave at friends during performances. If jeered when delivering a line he would break off to threaten the heckler with his sword. Either that or he'd pay them to leave, which of course made him a prime target for further baiting. Coates inherited an estate worth £40,000 a year, so when not onstage he'd be seen wearing coats with diamonds sewn into their seam, riding in a carriage in the shape of a conch drawn by white horses. His favourite role was the lead in *Romeo and Juliet*, a part he liked so much that he rewrote the lines to better suit what he felt was Romeo's true character. Coates was renowned for his death scene. At the moment of death he would produce a silk handkerchief, dust down the stage, place his plumed hat on the handkerchief and lower himself gingerly on to a prostrate Juliet. There would follow an ecstatic ovation. At which point Coates would jump up to acknowledge the applause before lowering himself back on top of Juliet. According to a review in 1811, 'In the school of Coates, dignity is denoted by strutting across the stage in strides two yards long; agony by a furious stamp of the foot at the end of every second line,' and to imitate 'Romeo' Coates accurately you 'must learn to commit at least three mistakes in every line of the play'.

Yet by far the most eccentric toff of the Regency period was John 'Mad Jack' Mytton, paradigm of the heavy-drinking country squire. His wardrobe contained 150 pairs of riding breeches, 700 boots and more than 1,000 hats. He owned a bear, Nell, on the back of whom he once rode into a dinner party in full hunting gear, roaring 'Tally ho!' as his guests dived for cover. The bear later ate part of his leg. This did not blunt Mad Jack's passion for animals and at one point there were estimated to be 2,000 dogs and 60 cats living in his house; the dogs were fed steak, or champagne. Perhaps both. His dining room, on the first floor of his house, was fitted with a trapdoor so that his pet giraffe could join him for Sunday lunch.

Having been kicked out of school in his teens, at the age of twenty-one Mytton inherited an estate worth £10,000 a year, with £60,000 in reserve. He proceeded to spend this at a dizzying rate on gambling, hunting and drinking. On average he would get through five bottles of port a day. The rest of his inheritance was lost around his estate. Piles of banknotes would be found hidden in hedgerows or buried in woodland from when he'd been out hunting, something he liked to do naked and accompanied by his pet monkey.

At one point Mytton was Tory MP for Shrewsbury, though he attended parliament only once and for less than an hour, concluding that politics was 'boring'. He'd rather be fighting. On one occasion he brawled with a Welsh miner who eventually conceded defeat after twenty rounds.

Mad Jack also liked pranks. One night after entertaining his doctor and local parson for dinner he dressed up as a highway robber and ambushed his two guests on their way home, firing two shots over their heads and chasing after them as they ran for their lives.

A friend riding with him in a gig once confided that he had never been involved in a crash. Mad Jack's reply was 'What a damn slow fellow you must have been all your life!' before steering the carriage into the bank and upending it. Throughout his short but explosive existence Mytton seemed hellbent on death by horse-drawn carriage. There are accounts of him pulling off a staggering number of stunts involving a gig, an obstacle and speed.

His life eventually unravelled and he fell inexorably into debt. By 1830 he was forced to flee the country. Holed up in Calais and drinking more heavily than before, he tried one night to cure a bout of hiccups by setting fire to his night-shirt. It went up in flames. Mytton was engulfed and would have died had his servant not been on hand to put out the blaze. 'The hiccup is gone, by God!' he exclaimed, before collapsing in bed, sodden, scorched and unable to feel. The next morning his skin was, according to his biographer, 'the same colour as a newly singed bacon hog'.

He later returned to England and was taken to King's Bench debtors' prison, where two years later, at the age of thirty-eight, he died of delirium tremens.

By modern standards, Mad Jack sounds barbaric, out of control and spoilt, but to a middle-class Victorian sensibility he was something worse. For them Mytton represented a memento of their recent past. He was an example of what an Englishman could become if left unchecked, like a drunk uncle at a wedding who by the end of the night you want nothing to do with but because he's part of your family you cannot simply ignore. Instead, you channel your prim disgust into a desire to make sure you don't end up like him. By the mid-nineteenth century this archetypal rake had been tamed by evangelicalism, betterment, and a more decorous Age of Cant. With 'the Game' training 'the Breed', a more restrained kind of Englishman was being cloned. If civilisation was 'built upon a renunciation of instinct', as Freud suggested, this Victorian paragon of English manliness was more refined, more civilised and much less driven by his innate animal-like id than his Regency predecessor.

The hunger for biographies of eccentrics like Mytton grew up in tandem with this moralising sensibility. For many, Mad Jack's story was a cautionary tale of how not to behave, yet for some it was a nostalgic reminder of a bygone age – one that must have looked more colourful, more tolerant of eccentrics and much more fun than the grey world the Victorians inhabited.

What amazed me, when I found him, was that there could be an Englishman in the twenty-first century who in any way resembled Mad Jack.

Like Mytton, Hew Kennedy is a Shropshire man. He is best known as the eccentric landowner who built a 30-ton medieval trebuchet which he uses to send sailing across his estate dead cows, small cars and defunct grand pianos with explosives attached. Why? 'Because it's bloody good fun!' he says.

By constructing a working trebuchet Kennedy had succeeded where most before him had failed. When laying siege to Mexico City, Cortés built a trebuchet that sent its missile straight up into the sky before it crashed down on top of the machine. Napoleon III's engineers couldn't manage it either, a failure that Hew Kennedy noted with relish. He doesn't like the French, you see.

I drove to the hamlet surrounding his attractive Georgian pile, its rose-red brickwork delineated by ivory-coloured pilasters and an empty pediment. Immediately it felt different to Longleat; its interior sun-stained rather than polished, and more homely.

Hew led me into the kitchen and boiled water on an Aga in between asking me about 'this dreadful book of yours', with a grin just visible on his face. He was tallish and dressed how you'd expect a Shropshire squire to: corduroys and square-patterned shirt topped off with a tweed flatcap when outside. He had bright, darting eyes that belied his sixty-eight years, though this youthfulness was offset by a temporary hobble. A few weeks earlier he had been involved in a car crash. Just as I began to say sympathetic things he explained how it had happened. He had gone to visit a friend with a drive that is long and ruler-straight. Whenever he visits he dares himself to go faster than last time. On this occasion Hew thought he had hit 130 mph, which he was quite pleased with. Unfortunately he did not hit the brakes in time, so when his car reached the gravel at the end of the drive it flew into the house. Hew's hips and upper legs were now giving him pain.

'What a bloody stupid caper!' he said in the slightly nasal bark of a public-school-educated man who lives in the countryside – roughly halfway between angry and joking. 'Such a prattish thing to do,' he went on. 'And I'm a cripple now! I was on painkillers, but I've stopped that now. Got bored of it. Don't like doctors much anyway. There's a marvellous book advertised in *Private Eye* about how to avoid being killed by your doctor. Have you seen it?'

I asked him about English eccentricity.

'Well, I think it's easy to be eccentric if you've got a lot of money,' he announced. 'All the more amusing things are done by people with lots of money. I mean anyone can dye their hair orange and parade around on a funny motorbike, but it's more difficult to maintain an *army* of people with orange hair, following you around on motorbikes.'

Hew is not one of these people, and generally leads a parsimonious lifestyle except for when it comes to his beloved trebuchet. He and a fellow enthusiast have sunk £12,000 into this medieval plaything the height of a four-storey building.

'Though it would cost a lot less to build a new one,' he explained, something he was tempted to do now that the original had gone. I hadn't realised this when we spoke on the phone. Two weeks earlier his trebuchet had been dismantled and transported to a theme park in Stratford-upon-Avon. It was falling apart anyway, he said. The wood had not been treated, and for the last decade or so he and his friend had been patching it up using bands of scrap iron as sticking plasters, knowing that one day it would disintegrate. I'd seen it in action on YouTube anyway, and had memorised the elegant parabola of each missile and the reluctant creaking sound the machine made as it launched each projectile skywards.

Apart from six years in the Army, during which there were 'never any foreigners in season', Hew has spent his working life as a landowner, farmer, antiques dealer and odd-job man.

'Odd-job man?' I asked.

'Yes. Odd-job man.'

'Doing . . .'

'Just that. Odd-jobs.' He sounded impatient. 'You know, I make armour for dogs, or elephant armour. Chandeliers.' Of course. 'I made an elephant out of fibreglass once. Repaired a mechanical elephant. Ran on diesel. Er. Ornamental shotgun covered in diamonds and gold, a tent in the medieval style like something you'd use at a pageant. Good fun that was. Four-poster bed with mother-of-pearl inlay, that was for Mrs Getty by the way. Had a Turkish headdress on top of each poster. Basically, I make things that someone wants to buy in the antiques market but can't, either because they're too expensive or there are none of them left.'

He showed me a suit of dog armour. The detail and craftsmanship were staggering and at first I couldn't quite believe he'd made it. He swotted away my compliments.

'Isn't it quite hard to create all these things if you've never made one before?' I asked.

'No, no,' he said, sounding a bit pissed off. 'Not at all. Just guess-work. Guesswork and common sense.'

He showed me a photo album with low-quality snaps of his finest creations. They were extraordinary, both in their exquisite finish and in the fearlessness required to make your first chandelier 18 feet tall. The professional chandelier-makers had laughed at him when he'd suggested it. Around its lower rung he had secured a ring of stag-heads to a central pillar made from old cooking pots. Most of his creations end up in large country houses owned by what he calls 'rich people' who have extravagant shoots and halls that need curiosities to make them look less cavernous.

From the pantry he took me on a tour of the ground floor, which turned out to be unlike any other sequence of rooms I had walked through in England. Clinging to the chandelier in the hall as if swinging in a storm was a stuffed baboon Hew had shot in Zimbabwe (when it was called Rhodesia, and of course for him it still was), while the main staircase was an overcrowded menagerie of stuffed animals. There was a giraffe that began at the foot of the stairs and whose head poked out on the first floor, tigers, stags, a hippo, warthog, walrus, bat, the skin of a boa constrictor, elephant feet and several freakish recast monkeys with parts of their bodies spliced away but sewn up again to look complete. Each monster stared blankly into the hall of Hew Kennedy's home as he continued his commentary on how and where each animal had died. Alongside the monkeys were dioramas that looked as though they'd been made by Walter Potter in a dark mood with taxidermied squirrels wearing medieval squirrel-sized outfits and re-enacting the apocryphal murder of Edward II by jamming a red-hot iron poker up another squirrel's bottom. The squirrel version of the king had its face contorted into a yelp. Other squirrels were getting drunk or vomiting over each other in a Georgian banquet. There were prints and paintings of otters being speared, foxes being tossed in large sheets, a popular sport in eighteenth-century Germany apparently, there were rabbits being thrown out of towers and shot at, dog-eating monkeys, abseiling pigs with fireworks up their bottoms, wolves, bears and hares being hunted. And more. It was exhausting. An overcrowded Noah's Ark of stuffed animals, animal skins and pictures of animals being either hunted, blown up or buggered.

'And that's what they used to do in the eighteenth century,' Hew explained.

'Why do you think people's attitudes in this country towards animals have changed so much?' I tried, slightly dreading the answer.

'Ignorance, I suppose. Lack of religion plays a part too. Animals did not have a soul before. They were given to us by God to do what the hell we liked with.'

That was in line with quite a few things he said that day: words or phrases that when you wrote them down sounded puerile, like 'I love racial prejudice, it's bloody good fun.' Or 'Fuck the Frogs.' Mongolia for him was 'Wogland'. Later, 'I like cruelty to animals.' Pause. 'I quite like that cruelty-to-animals stuff.' In case I hadn't got the message. He went on to share his thoughts on 'All this crap about women being equal to men. It used to be much more sensible, didn't it? The medieval idea was that man was made in God's image, whereas the woman was only made of spare parts. So the woman didn't have a soul, nor did she have a bank account.' He started to laugh. 'Excellent wheeze!' This was meant to wind up the townie–liberal–pinko in his midst. It was a bit like a schoolboy drawing a phallus in a textbook.

'Why did you build it, the trebuchet?'

'Oh, to give people something fun to look at, I suppose. Every time there was a throwing the word would spread locally and at least a hundred people would turn up. And when we threw dead animals, everyone loved that.'

As well as the RAF Stunt Parachute Team, and Johnny Knoxville from the MTV programme *Jackass*, someone Hew really liked, saying he was 'a real nutter', which, from Hew, was the highest compliment, he's had film-crews from all over the world who pay a few thousand pounds to record his machine in action. He's never seen any of these clips on television, though, because he doesn't own one. Nor does he have the internet, which was interesting. It suggested a degree of solipsism that no one I had met apart from Tom Leppard would understand.

Both the RAF and *Jackass* wanted to use his trebuchet to send a human flying through the air which, as Hew made clear, you could do, but the body would fall to the ground dead. The gravitational pull involved in take-off would tear the stomach from it. The *Jackass* people begged Hew to let them try all the same, but he refused. They compromised by firing a crossbow at a member of their team wearing a breastplate. Hew thought this was great. If he did own a television, I could imagine him watching a lot of *Jackass*.

Towards the end of our conversation he told me that what he liked to catapult more than anything else were 45-gallon drums of petrol with detonating equipment attached.

'I've got an excellent explosives man,' he said. 'And he fits a radio receiver into the bomb and then you just sling her up in the air, and there's a little thing not much bigger than that Dictaphone of yours.' He gestured with a stab at my machine. 'You press the button when it's in the air, and it's bloody marvellous, it goes whoom!' His face lit up and his arms flailed. 'Just shows what fun it must be to be a terrorist, be bloody brilliant!'

It is tempting to leave him there. Tempting but misleading. Beneath this veneer of racism, sexism and general political incorrectness I was surprised to find a complete lack of arrogance or snobbery. He was not Toad of Toad Hall, and beneath his exterior was humility and a brilliant, childlike curiosity. It was only when I heard him mention that he was a fan of Charles Waterton, England's original animal-lover, that I understood something more of his character.

'What about Waterton's love of animals?' I had asked, puzzled. 'And his hatred of cruelty to animals?'

'Yes, he was unusual in those days.' Hew had pondered for a moment. 'Perhaps he did it just to spite them?'

And this was it. Hew Kennedy loved to spite *them* – mainstream society and all its mollycoddling Eurocentric nannyish ways. Had he lived in the age of Waterton perhaps he would have built a wildlife reserve. As a characteristic, that slotted with a satisfying clunk into my understanding of what made someone eccentric with a small e.

Behind Longleat lies a settlement of canteens, shops and a self-service buffet that smells and looks like a food hall in a motorway service-station. They are there to service visitors to Lord Bath's home. Everywhere you look you can see families. They move slowly – slowly because of the setting, the sunshine, the subdued holiday feel of the place, and to accommodate the oldest or youngest member of their group. Most have a toddler or grandpa in tow. The rhythms of speech have slowed as well. 'You, gonna, eat, your, chips, then, Matt?' 'I, knew, I, should, have, brought, a, hat.' Men wear tinted glasses. Women over the age of forty have their hair short, about the same length as the men's, because it's less bother that way, only it is more thin. Otherwise, above a certain age, the men and women have comparable faces with traces of the same scowls worked into the flesh around their mouths and eyes while the same jowls have begun to hang hopelessly from their jaws.

I meander past signs advertising food, ice-cream, sweet drinks, or the ones that warn you about a looming danger like the uneven slabs of paving in front of the house that are described as 'Historic Paving'. You step on to these at your own risk. Another sign warns you that the toilets are, on occasion, cleaned by a member of staff who could be either male or female. The message is printed on to a sheet of A4 in bold font and has been stuck on to the door with sellotape. Someone must have complained.

It is a scene I would try to keep Hew Kennedy away from. He would explode. It is also a very English vignette. This is the centre that I have had my back turned to as I've journeyed through the eccentric margins, and it looks different now. I dare to think that I am seeing it with fresh eyes.

Beyond the canteens there is a man in his early twenties with a shaven head and wearing an England football shirt. He is stretched out on the lawn next to a woman with streaked blonde hair scraped back over her skull. They have between them a pair of speakers that pump into the Wessex sky a tinny version of Baby D's 'Let Me Be Your Fantasy'. There is a baby between them. He, she is silent. The three of them are in the shade of an enormous oak, and beyond them in the landscaped parkland are more of these trees standing sentinel over a carpet of grass kept at a picturesque height by sheep.

It is early June now and you can see the lambs nibbling at the grass, a flock of them. Each lamb frolics less than it might have done four weeks ago. Slowly he, she is assuming the shape and mannerisms of its parents and so it continues, it evolves: an idea, an -ism, a -ness, as it is transferred from one to the other, parent to child, and in a blink-and-you'll-miss-it moment of transmission it shifts shape ever so slightly.

I try to spot the black sheep of the flock but can't. It is strangely unsettling. I'm not sure if I would have found it unusual half a year ago.

10

THE NEW ARISTOCRACY

I've come a long way from the Serpentine on Christmas Day. The foothills of eccentricity are behind me now and I think I might need crampons soon, or maybe some mountaineering rope. I've met part-time eccentrics, an eccentric collector, an animal-loving eccentric – though he was a hermit as much as an animal-lover and was confusing in terms of my eccentric taxonomy – I've also met a trickster eccentric keeping alive a peculiarly English mythology, Captain Beany was an eccentric exhibitionist and, more recently, in Lord Bath and Hew Kennedy, I have found two versions of the eccentric toff.

But were any of these people England's leading eccentric? I was not sure. Tom Leppard's existence was certainly the most unusual experiment in lifestyle I had encountered, and Hew Kennedy was unique in the way he combined indifference to mainstream society with creativity, curiosity and a resemblance to the literary caricature of an English eccentric, yet neither seemed to be the contemporary incarnation of the English eccentric that I was after. And this was something that had changed. No longer was I looking for the leader of the tribe. That didn't make sense in light of what I understood now about the history of the term. Instead I wanted to update this label, because as far as I could tell this had not happened for the last hundred years. I wanted to find an English eccentric for the early twenty-first century, someone who personified the modernisation of the term that I had in mind.

Having looked briefly at the traditional heartland of eccentricity, the English aristocracy and landed gentry, it was time to move on to the new aristocracy of twenty-first-century England: celebrities. I needed an eccentric celebrity for my collection.

The similarities between the toff of old and the celebrity of today are striking. Just as the typical landed aristocrat and gentleman of yesteryear might have spent his days surrounded by servants, housekeepers and gardeners, the modern-day English celebrity has a cabal of managers, agents, publicists, stylists, all King Canute courtiers more keen on the word yes than no, who surround them and provide a semi-opaque cocoon. The life of both celebrity and toff is similarly underwritten by wealth, which might allow them to become uncoupled from the conventional tools and structures with which society metes out morality. Instead they have the press to tell them when they have got it extremely wrong or extremely right.

Another unavoidable part of being an English celebrity in the early twenty-first century must be the temptation to think that you're in some way more important than the hoi-polloi who buy your records, watch your films or pay to see you run around a field. And why wouldn't you? When the event of your journey to, say, a local shop is photographed, captioned and disseminated to millions of readers nationwide in a *news*paper then you are *de facto* more important. You exist within an upper stratum of English society. If you are described as 'down-to-earth' it's noteworthy because it requires exertion on your part. Who knows, you might even try to maintain that sense of apartness by giving your children unusual names like Moon Unit, Diva Muffin or Dweezil, as the 1970s rock-god Frank Zappa famously did.

These are the bare bones of English celebrity, but how does one go about becoming an eccentric celebrity?

It takes all of the above and, ideally, an unusual childhood spent trying to excel at whatever it is you have become famous for which means that as an adult you need to act out the childhood you never had; or, just as important, the experience of having been in the limelight before being removed from it. That would be enough to turn all but the most down-to-earth celebrity into an eccentric. Not only would you miss the cushion of attention that once supported you, but you no longer exist under intense media scrutiny so it becomes easier to inhabit a world of your own.

As an eccentric celebrity you might even sense this link between the English toff of old and modern-day celebrity and buy a title such as 'Lord of the Manor'.

I'm up on high next to the Lord of the Manor of Brighton and it's like being on a throne. I need a crown. So does he. The street below is distant, a backdrop, and we're grumbling down London's Grosvenor Street in the cab of a 7-ton, 32-foot-long American Peterbilt 379 truck. The interior is upholstered in nut-brown leather, and the cab jerks and jiggles as he crunches up a gear. His hand flies to the black cord dangling from the ceiling and he gives it a heave. It is the horn. It booms, and everyone on the street looks up. *Up*. It feels better that way. The past fifteen years they've been looking up, so why stop now? When they see who it is they grin, wave and give him the thumbs-up. Tourists or sunglassed wives of European investment bankers don't recognise him. He's not part of their celebrity family. He's part of ours. Cabbies, builders, doormen outside Claridge's, lads on scooters, van drivers, they recognise him. He smiles, leans out of the window and says, 'All right' or 'Cheers' and gives them a royal wave, then we're off again down Grosvenor Street, right up Davies Street, right again on to Brook Street and on through Mayfair.

Everywhere people are waving and smiling at us. Well, not us, him: Chris Eubank, former world champion boxer with a taste for jodhpurs who was voted Britain's most eccentric celebrity in a 2006 BBC poll. Just the man I was looking for.

Born in poverty in south London, Chris Eubanks (he dropped the s later, a bit like Bath dropping the e from Thynne, Barry Kirk becoming Captain Beany, or Tom calling himself Tom Leppard) was thrown out of almost every school he attended. He was suspended eighteen times in a year from one before eventually being expelled. His parents separated, he went into care, and for several years he was shunted by the Social Services between different institutions before being spat out in his early teens, adrift, a boy living rough in London with a taste for shoplifting, alcohol and marijuana.

Plate VIII a

H. Hemming   C. Ewbank

The Celebrity

Aged sixteen he went to New York to live with his mother. He stopped drinking, went to church and got into boxing. He trained with the commitment of a zealot. Eubank had both natural agility and power, and before long was winning fights and trophies. He got noticed, and in his early twenties returned to England a changed man.

He soon became a professional boxer and in 1990, at the age of twenty-four, Christopher Livingstone Eubank became WBO Middleweight Champion of the World. The following year he moved up a division to become WBO Super-Middleweight Champion. To do this he beat Michael Watson in a fight that has been described as 'one of the most extraordinary exemplars of human desperation that sport has ever produced'. At the end of this epic bout, Eubank's opponent fell into a coma and suffered brain damage. This happens in boxing, and Eubank was not vilified. Besides, he was world champion and he was English. He became a celebrity.

This, the early 1990s, was his heyday. Chris Eubank was famous not just for his boxing, but for his style and personality. He would be photographed arriving at premieres wearing Edwardian suits, spats, monocle and cane. He spoke with a lisp, quoted poetry and modelled himself on 1950s filmstars like Terry-Thomas, a man famous for playing the cad in a silk dressing gown with cigarette holder and delivering catchphrases like 'Good show!' or 'You're an absolute shower!' Eubank felt these people knew how to dress, that their style was 'spot on'. Plus, he was black, so these clothes looked exotic on him and that made him even more photogenic. He began to be affectionately labelled an eccentric which, among other things, suggested that the term was not rooted to a racial stereotype. You did not have to be white to be called eccentric, though dressing that way certainly helped. His clothes might sound like pantomime, but he wore them with genuine style and panache and was twice voted Britain's Best-Dressed Man.

Eubank's last fight was in 1998. Seven years later he was declared bankrupt. So I was a little surprised when he said we should meet at one of Mayfair's most expensive hotels, where he was staying.

'Henry, isn't it?' He offered a hand. I felt the pang of embarrassment that accompanies meeting someone whose face you've seen hundreds of times on television. It was as if I had been spying on him all these years and he'd just caught me red-handed.

He was broader than I had imagined, and taller. His pate was clean-shaven, and his demeanour dignified. He was immaculately turned out that day, and wore a pale-olive suit, brogues and a white shirt with a high collar that was crisp and looked like porcelain in the way it curved. I got up to shake his hand. I'd never shaken the hand of a boxer before; it was a handshake that could crush granite.

In a lisp much less pronounced than that of his puppet on *Spitting Image* he said we should go somewhere to get coffee. We got into his truck, drove to a nearby Starbucks and took a table outside. He sat at right-angles to me, looking resplendent in his tailored suit. I'd now had more time to take in his nose that was testament to a decade of being hit. It was wide and knobbly and from certain angles looked like a half-chewed sweet.

Our conversation got off to a bad start. For about fifteen minutes he spoke cagily in an argot of sports psychology mixed with light philosophy – all negatives, positives and a succession of pauses that would put a stylite to shame – and just as he was beginning to open up, when talking about how he might have lost his dignity when in love, he stopped.

'So, hang on a second. These things I'm telling you are very important to me.' He was agitated. 'We need some kind of contract.'

I stared back at him blankly.

'We need some kind of contract,' he said more forcefully. 'This can't end up as anything other than for your project.'

'Um. I don't have a contract.' I tried my own sports-psychology-speak. 'All I can do is look you in the eye and say that I have no intention of using this anywhere else.' I then looked him in the eye and made a pathetic, I'm-not-capable-of-selling-this-to-a-news-paper-I'm-barely-capable-of-operating-a-Dictaphone expression.

'It's not you I'm worried about. It's life. Call your agent. Get him on the phone.'

It being Yom Kippur, Jonathan's phone was off, so I left a slightly theatrical message on his answerphone telling him to call me right away.

None of the other people I had spoken to had been this wary, I suppose because none of them were celebrities like Chris Eubank and consequently forced to see the media and its ambassadors – people with Dictaphones or telescopic-looking cameras – as the untrustworthy class gossip and bully rolled into one, the person who pretends to be your friend, twists your words and spreads malicious rumours about you.

Chris went to get more coffee and returned with a slice of carrot cake that he cut in half using a Starbucks fork, generously pushing the larger half towards me. I wrote my address on a piece of paper and handed it to him.

'If what you're telling me appears anywhere other than my book, here's my address, so you can firebomb my house,' I said.

He laughed reluctantly, and said it was all right and that we should go back to the hotel. We got in the truck and flew down the street. Once again everyone waved and it felt like a high-speed parade.

Back at the hotel we settled in the bar where Chris ordered a cappuccino. No froth.

'Isn't that a latte?' the waitress asked.

'No. It's a cappucino with no froth.'

The waitress sucked in her lips.

The room was decorated in manly greys and browns and smelt of last night's alcohol.

'So carry on,' he began, his body language more open than before.

'When you said', I scanned my list of interesting Eubankisms, 'that as a boxer you partake in a tragic form of entertainment, do you think that's what you're doing now, as a celebrity, that you're partaking in a tragic form of entertainment?'

The CD began to skip. It was the Brazilian song from Nike's football adverts, 'Mas Que Nada', with the chorus going la-la, la-la, la-la, la-la, over and over, locking the room in a sunny Latin loop.

'That's not true,' he said crisply. 'Boxing tragic? It is not tragic. It is uplifting. It is awesome, because it is real. And in a utopian world it would be tragic, but in this world, the world we live in, it isn't tragic. I would have said that in '94 when I was doing far too much. But I was in love with that time. I loved and I was in love, so I fantasised and I adored, but at the same time when you love something you can also hate it at times. It's a love–hate relationship. So it's not about regretting, it's about looking at the positives in the particular phase of the life that you're in – because there'll always be positives and negatives. Nothing is always good. But I choose not to dwell on the negatives in my life. I only look at the positives.'

I have never read a self-help book, but at times listening to Chris was what I imagined one to be like. The power of what he said seemed to lie both in its learned simplicity and its repetition.

'Can we talk about your relationship with the English public?' I said. 'You as a non-conformist. Do you think English people have an engrained affinity for a non-conformist?'

'Let me see. You're talking as though my fellow countrymen are . . . Lord Bath is an eccentric. Let's talk about the word "eccentric". Because I think that's what you're looking for here. You tell me what the difference is between a non-conformist and an eccentric.'

'I think they're very similar, unless you're using non-conformist as a religious term. The word "eccentric" has a history of its own, whereas I think the word non-conformist today has less baggage. I like the word eccentric. I think it can be used as a compliment.'

I talked for a while about John Stuart Mill and the way he had construed eccentricity as something less frivolous than it is today.

'So if someone calls you eccentric, what do you feel?' I asked.

'Well, they're looking at the fact that I intellectualise everything. And why wouldn't I? You should. It's the media who calls me eccentric, and they'll look at the dress sense, the cane, the poetry, the philosophy, the pacifist who is a fighter, a boxer, a former world champion, and they'll say, "Well, he's an eccentric." The only time they can really look at me and say, "Hang on, this man's a non-conformist," is when I protest outside Downing Street.'

Chris had been arrested twice in the previous six months for campaigning near the Houses of Parliament with anti-war slogans emblazoned on his truck. While I agreed that if you pose a threat you are unlikely to be called eccentric, there were certainly reports of his arrests outside Downing Street that labelled him as an eccentric, so he was not necessarily posing the threat that he insinuated.

A text message buzzed into his phone. On reading it he began to laugh: a lovely, deep chuckle. I asked him what it was. He shook his head.

'How old are you?' he asked.

'Twenty-seven,' I said.

'Do your writing,' he said in a fatherly tone. 'Write, and have serious love affairs.'

'Okay.'

'Have serious love affairs.'

'But I'm already in love with someone. Should I have affairs with other people?'

'Well.' He allowed his head to do the upwards half of a nod. 'Just don't waste your time not being in love.'

'Are *you* in love?'

'Yeah,' he said definitively. 'But have serious love affairs. Make of that what you will. I'm not steering you down one track.'

'Do you wish you had had more serious love affairs when you were my age?'

'A gentleman never speaks about love.'

'But he can talk about it in abstract terms, can't he?'

'I can give you lessons, as I just have. Again, have serious love affairs. That is the most important thing in your life. Everything else should be designed to make the love affairs more fanciful.'

He would tell me nine times during our conversation to have serious love affairs, fanciful or otherwise.

'Can you talk me through a day in the life of Chris Eubank?'

'There's no form to it right now. So no. I'm not following anyone.' He sat up in his chair. 'Well, actually I am following in someone's footsteps . . .' He paused.

I admired the music, took in my surroundings, had a sip of tea, thought about what I was doing later that day before – oh all right then: 'In who's footsteps?'

'You could say Mandela,' he said, before the words were out of my mouth.

'Right.'

'But it's very hard today for anyone to make an example, because the media, they're like the Gestapo.' He broke into poetry, "'If you can bear to hear the truth you've spoken twisted by knaves to make a trap for fools." Rudyard Kipling's *If*,' he said perfunctorily, as if answering a question on a quiz. 'So they take your truth and taint it, and make a trap for anyone foolish enough to pick up a tabloid and say, "I believe that."'

'In the past you've described yourself as a warrior, and you've just mentioned following in the footsteps of Mandela. I get the sense you want something to fight against.'

'There's always a fight to fight. Big or small.'

'But you'd prefer a big fight?'

'Well, it would be folly to say that. The question is, will I have the courage to act? Or will I realise the opportunity that is in front of me when it comes? Getting arrested, going to the jailhouse for nine hours with my truck and its slogans on the back. It's not nice in the jail.' He shook his head stoically. 'But this can only credit me.'

'Do you admire Brian Haw? The protester who has spent six years outside parliament?'

'Yes. Of course.'

'And was the point of your protest to get arrested?'

'Yes. It's not a protest if you don't get arrested. It's just a gathering that won't be reported. This is why I've tried to point out that being arrested for the right thing is *good*.'

Here was a man who badly wanted something to struggle against. I could feel it in the way he spoke. A chance to be heroic, or anything more epic than being on *Celebrity Big Brother*, as he was in 2001 (he was the first to be voted off, which he saw as a victory).

'For you, what does it mean to be English?'

'To be decent. That's what.'

'And in England today, do you think it's more difficult than ever to be an eccentric?'

'Yes, because of the media. If you are just a little different and you make that known then they point their finger at you. So those responsible for the decline of the non-conformist are the media, especially the tabloids.'

'But it seems they haven't really succeeded. I mean there was so much public affection for you when we were outside just now, the way everyone greeted you.'

'Yes, they are inspired by me. And why do you think that is?'

'Because the public like a non-conformist, an eccentric?'

'Exactly. So they ask me, "Why do you carry a cane, why do you wear jodhpurs, why do you drive a truck? You shouldn't." But the more they say that the more I do it. And that's why I have the affection, because I stick to my guns. There's a quotation that goes, "The only way to know a man's true worth,"' he slowed down for effect, '"Is his capacity for sticking to his guns".'

He said it with the lilting rise and fall of a well-worn homily. I racked my brain to work out where, or if, I'd heard it before. Perhaps it was from Kipling, Rumi, Blake or another semi-quotable mystic. But no. It didn't sound right, just as it didn't sound right to call Chris Eubank a twenty-first-century English eccentric.

He was a celebrity and, as he put it, a showman. He was also a very *good* person. The way he greeted passers-by on the street was fantastically sincere, warm and open, and the fact that he gave me advice on how to live my life was significant – it was something none of the others had done. But at the same time Chris Eubank seemed to take badly to the prospect of relative anonymity after his time in the spotlight. Perhaps an eccentric would not have minded so much.

Chris Eubank was not really an eccentric by my reckoning, but I was intrigued by the fact that he was labelled as one.

If every group needs an eccentric and ends up unbalanced without one, within the pantheon of English celebrity Chris Eubank was the closest anyone could find to this character. So his actions were made out to be more dotty than they really were. What's more, he dressed anachronistically, which also placed him within eccentric territory.

Once he had become this cartoon character, Eubank the eccentric celebrity served another purpose. Along with his fellow celebrities, through his deeds and misdeeds, he helps us articulate our collective morality. In the sense that each society's morality is fluid, and what is acceptable now is different to what it was ten years ago, or a hundred years ago, this morality requires regular probing and redefinition. Only when it is tested like this can it be reasserted. Unless a taboo is broken, or seen to be broken, it does not exist.

Traditionally in pre-industrial societies it was the role of mythology to help define a group's morality. Contemporary soap operas, novels, plays and films perform a similar role today: through the moral or immoral actions of their protagonists you, the viewer, unconsciously redefine or reinforce your sense of what is and is not permissible. In an identical way the fragments of celebrity gossip that we consume each day are equivalent to a soap opera. When you read about them you do so in the language of moralistic judgement: what they get up to is either right or wrong, thumbs up or thumbs down, so if a celebrity gets riotously drunk it is made clear in the caption whether or not they have gone too far – perhaps this is the beginning of a familiar fall from grace and subsequent slide into addiction (while in the next-door photo a different young hero begins their equally archetypal rags-to-riches ascent) – or maybe this drunken night out was acceptable and they were just having fun and they deserved it after all their hard work because it's all right to let off steam once in a while. If a male celebrity sleeps around a lot it's impressive and funny and he might win the *Sun*'s 'Shagger of the Year' award. When a girl does the same it is less so. This is a boring example because it feels sanctimonious, but it's useful in the sense that it illustrates the extent to which our morality is received, and how much we rely on disposable contemporary culture for our sense of what is right and wrong to be reasserted.

Within this constantly evolving cipher of morality the eccentric, whether real or cartoon-like, becomes the limit of what is acceptable. He or she embodies as-far-as-you-can-go. To stray beyond this eccentricity is to go beyond taboo. So the eccentric acts as the boundary-marker.

Beyond taboo. These two words have appeared together in my head so often that they have become an inelegant dyad, entwined, the one looking incomplete without the other by its side. Beyond-taboo is the Atlantic Ocean in the eyes of a medieval Arab, forbidding in its immensity and left blank on a map except for a cartoonish monster or two. Medieval Arabs would call the Atlantic *Bahr al-Zulamat*, 'The Sea of Darkness'.

To have any meaningful understanding of eccentricity I had to explore what lay beyond it. I needed to find people who lived in a land called insane, perverted, immoral, dangerous or just illegal.

I needed to take my journey somewhere less light.

PART TWO

CROSSING THE LINE

11

BEHIND CLOSED DOORS

If paying for sex is a bit like paying someone to let you win at tennis, then what is it to pay to be whipped, caned, tied up, flogged and anally penetrated with your genitalia wired up to an electric current? I had no idea, but for £120 you could buy an hour of this with Mistress K and find out for yourself.

I had clicked through her website slowly, and nervously, on account of the day several years earlier when I'd ventured into the world-wide web looking for porn and my computer had become infected with a spyware virus. I had taken it to a computer surgery on the Tottenham Court Road to get it fixed. Set towards the back of a larger shop, it had the feel of a backstreet abortionist. The expression on the face of the Bangladeshi man who asked what I had been looking at to cause this infection lingered like a verruca long after the event. It was a mixture of pity and disgust. I wanted never again to be on the receiving end of it.

This feeling was compounded by having to pay £200 for his services. That, I thought to myself on the bus home, felt like a draconian fine for sexual curiosity. Yet being punished like this was strangely apt. It fleshed out an axiomatic link between sexuality and guilt, one that in some ways is a hangover from Victorian times but is also something you can trace back to the classical age.

Two years later I was in internet-virus-land once more, only this time, I told myself, if anything went wrong I'd be able to look him in the eye. I'd tell him it was in the name of research. He wouldn't believe me of course, so I'd go to the surgery with my contract to write the book and drafts of the first few chapters. Then he'd pull that face again and I'd be putty in his computer-fixing hands before handing over £200 and muttering a prayer to the god of internet porn that this really would be the last time.

Or perhaps he'd look at the chapters I had with me and ask what any of this had to do with an attempt to understand English eccentricity? It was a long story, I'd tell him. Then I'd tell him the long story.

Sexual non-conformity is a lacuna in the literature of eccentricity. Almost none of the nineteenth- or twentieth-century eccentric biographies mention it, partly because these books were intended for a family audience, but also because sexual deviation posed a threat to Victorian probity – which explains why 'Byron could not possibly be an eccentric. He was too dangerous,' according to the historian Paul Langford. I wanted to explore this gap, and to do that I had to find someone who led a sexually eccentric life.

The most difficult part of deciding who or what was sexually eccentric was working out at what point sexually unusual becomes sexually depraved. Eccentric was, as ever, the poorly lit no-man's land just this side of taboo. And therein lay the problem – which version of immoral should I be guided by? As a professional dominatrix Mistress K was breaking the law, so she existed beyond legal taboo. Yet for a growing number of people what she did was morally and socially acceptable: she did it in her own home and the participants were adult and consenting. It incurred a very English notion of MYOB that you can trace back at least as far as the mid-eighteenth century when Tristram Shandy summed it up: 'So long as a man rides his hobby-horse peaceably and quietly along the King's highway, and neither compels you or me to get up behind him, – pray, Sir, what have either you or I to do with it?'

This applied especially to sex.

Any ambiguity about the acceptability of Mistress K's lifestyle was testament to how much English attitudes to sex had changed over the last 250 years.

Although it's tempting to caricature the nation's sex-life during the eighteenth century as a sodden orgy of libertinism and Enlightenment-fuelled free love, it was not. The sex-lives of most Englishmen and women during this period were reserved by modern standards. All the same this was an age when you could talk about sex in public, laugh about it and openly look at pictures of it without being labelled a pervert.

This changed during the Victorian era, when sex moved indoors. A silence was cast over it, the metropolitan demi-monde of courtesans was forced underground, turning it into a subterranea of brothels and pimps, and reinforcing the link between sex and shame. Moral respectability was attached to the suppression of one's primal urges. Bodies were no longer there to be enjoyed or laughed at, but disciplined and restrained.

In 1858, the year before the publication of *On Liberty*, the art critic John Ruskin, the personification of Victorian fastidiousness, was sorting through Turner's bequest to the Tate when he found a series of erotic watercolours Turner had painted fifty years earlier. He recorded his shock, concluding that these works were 'drawn under a certain condition of insanity'. He kept a few, but in order to protect Turner's reputation had the rest burned. Not only does this illustrate the degree to which English attitudes to sex could change in the space of fifty years, it is interesting also because of the language Ruskin uses. Instead of 'perversion' he puts it down to 'insanity'. In the crepuscular hinterland of the immoral or the illegal, terms like 'insane', 'perverted', 'sick' and 'treacherous' could be interchanged or piled on top of each other for added effect. The asylum, the brothel and the prison were being shunted closer together.

During the twentieth century, English attitudes to sex continued to shift, though thankfully in the opposite direction. A pioneer in our contemporary understanding of sex was Havelock Ellis, a shy and eccentric doctor from Croydon who saw the world differently. He became the founder of sexology. Ellis was notorious during the last decade of the nineteenth century for his idea that Christian sexual morality was 'profoundly antagonistic to the art of love', and that homosexuality was neither immoral nor mentally unhinged and should therefore be decriminalised. The book in which he explained this, *Sexual Inversion*, was banned in 1897. Ellis was also the first writer to discuss the power of a sexual fetish, furnishing his analysis with an account of his own weakness for watching women urinate, something he linked to seeing his mother lift her skirt in London Zoo (she wasn't on display, they'd just gone there for the day). By the 1960s, sexuality had been reinserted into the public sphere. Fuelled by the development of more accessible birth control, popular understanding of what was sexually outré or permissible continued to evolve.

By the dawn of the twenty-first century the stereotype of the English as a sexually frigid nation was no longer apt. According to the National Survey of Sexual Attitudes and Lifestyles nearly a third of English teenagers in 2000 had had sex by the age of sixteen; England had the highest rate of teenage pregnancy in Europe; statistically English people were sleeping around more; they were also having much more anal sex than previously; gonorrhoea was on the rise; and sex toys were being sold at parties in the way that Tupperware once was.

As a nation, we might still have been crap in bed, but we were at least getting into bed in order to be crap more frequently than our grandparents and with a wider vocabulary of things to try once there.

Sadomasochism, bondage and fetish-worship, once thought by psychiatrists to be parts of a pathological disease, have become increasingly popular in England thanks to the internet. Since the 1990s the English BDSM community (BDSM stands for Bondage, Domination, Submission and Masochism) has grown exponentially, and although increasingly normalised, the scene remains marginal. This was perfect. It seemed to be parked right in the spot usually reserved for eccentricity. All I needed to do was find an eccentric practitioner of BDSM.

Of all the sites I looked at, Mistress K's was the most unusual. It included a lucid rather than lurid description of why she loved to dominate, boasted 'intelligent domination', and had artful black-and-white photos of various clients spreadeagled on bondage benches with wires attached to their scrotums. Mistress K also had a degree in English. I emailed her.

For several weeks there was no response, so I called. She picked up. I was nervous. I explained what I was doing and eventually she said she'd be happy to meet, on the condition that I concealed her identity and called her K. Her parents didn't know that this was her profession and she planned to keep it that way. We agreed on a date.

'I'll be free from about ten o'clock,' she said, in a flat voice with little accent. 'We shouldn't be disturbed then, although I should warn you my transsexual maid will be coming in that morning, but she's very quiet. I might have to break off to give her a quick caning but that shouldn't get in the way of anything. I'll see you next week.'

I parked in a leafy street in the town where she lived. Let's call it Bracknell. It's in a similar part of the country and is made up of equally quiet, suburban streets, lean gardens and absurdly fat cats waddling across the street trying to look as though they are off for a spot of hunting.

Like the others in the street, Mistress K's house was detached and double-glazed. The bell played a ditty and three seconds later the door opened. She was taller than I had imagined and in her late forties. She had powerful legs, longish dark hair and eyes that were warm and worn.

'You must be Henry,' she said, ushering me into a magnificently clean sitting room with cream-coloured walls and Ikea furnishings: not the cheap student stuff but top-of-the-range deluxe Ikea. Through the window at the bottom of the garden she pointed out her dungeon, or playroom as she called it.

'Now, would you like tea or coffee?' she said, taking control of proceedings with wonderful ease, both with her delivery and the word 'now'.

'Coffee please,' I mumbled, taking a seat next to her.

Christine the transsexual maid entered, quivering slightly. She was in her sixties and wore a 1930s maid outfit somewhere between the real thing and a rubber one you'd get in a King's Cross sex shop. She was broad-shouldered and slender with hands several glove sizes larger than mine. She had known Mistress K for a few years now and would pay to come round to do her housework.

'She's a submissive,' K pointed out, as if telling me her star-sign.

'Right,' I said.

'Is that all?' Christine chirped in a pantomime servant voice.

'Yes, that's all for now, Christine. Thank you,' said K with delicious authority. 'Right.' She turned to me. 'So what would you like to know?'

'Well.' I scrabbled with my notes, trying not to look flustered. 'First of all, I wanted to ask how it began. How you got to where you are now.' I gestured at the well-appointed room, at Christine making coffee in the kitchen and at the dungeon towards the end of the garden.

For Mistress K it began with John Wayne. She was about four and a half at the time, and as usual had been left in the front room to play. She remembers sitting cross-legged on the goatskin rug that her parents had brought back from Spain where they'd been on holiday the year before. She loved that rug and would spend hours on it, parting its hairs, ploughing pathways through it, rearranging her dolls within its willowy folds, or just lying back and letting it tickle her skin. Next to the rug was a gas heater that hissed and filled the room with the tang of leaking gas. It made the air damp. Behind her in the kitchen was her mother, and opposite was a small black and white television, which for K, aged four and a half, was by far the most interesting thing in the room.

One day she looked up, and there, on television, was something that made everything else in the room step back momentarily. Her mother called. She did not register; it was as if she was calling someone else. The only thing K could hear just then were the jeers of the crowd and the ping of the coal shovel as it came down on Maureen O'Hara's backside, her flesh protected only by a damp petticoat.

It was an epiphany. That scene and everything it stood for became her lodestar.

The film was *McLintock!* – The Taming of the Shrew set in the Wild West – and K had just watched the final scene when Maureen O'Hara is spanked into wifely submission by John Wayne. Apparently the Duke used such force during the filming of it that O'Hara considered suing him for assault and battery.

K didn't know what she liked about it, other than that there was something to do with power and its exchange that was very interesting.

Standing in her dungeon forty years later surrounded by a smorgasbord of whips, paddles, riding crops, lubricant, chains, leather bondage stools and a bondage rack made from a Homebase gazebo that had been screwed into the floor, along with various other tools of her trade as a dominatrix, the rest, you could say, was inevitable.

She described her fascination with corporal punishment at school. As one of the prefects she got to witness a lot of this, and it was through these canings or rulerings that she realised discipline or punishment was about much more than physical pain. It relied upon humiliation.

'Did you ever want to be one of the teachers administering the punishments?'

'Not sure,' she said, her light East Anglian accent coming through for the first time. We were back in her sitting room now. 'But it's interesting that a lot of the men who see me now will say that for them it began with a teacher doing something to them when they were young, or a matron, or a mummy.'

'And what kind of men come to see you?'

'Oh, powerful men. Journalists. Actors. Sportspeople. That sort of thing.' She sounded proud as she said it, straightening her back in the voluptuous folds of the sofa. 'I used to see a chap who was in the police, someone capable of being extremely aggressive and assertive, but when I stood in front of him and basically barked at him, well' – she began to shake her head – 'he would melt.' Her voice became breathless. She crossed her large legs so her body was now at 45 degrees to me. 'All of his masculine mask would just disappear and this softness would just kind of *emanate*, and that's an incredible feeling for me. There is definitely a type of person like that who comes here. People who are high-profile or famous in their everyday life who need a release.'

'When you say famous, how famous?'

'Oh very famous.'

'And who—'

'But I am utterly discreet,' she said, her lips curling inwards.

'How old are they usually?'

'They're generally older than me, I'd say. Forty-five to seventy-five on average. Though some of the older ones, obviously, can't partake physically the way they used to . . .' She trailed off. There was something lovely about the decorum with which she phrased this. Even in their anonymity and absence she was protective of her clients. 'I used to have one who was eighty-seven,' she went on. 'He'd been caned first by his matron, then his teachers at school, then he married and his wife was amenable to caning him, so she gave him a regular seeing to, then his wife died, and he had a live-in housekeeper, and bless his soul, he got her to do it. Then she died. So, by now really missing his caning, he came to see me. I saw to him about three or four times and then there was no more contact.' She sighed. 'To this day I wonder whether he passed away happy that he got the discipline he needed. Who knows?'

'What's the strangest thing anyone has asked you to do?'

'Ohh. Let me see,' she said, as if she was working in a second-hand bookshop and I'd just asked for an obscure book. 'There was one man, hmm, who wanted me to throw custard pies at him. Then . . . another who wanted baked beans squashed all over his body.' I thought of Captain Beany. 'But perhaps the most unusual was the guy who found it deliciously humiliating to be made to wear women's knickers with just enough pebbles in the crotch to weigh them down. So they were at the point of falling off. It gave him a sense of precariousness, I think, which probably went back to defecating into a nappy.'

'And what would you do while he was in the knickers?'

'I'd stand there.'

'And he'd . . .'

'He'd stand there as well.'

'So have you ever said no to a particular request?'

'Well, I don't do age-play. You know, men who like to dress up as babies. Gives me a bit of a squick.' She grimaced accordingly. 'I did have one guy though who got me to beat him until he bled. That was the first and last time that happened,' she harrumphed. 'He bled everywhere. I had to disinfect the whole room and repaint the walls.'

'I bet he liked it.'

'Oh he was as happy as a lamb! But no, he was *not* invited back,' she smiled.

'No.'

'You see, with most clients I can't leave a mark.'

'Why's that?'

'Because they're married.' Her voice dropped in pitch.

'Of course.'

'Although most of the time they're in such deteriorated relationships that their partner no longer sees them naked, so it doesn't matter. Other times, the partner will be away for a few weeks so they'll call up and say, "We can really go for it this week."' She said this with a friendly relish. 'Most of the time, though, the challenge is how to create pain – which is what they've come for – without leaving marks. Which is great fun. You get to use your imagination a lot.'

K tailors each session to her customer. Once she's got an understanding of what they're after and they've agreed on certain safety words that will bring everything to a halt, the game will begin and she becomes She, the goddess–mistress–tormentor. He transforms into the slave who can answer only, 'Yes, Mistress,' 'No, Mistress,' and both mistress and slave, or 'dom' and 'sub', suspend disbelief. They slip into invisible costumes that only the other can see as they act out separate parts of an elaborate and mostly improvised game that is also a performance. Both turn their world upside down for a set period of time, knowing that at the end the real world will come rushing in like a draught, but until that moment they can lose themselves entirely in these characters. They are acting, in the way that perhaps all of us are when we have sex, mimicking what we've seen, becoming the person we want to be but can't, yet it's rarely acknowledged as acting. It is acting in the pervasive sense of the word where all of our actions become avatars of something more real. They are so fake they acquire their own patina of reality.

During the game the client will be stripped, tied to a rack, flogged, whipped, blindfolded, cuffed, hooded, placed in a straitjacket, wired up to an electric current and have different tools inserted into him until he is both physically and psychologically reduced to a frightened schoolboy desperate for approval from his mistress. He will worship the woman I was sharing a sofa with in whichever way she sees fit. He can come only when she says so, if she says so; and if all goes well, which I sense it does as K is clearly very good at what she does, he will enter what is known as 'sub space'. This is a state of euphoria brought on mostly by an endorphin high: a feeling of gorgeous helplessness heightened by the fact that he's been put there by this loving mother–punisher figure.

So it's a beautiful thing K does. She was keen to make that clear. Neither violent nor man-hating. And what sets her apart from the other 'doms' is not only that she doesn't dress up in PVC or leather, nor operates out of a purple-walled dungeon – *so* '80s, she groaned – but she does this for her own well-being. She has a deep-rooted need to dominate.

'So sometimes I'll reach what is known as "dom space". Which is absolutely amazing.' Her face softened. 'It happened to me the first time I made a man cry. What made it better was the fact that this man was very successful, very masculine, almost arrogant, and I'd stripped down layer after layer until I got to a point where he was as soft as a kitten . . . Hard in other ways!' she grinned. Her face became reverential once more. 'But in the sense of being open and receptive he was just . . . It was fantastic. A real headrush.'

Just as interesting as people paying for pleasure born of pain was the idea that to reach this high they were acting out a dictatorial calculus of crime and punishment, obedience and reward. It was a crude facsimile of school, the structure that for so many of Dr Weeks' eccentrics was the starting point of their non-conformity. It was fascinating to think of this base system of discipline and conformity, the place where eccentricity begins, being acted out and reinforced again and again in Mistress K's playroom at the bottom of her garden. It's probably going on right now. Perhaps there is something about this structure that we *need* at a primal, even animal, level.

For the client, pretending to exist within this make-believe land of rules and sexual torment also allows him to follow a leader slavishly. If this too fed some kind of instinctive need all of us have, then it made sense that so many of her clients should be powerful or famous, men who would not be following anyone otherwise. Yet here they were paying for the chance to worship unreservedly at the feet of a sexualised amalgam of mother, whore and headmistress.

Bearing in mind this emphasis on rules it came as no surprise to hear K talk about how much she hates breaking the law. She declares every penny she makes. The only real fib in her tax returns was regarding the nature of her profession (she also has to perform some acrobatics with receipts when it comes to writing off the expense of her £500 bondage rack for example).

'How rigidly are laws against you, or rather the BDSM community, enforced these days?'

'Well, it comes in waves. There'll be a moment of moral outrage in the *Daily Mail*, the *Daily Express*, and things start happening. New laws will be proposed. Clubs will be busted mainly. Then it will cool off. The place I have to be most careful is in the area of damage done to people.' Her expression changed. 'If I took my fingernail and scraped it down your arm' – she raised her hand and let it hover above my forearm – 'and made a mark that lasted for more than a couple of hours, by law that would be assault. So you would, in fact, be able to charge me for assault.'

'Really?' I said, as she pulled her hand away. 'And has that ever happened to you?'

'Oh no. Never. In reality no man is going to go to the police station and offer his bleeding bottom for inspection. Also their wife would find out.'

'Of course. And do you ever feel guilt about that, that most of your clients are married?'

'It's something I might have felt, once, but now I realise it keeps relationships together. Most of the people I see come out of a session reinvigorated and ready to face the vanilla world, as we call it.'

'Vanilla?'

'Ah,' she said apologetically. 'That's what we call straight sex in the BDSM world. The straight life. You know, vanilla being the most bland ice-cream.'

We. She had used the word a few times now and it made her sound suspiciously uneccentric. Although the BDSM community was not a cohesive unit, it was a group with its own jargon and idiosyncratic centre and margins, and while K was clearly on the edge of this group, was she really an eccentric?

In recent years the BDSM scene has become, as she put it, huge, mainly because of the internet. Not only does the worldwide web allow someone from outside the world of BDSM to get an idea of what it's all about from the onanistic privacy of their bedroom, but it lets that person feel security in the fact that others get turned on by the same thing. It's not just you, this is something you can explore, enjoy, express. Please enter your card details. The internet has changed the dimensions of English sexuality as well as narrowing the possibility of eccentricity throughout our cultural landscape. It has made solipsism rarer because wherever the internet goes it leaves in its wake e-groups, communities and virtual societies of shared interest. It can't help this, yet the more it happens the harder it becomes for anyone to exist in a cocoon of eccentric solipsism. The internet represented one of the biggest threats to English eccentricity.

'In a similar way,' K added in between sips of tea from a fresh mug Christine had just set down beside her, 'the internet creates communities of paedophiles, and by getting paedophiles to talk to each other you could say it normalises what they're doing. But there's also a chance that by talking to other like-minded people it's harder for your urges to become violent or explosive. So overall I think the internet is helping people sexually. It's educating them, and as long as there's less joyless or meaningless sex in the world, I'm happy.'

There was a skewed logic here, and out of a mixture of politeness and feebleness I did not point this out to K. I should have done. The effect of paedophilia becoming normalised within marginal internet groups was clearly much worse than the possibility of a paedophile's urges becoming violent or explosive. In any case, the former did not rule out the latter. With selective normalisation of paedophilia you'd end up with an established market of online punters eager to purchase or view fresh e-images of children being abused, and until CGI technology becomes sufficiently cheap and accessible this would of course require greater levels of abuse in order to generate the new images.

Christine returned to ask if there were any other chores that needed doing. She stood demurely with her outsized hands crossed in front of her like a pair of entwined elephant trunks. Mistress K told her about some clothes that needed washing.

'Do you think', I began, as Christine tiptoed out of the room, 'that part of what makes BDSM exciting is the idea that what you're doing is taboo, or risqué? So if everyone walked around in leather and chains whipping each other in the street it would no longer be a turn-on.'

She smiled. 'Well, boundaries and repressions definitely create frissons, and out of those things come the greatest expressions of passion. So you couldn't really, ever, remove from sex that sense of taboo, of shame, and repression. If you did there'd be a kind of blandness which would bring about the death of sex. It's the same as the idea of having sex where nobody's in charge. So dull!' she exclaimed. 'But there are some people for whom these things will always be a turn-on, no matter how taboo or tolerated they are. You see, most of us do it in a very law-abiding way. We have no desire to shock or alienate mainstream society.' For an instant, no more, she sounded like a major's wife talking about a book club or a coffee morning. Her delivery was parochial and suburban. 'An important part of the BDSM community is about not shoving your kinks down someone else's throat. We're not at the stage where, like gays, we feel we have to be out and proud. Maybe we never will be, because we can do everything we want behind closed doors.'

'So do you worry about your neighbours finding out?'

'God yes! Everything in this neighbourhood is very *nice*, people are friendly as long as nothing causes any ripples. There would be a serious backlash if anyone found out.' I shuddered at the thought. 'So I am extremely careful. If anyone asks, I'm a grief counsellor. And you see nobody, but nobody, wants to talk about your work when you say that.' She grinned. 'If someone's been recently bereaved and they want to talk I'll say I only do it on referral. That took a little bit of thinking up, but it seems to work.'

Here was the Englishman or Englishwoman's home as their castle. It was defensible, private and beyond the reach of nosy neighbours or of a centralised state. Neither had any business there. As J. S. Mill told Alexis de Tocqueville when asked if he thought England would ever be run by a centralised government, 'We have never considered government from such a lofty point of view.' For several centuries now the English have operated and maintained a society that exalts both the property of the individual and his or her civic rights. You can see this even in the layout of the capital: while European capitals are calibrated by broad streets lined with monumental buildings, London, with its higgledy-piggledy lanes, relative lack of grandiose or extravagant royal palaces and array of different centres, to an outsider at least is an exercise in decentralised society with the individual at its heart.

That K has been able to do what she has for ten years without any of her neighbours catching on – or if they have, they have kept it to themselves – was a monument to the sacred and private position of the home within an English way of seeing the world.

Mistress K's home is where her dominating self remains. You could share a pavement with her, a shop, a train carriage, perhaps you are doing so now as you read this, and you would have no idea that you are standing next to a queen of sexual domination – unless you were one of her clients, that is.

While at one point in our conversation she said she'd be happy to be called eccentric, and the idea of it had made her laugh, Mistress K was not the silver-bullet answer to my quest for someone with all the qualities of a twenty-first-century English eccentric. If nothing else, her anonymity seemed to jar.

The hunt would continue, and I wanted to keep it in the land of the partially illegal. I liked it there. I decided to interview someone who also inhabited a grey area between legal and moral taboo, yet he did so in such a way that he was championed. It was time to track down the country's best-known and most colourful dissident: a man at the sharp end of political eccentricity.

12

THE DISSIDENT

'Oh I'm weary,' he began. 'I'm just so tired of this, I can't tell you, it's been six years, I can't believe it's been six years and still they don't listen, still the suffering goes on. Liar Blair, Murderer Brown, Killer Bush, they're war criminals, the lot of them, they're mass-murderers and they're killing our babies, our children.' The word 'children' fell apart in his mouth, so it was more like 'chilled wren', which made him sound like a blinking, avuncular vicar. 'You think about what they're doing, killing the child-ren, and you compare it to what I'm doing, and they're calling me a criminal?' He gave me an incredulous look. 'Well, it's a travesty, it's an outrage and it's happening here in England, but no one wants to know.'

Brian Haw has been angry for some time. His face looked run down from the strain of his one-man rebellion outside the Houses of Parliament that has consumed the last six years of his life. For most of this vigil – directed against, variously, war in general, British foreign policy, the invasion of Afghanistan, the invasion of Iraq, genocide, and the killing of children – he has protested alone. It's only during the fifth year of the protest, from early 2006 on, that a band of followers made him their leader. They speak about him in reverential tones and will form an irregular cordon of courtiers around him when you approach.

He's an unlikely icon – no Savonarola demagogue, and he certainly doesn't go out of his way to be liked – yet in the year that his supporters began to pitch their tents alongside his, Brian Haw was voted Most Inspiring Political Figure of the Year 2006 by Channel 4 viewers. He won 54 per cent of the vote. Tony Blair received 8 per cent. In the same year an exhibition by Mark Wallinger opened down the road at Tate Britain, featuring a 40-metre-long simulacrum of Brian Haw's 'peace wall' that had been removed by seventy-eight policemen in the middle of the night as a result of a new law prohibiting organised protests within 1 kilometre of parliament. Brilliantly, Wallinger had worked out that the perimeter of this exclusion zone bisected the Tate's Duveen Gallery and had Haw's wall of banners, flags and placards meticulously recreated and positioned along this boundary.

Following the removal of his placards Brian Haw was lionised. In the eyes of the public he had been transformed from embittered lone protester into an underdog, and just as hell hath no fury like a woman scorned, the English public has no hero like a man wronged by the state.

Yet by the summer of 2007 the future of this committed Christian's one-man protest was in jeopardy. The loophole that had allowed him to remain in Parliament Square was beginning to tighten like a noose around his neck and it was hard to know how much longer he'd be there.

With his high cheekbones and trademark hat covered in badges, their anti-war sloganry softened by the sun into blobs of ice-cream colour, he was easy to spot. Brian Haw was squatting next to what remained of his shanty town of placards with pictures of disfigured babies or slogans slagging off Gordon Brown. The '-lair' of 'Blair' had been altered in the last few months to '-rown', marking the accession of the new Prime Minister. On the ground were two teddies that had not been cuddled in years, each one rotting and caked in mud, its eyes covered in grit. There were baby clothes hanging from a line, each one daubed with red handprints. They reminded me of the Shia ceremony of Ashura, perhaps a reference to the Shia Iraqis massacred by Saddam Hussein, I thought, before realising the anti-Saddam and perhaps interventionist implications of that.

I came in close and knelt beside him. He was sucking on a hand-rolled cigarette. The fingernails on the hand that held the cigarette were long and clean. His skin was tanned a reddish, nutty colour. Below his neck was a dog collar of white flesh that the sun had not reached; elsewhere it had been busy mapping out a topography of tramlines, indents, loops and whorls over his open and symmetrical face. His eyes were a watery blue and he was good-looking in a wholesome and unthreatening kind of way. There was something also about the shape of his hat combined with his square jaw that made him look like a medieval archer. I have no idea why, but I kept imagining him firing a longbow at Agincourt.

Brian the Archer.

I had been squatting next to him for some time now. Still he gazed at the Houses of Parliament. They were in recess. Behind him the plane trees fussed and shook as the wind buffeted their branches. Above, the clouds raced by as if in fast forward. At last he turned in my direction.

'Er, hello, Brian,' I said. 'Can I ask you some questions?'

'Can I ask you some questions?' he repeated quietly. 'That's a stupid fucking question. That's what it is. Stupid fucking question.'

A cabbie drove past.

'Oi, Brian, nice weather, isn't it?' he called, leaning out of his taxi.

'That's a stupid fucking question,' he growled back. Not a good start. 'What do you want to ask?' he said, turning to me.

'Um. I wanted to ask if you had seen Mark Wallinger's exhibition, the one in Tate Britain?'

'That's a stupid fucking question.' His eyes darted towards me with the venomous alacrity of a viper's tongue. 'What do you think?' he asked sarcastically. 'When I'm living here and it's just down the road? Course I did—' A bus roared past, cutting out what he went on to say. I asked him to repeat it.

'Oh God! It's unbelievable!' He sprang back from me. 'No matter how long I talk, how much I say, people don't hear me. They're always saying, "Pardon?" Or "What?" "We can't hear you, Brian!" I've shouted so long my voice's gone hoarse and still no one hears.'

'I'm sorry.' I waited a moment.

'What else?'

'I wanted to know what it was like to see the replicas of your placards at Tate Britain.'

'Another stupid fucking question,' he tutted, without bothering to look at me.

Plate II a

The Peace Protester

Time to beat a retreat.

This wasn't my first attempt to speak to him. It was the fifth, though it might as well have been the first because he never seemed to remember me, and each visit would end either with him going silent on me or his supporters closing ranks and telling me today was not a good day for Brian.

I'm familiar now with his ups and downs. When he's down he is very down and there's no way in for someone like me, an outsider. Like John Bull, whose 'spirits rose and fell with the weather-glass', his mood seemed dependent on the weather. If the sun was out and he had a crowd of supporters with him he'd be upbeat; a backbench councillor might drop by, perhaps there'd be a journalist jotting down his *bons mots*; well-wishers from abroad; or ripe female students he could put his arm round and be photographed with and perhaps catch a whiff of their just-washed blonde hair. Those were the good days, yet they were rare.

More often it would be raining when I went to see Brian Haw and he'd be alone, under his umbrella, deep in contemplation of the building opposite and dreaming like Captain Ahab of the day he'd get his whale, and he was going to get it all right. He knew that. He was going to get it because he was right and they were wrong and they couldn't kick him out, they had no right, he'd say, no legal precedent.

Brian Haw believed in the law like he believed that night followed day. He would tell you he knew his rights, and while he did not trust the police, the politicians, the ministers or the high court judges – they were a bunch of crooks as far as he was concerned – the law was different. The law would not fail him, and while this intense belief in the rights of the individual before the law of the land was not a unique national characteristic, it was rare. Haw was an English political protester who believed in his right to protest at the heart of the nation's political geography as if it was sacred. But was he eccentric? This was what I wanted to find out. I decided to return a week later.

It began to rain so I edged in underneath his umbrella. This was the closest I would ever be to him. He had a troubled look on his face.

The umbrella was red and capacious and its acoustics magnified his voice so he spoke in a hushed tone.

'Lots of things in my head I need to sort out,' he muttered, gazing at the white whale opposite. It began to rain harder. He turned to me. 'So what's this book you're writing?'

'Well,' I began, 'it's a journey into English non-conformity and creative individualism, focusing—'

'Listen,' Brian said. 'If you call me an eccentric in your book, I'll tear your bloody head off.'

I gulped noisily.

'Okay. Why don't you like that word?'

'I just don't.' He screwed up his face. 'I don't like the way people use it. It's belittling. But I mean it. You call me eccentric and I'll tear your bloody head off.'

Jayne Dowle, in the *Yorkshire Post*, once wrote, 'Mr Haw is an eccentric, no doubt.' Bruce Kent, president of Campaign for Nuclear Disarmament, called Brian Haw 'an enormously courageous eccentric'. In the *Mail on Sunday* he is 'Britain's most eccentric protester'; in the *Daily Telegraph* Haw is a 'lone eccentric'; the *Sunday Herald* called him 'a bit eccentric'; the *Camden New Journal* has him down as an 'extraordinary eccentric one-man peace protester'; in a letter to the *Independent* from a former police officer Brian Haw is described as 'slightly eccentric but totally harmless'; the North Wiltshire Conservatives, meanwhile, decided Brian Haw was 'an eccentric figure'.

It was easy to see why he hated this label. Just as Chris Eubank suggested that he was called eccentric only when he posed no threat, in a political milieu the word can imply amiability and harmlessness. Brian did not want either. Like Herbert Spencer in the mid-nineteenth century, he worried that 'If you show yourself eccentric in manners or dress, the world . . . will not listen to you.'

So what was he if he wasn't an eccentric? Brian was a committed protester who wore an unusual hat, yes, a dissident and a rebel, though he was not a revolutionary. A revolutionary would bring with him a new order that he hoped to impose. A revolutionary cannot be an eccentric because of this desire to have people follow him and his rules. Brian wanted only to alter the section of the status quo that he disliked.

The longer I spent with him the more interested I became not in why he was doing this, or in how best to describe him, but in the fact that he could do it at all. I was fascinated by the possibility of an English national spending six years camped outside the country's legislature (during what was apparently a period of heightened security), waving banners that described the democratically elected head of government as a liar and mass-murderer and for part of this period using a loudspeaker to project murderous vitriol towards the same legislature – including his feelings about the prospective death of that same head of government, the most politically powerful man in the country. The fact that he had been able to do this where he did it, for six years, was extraordinary. And inspiring. It's unlikely that it could happen anywhere else in the world, and that, more than what drove Brian Haw, reveals something about England and its relationship to eccentricity. It rams home the idea that the right of unfettered individualistic protest is cherished in England, by judiciary and public alike. In many ways the life of an eccentric is a protest in itself. The eccentric is a protester against conformity, authority and any attempt to alter his or her existence. By definition, the eccentric succeeds in this protest.

The most colourful protester to make his mark on the English political landscape before Brian Haw, a man who in some ways helped make Haw's vigil possible, was the dissident, libertine, journalist and campaigner for civil liberties John Wilkes. He died in 1797.

Rather like Haw, Wilkes lived his political life on the cusp of legality. He was a man who felt inhibited by convention only very rarely, and when he perceived a political injustice would attack it with all his wit and vim, whether from the floor in the House of Commons or in the pages of his radical journal the *North Briton*. Wilkes was the joker in the parliamentary pack, and as a thorn in the side of the political establishment he became a cult figure. During the 1760s and 1770s his was a household name, and had there been a Most Inspiring Political Figure of the Year award in the 1760s or 1770s Wilkes, surely, would have won repeatedly.

Something Brian Haw did not share with John Wilkes, as far as I could tell, was a spectacularly debauched lifestyle driven by his mammoth appetite for sex. Wilkes spent most of his adult life moving into and out of marriage, prison, debt (including a stint in the debtors' prison where 'Mad Jack' Mytton died), the Tower of London, and a Byronic number of different women's bedrooms. Although hideous – he was once described as the ugliest man in England – Wilkes claimed it would take him just ten minutes to get a woman to see beyond his wonky jaw and cross-eyed squint to jump into bed with him. In all my attempts to interview Brian Haw we never got on to his sex life.

A cad and a rake, Wilkes would swagger about mid-eighteenth-century London dressed as a pirate with a sword by his side wearing a three-cornered hat. Just as he had admirers he had dedicated detractors, including a fellow member of the Medmenham Monks, the Earl of Sandwich. A bitter enemy of Wilkes, in an attempt to defame his name Sandwich once read out in parliament several lines from a poem Wilkes had written as a young man. It was a parody of Pope's *Essay on Man* called *Essay on Woman*, including the line 'life can little more supply / Than just a few good fucks and then we die'. On hearing this several peers almost fainted. Later, Lord Sandwich set up Wilkes for one of the greatest put-downs of all time, saying: ''Pon my honour, Wilkes, I don't know whether you'll die on the gallows or of the pox.' To which Wilkes replied, 'That must depend, my lord, upon whether I first embraced your lordship's principles or your mistresses.'

None of this should overshadow what he achieved as an activist. As well as the right for printers to publish verbatim accounts of parliamentary debates, John Wilkes presented the first parliamentary reform bill in 1776, in between providing relentless opposition to the King and his government whenever he felt they were infringing English civil liberties. This later led to him libelling the King, which in turn forced him into exile in France, a country he loathed.

One of the most interesting things about Wilkes is the extent to which his political opposition was based on satire. In many ways this Gordian knot of political protest and humour seemed to be English political opposition at its most powerful. It appealed to the two most sacred parts of the contemporary English character: the ability to laugh at yourself or make a joke, and the right to individual protest.

As political campaigners who have been called eccentric, both Wilkes and Haw are part of a long English tradition of individual protest that has its roots in Magna Carta, trial by jury, habeas corpus and the Toleration Act of 1689. It has produced groups like the Tolpuddle Martyrs, the Chartists, the Suffragettes, the Levellers, and radical dissidents like 'Freeborn John' Lilburne, John Pym, Algernon Sydney, Thomas Paine, John Hampden, Major John Cartwright and Emmeline Pankhurst. Each was a rebel rather than a revolutionary – not only did they work *with* the established order of things, they didn't try to kill people to make their political point, unlike Guy Fawkes, for example, or the 7/7 bombers of 2005, both of whom exist outside this tradition.

If at first these English protesters were suppressed, none were executed for their activism and most were ultimately successful insofar as the issues they sought to reform were addressed, eventually. In the years following their death statues were erected to commemorate their protest, plaques attached to the walls of buildings, or streets named after them. This suggests a desire on the part of the state not only to tolerate individual protest, but to set it up on high and have it revered retrospectively.

While this desire to accommodate protest might have been either unconscious, accidental or pragmatic up until the late eighteenth century, in the years after the French Revolution it became a proud hallmark of English liberty. This was a shift that took place at exactly the same time as the label 'eccentric' came to be seen as a particularly English designation.

Several weeks later I returned. Again Brian Haw began by saying he was sick of people fucking well coming up to him and fucking well asking him questions. They ask him questions and then he has to answer and he gets carried away and he starts talking and once he starts talking he's got to tell them about the atrocities that are going on in Iraq, in Afghanistan, in Palestine, and that they're killing our children, our babies, that they've got blood on their hands and they won't admit to it, that they're criminals and they all need to be tried and . . .

At that moment light relief arrived in the form of two frazzled

Mancunians. They stopped in front of Brian's posters with their feet at a quarter to three. Both were clad from toe to head in shellsuits that had been accessorised with sunglasses. The sun was most definitely not out that morning, and both looked like men who had, in their time, dropped a pill or 800 too many.

Using a can of Tennants Super as a pointer, one gestured at Brian.

'Eh look,' he said, turning to face his friend, something that took several seconds. 'It's Brian Haw!'

'Wah-hey, so it is. All right, matey!' said the other one.

Brian did not flinch.

'This man here, right,' the first one carried on, addressing the trees and Winston Churchill before them. 'He's a fucking icon, right. Wah-hey. Fucking icon, mate! Here, shake my hand.'

He lunged his non-can-holding hand at Brian who was crouched on the pavement, on his marks. Brian ignored him. I could almost hear the anger hissing out of his vitreous non-expression.

'Fucking icon!' he tried again. Still Brian wouldn't look at him. Eventually the man bent down to touch Brian's hand with the back of his. Brian recoiled as if he'd been bitten.

'Just back off will you!' he cried. 'Take your drink. Go on. Take your drink and come back when you're sober. All right?'

This was my moment.

'Yeah. Back off,' I said, standing up as Brian moved away.

'What?' said one, looking at me in complete bewilderment, as if I'd just asked him to imagine an elephant pole-dancing in a tutu. There was a silence.

'Um. I just don't think you should speak to Brian like that,' I yelled over my shoulder in Brian's direction. The two men continued to look at me in utter confusion, pausing several times to look at each other for confirmation that this was actually happening. Eventually, without another word, they shrugged their shoulders and padded off towards St James's Park, one of them turning round to shout at me, 'It's about the kids!' while pumping his fist in the air.

Brian returned, warmer this time.

'They keep sending them,' he said wearily.

'What do you mean?'

'People like that, they get sent here by the government to come and distract me. All I'm trying to do is protest peacefully, to bear witness.'

At last he was starting to talk, something that had barely happened in my previous visits. 'Don't screw it up,' I kept thinking to myself. I decided the best thing to do was keep quiet. So I went mute. Slowly, lips bitten in to remind me of this, I knelt on the pavement next to Brian to be at the same height. I thought this was a good move, like something they'd teach you in the army after the one about taking off your sunglasses to calm down a man whose village you have just destroyed. Brian continued to stare at the Houses of Parliament. I turned my gaze in the same direction and worked a steely look on to my face. He glanced over at me.

'What the hell are you doing?' he cried.

I made a silent gesture to say, 'I have no idea.'

'You're in front of the pictures of the child-ren!'

Crap. He was right. I was squatting in front of a poster of a baby.

'No one's going to see them if you're sitting there! This is the evidence, the evidence of what they're doing to the child-ren, they're killing our babies, murdering them before they've even grown up! That's not right, is it?'

I shook my head and clambered over to his left-hand side. He continued to talk, and now there was no stopping him. A powerful monomania drove the words out in an unending singalong sea-shanty shower of invective. Twenty minutes later I understood something of the scale of his frustration. There were times when he couldn't sit still for the intensity of it. He'd been chasing his white whale for so long, and he'd spit his last breath at it, I was sure of that. There is no word that can describe this depth of feeling. It's equivalent to seeing a large tree that is about to fall on top of someone you love, and you try to warn them about this but they don't listen, they think you're joking, you tell them again that this tree is *about to fall on their head*, but they turn away as if there's nothing to worry about. You scream at them, and they turn back at you and start to tell you you're mad, but you don't care, the tree's seconds away from falling on their head so you couldn't give a toss about whether they think you're mad. You shout at them some more because surely there will come a point when they look up and see that what you are saying is so blindingly obviously true that they'll kick themselves for not seeing it in the first place. But they don't look up and they don't see what you're saying and it hurts. Then they try and have you moved on.

Towards the end of the summer I went to visit Brian Haw for the last time. It was warm and there weren't too many people around. The sky looked like an Etch A Sketch board that had got into the hands of a couple of bored drunks and was madly crisscrossed with vapour trails. The traffic continued round the square past the statues and the plane trees. A river of sound. Brian used to think the government sent cars round at night to stop him from sleeping. His ramshackle village of banners, flags and tents slung low to the ground looked like a guerrilla encampment. Just beyond was the statue of Winston Churchill, 'the old gas-bag' as Brian liked to call him. He scowled at the section of road between parliament and Brian's camp. Standing sentinel over the rest of the square were fractionally less titanic political figures, all totems to innovation, respectability and stubbornness, men like Robert Peel, Palmerston, Disraeli, Abraham Lincoln and, since earlier that day, Nelson Mandela. A bronze statue had just been unveiled in the south-west corner of the square showing Mandela in mid-speech with his arms raised as if subduing a crowd.

For the unveiling there had been a ceremony with African music and mawkish speeches by white politicians who described Mandela as an inspiring figure and eulogised his political achievements, including his twenty-seven-year stint in prison. He had refused to change his political stance during this period. Most of the people speaking saw this stubbornness as immensely heroic.

Brian Haw was not invited to the ceremony, which he argued was illegal anyway. He had sat with his back to the event and gazed at parliament.

The statue was unveiled, they cheered, the traffic continued to roar past, and later the stage was dismantled by men in shorts and DayGlo jackets with screwdrivers in their belts. Evening fell and a relative quiet descended on the square as the normal order of things returned. The family of statues had a new arrival, and it was only then, once the square had thinned and there were no longer people lingering to peer at the new addition, that Brian Haw became a monument in my mind. For the last six years he had not moved. He had been rained on, hailed on, snowed on, shat on by pigeons, and throughout had been as stubborn as a heifer. In doing all of this he had become a living monument to English bloody-minded protest, more so than Mandela. He was a protester at the heart of a Protestant nation. And this was it. The location of his vigil was uncannily apt. Although one of its most obstinate and colourful enemies, Brian Haw was encamped at the very heart of the English political machine. In this sense he was a centric eccentric, an embodiment of what Jeremy Paxman once called a 'sense of I-know-my-rights', as well as testament to the English toleration of dissent. He was also, from where I was sitting, an eccentric with a small e. He did not pose a threat, yet I don't think he realised the power of this. Seeing him there I began to believe that English society was shaped in such a way as to accommodate this kind of useful and constructive eccentricity at its very centre.

The statue was unveiled, they cheered, the traffic continued to roar past, and that evening, with the lawn lit gold, I asked Brian if one day he'd like a statue erected in his honour.

He smiled, at last.

'I wouldn't mind something, perhaps not a statue though.' He finished rolling another cigarette. 'What I'd like is a bed of forget-me-nots. Just here.' He pointed behind him at the spot where he had been camped for the last six years. A coach roared past. 'A bed of forget-me-nots would be just right.' He smiled again, before turning back to parliament.

13

SECTIONED

During the years Brian Haw has been camped in Parliament Square there have been times when a pair of passing police officers will taunt him, lightly, ask him if he's starting to lose it, going mad, hearing voices. They know and he knows that, although the police do not have the authority to kick him out on account of his political protest, if it was adjudged that he had lost his mind and consequently posed a threat to himself or others the police have the power to take him to a hospital, have him looked at by a psychiatrically qualified professional, and if they agreed that Brian was suffering from a mental illness he'd be sectioned. The police can do this to any UK citizen. The prerogative here lies with the medical professional because of the loose definition of the term 'mental illness', on which a sectioning hinges.

Once sectioned Brian Haw would be detained against his will and forcibly given certain types of medication. In theory he'd be released as soon as the doctors concurred that he was better, but the chances are he'd be there for some time. The mental health facility becomes – as Beau Brummell howled when led into the asylum where he later died – 'A prison, a prison.'

This is the domino-like sequence of events and procedures set in motion when society *feels* that someone has strayed beyond eccentricity into the land of insanity. And it is often *feel* rather than *know*. Rarely will a sectioning be the result of a criminal act – a study published by the Royal College of Psychiatrists in 1999 estimated that as a UK citizen you were more likely to win the national lottery than die at the hands of a mentally incapacitated individual. Sectioning is based instead on what we find strange or threatening. It is about hunch, instinct and projections into the future: it elucidates the isthmus in our minds between the perception of danger and its reality. Fear is the lighthouse that guards this channel.

Next to the idea of the 'harmless eccentric' that had been invoked throughout my journey was this, its deductive extension: the unharmless non-eccentric. The madman or madwoman. I could have no decent understanding of eccentricity without a sense of what happens when a man or woman is thought to have slipped beyond it.

Compared to other nations English law is freakish in the way it legislates mental illness. By the early twenty-first century there remained many parts of the world with no mental health legislation whatsoever, let alone laws that granted police the power to scoop off the street anyone who has what to an untrained eye looks like a psychiatric disorder.

Jenny, or Jen to her friends and family, is a police officer based in York who administers the Mental Health Act of 1983. She sections people. She's a devout Christian as well with hair the colour of liquorice. We arranged to meet in a Costa Coffee near her police station.

'How do you section someone?' she repeated, leaning forward against the acoustic-guitar coffee-shop music. 'Well, it starts with the police being alerted, usually by a neighbour, a relative, carer, that sort of thing, and they tell us there's someone who appears to be mentally ill who is putting themselves or another at risk. Often it's an immediate-response call so we have to be there in twelve minutes.' She glanced over my shoulder. We were at the back of the coffee shop. I was to pretend to be an old friend if one of her colleagues spotted her, rather than a writer interviewing her about sectioning. 'Now, once we've picked them up,' she said, addressing me again, 'we take them to the main ward of the hospital – you know, your normal NHS hospital. Take them to A and E where they're seen by a hospital member of staff who'll assess them. Though I should say the assessments I've seen are not at all thorough. They'll literally just . . .' She mimed looking someone up and down and put on a medical voice. '"Yes, they can go."'

'Go where?'

'To the nearest mental health unit, where a psychiatrically trained doctor will assess them. But again, in the cases I've seen, like the one where a woman takes off all her clothes and starts running round the room screaming, the doctor just pokes his head in and goes, "Yes, that's fine. We'll take her." It's not like they have a checklist necessarily.'

Once the individual has been detained in the hospital they are referred to as a patient, a label that forces them to see their current mental state as an aberration in need of correction. The relevant section of the act is applied. It might be a section 3, a section 4 or, the most common, a section 2 – though this depends on whether or not they have broken the law. Between 1998 and 2004 on average just under 27,000 UK citizens were sectioned every year, and in each case a doctor would ascertain that their illness was curable; otherwise it was impossible to have them sectioned.

'Yeah, that's the treatability clause,' Jenny went on. 'I had a situation where someone ran at me with a carving knife before trying to set me alight.' She sounded nonplussed. 'And because this woman was sufficiently mental, they couldn't section her.'

'Because she wasn't curable?'

'Right.'

'Then what?'

'Then she carries on causing havoc basically until she's bad enough to go to prison. Or, until she's deemed not mental enough that a doctor can cure her.'

This loophole is no more. A few days after I went to meet Brian Haw for the first time, across the road in parliament the Mental Health Act 2007 was passed. It followed nine years of bitter wrangling by politicians, doctors and mental-health lobbyists, and among other changes this act abrogated the treatability clause. So it was easier now for Jen to have someone sectioned, though the act also gave the patient's opinions on treatment greater weight and added several items to the list of procedures and chemicals a doctor was not allowed to inflict on a detainee. One of these was the use of sex hormones, once used to try and alter the sexuality of gay men by reducing their sex drive back in the days when homosexuality was considered a mental illness, something it continued to be up until 1967. This in itself hints at the startling changeability of what the words 'mad', 'insane' or 'mental disorder' can imply.

Alan Turing was one of the most original, far-sighted and mathematically gifted Englishmen of the twentieth century. Described as 'an eccentric don' while at Cambridge University, he's seen now as the father of modern computer science as well as being the first scientist to propose Artificial Intelligence; he was also gay at a time when homosexuality was not only classified as a mental illness but subject to criminal sanction (you'd think one would be enough). In 1952, after letting slip to a policeman that he was in a relationship with a man, Turing was arrested and given a choice of prison or hormone treatment. He chose the latter and underwent a year-long bout of oestrogen injections to 'cure' him of homosexuality. The criminal record that followed meant he could no longer work for the government at GCHQ, where he had been employed after his stint at Bletchley Park during the Second World War helping to crack the apparently indecipherable Enigma machine. A year after this treatment finished, at the age of forty-one, Alan Turing committed suicide. Snow White in her lair, he bit into an apple laced with cyanide.

'Men will always be mad and those who think they can cure them are the maddest of all,' Voltaire wrote in a letter to a friend in 1762.

While men may always be mad, what we define as 'mad' clearly shifts. It is a relative term, as is 'eccentric'. In English society madness and eccentricity sit side by side, although their relationship is always lopsided: like a nervous aide, eccentricity follows madness wherever it goes. Madness never follows eccentricity. You deduce the meaning of the word 'eccentric' by looking first to society's understanding of 'insane' or 'mentally disordered'. As English society navigates the chicanes of fear, repression, toleration and hope presented by history, so the authority within that society will change its application of the word 'mad', and while this is entirely natural, and this particular word can never have a permanent meaning, the desire to alter the mental functions of an English citizen who's been labelled 'mad' or in any way mentally disordered is new. For most of the last two millennia that person would instead have been either tolerated and cared for by the Church, ejected from society, isolated or turned into a scapegoat and killed.

Not only is this person whose lifestyle has slipped beyond the tramlines of eccentricity subject to well-intentioned yet by their nature clumsy attempts to change the way his or her brain works, but they are kept apart from society in a place where they can't be seen. In this sense the medieval principle of expulsion or isolation persists. That way they cannot interfere with our daily existence, even if it is paradoxical to the point of irony that a man in the street talking to *himself*, for example, could be considered an intrusion on the lives of his fellow pedestrians.

Once this person has been set aside, doctors will try to recast the workings of their brain in a form that's amenable to the England from which they've been kicked out. The detainee would once have had lobotomies or leucotomies forced upon them. Electroconvulsive therapy is still used today. Otherwise the sectioned patient will be on the receiving end of an exotic but grim-sounding cocktail of stimulants, anti-depressants, neuroleptics and tranquillisers such as chlorpromazine, Librium, Largactil or lithium, the latter a drug that was and still is used to combat bipolar disorder.

'Cured, I'm shrivelled, stale, and small,' the poet Robert Lowell wrote after completing a course of lithium.

These drugs will almost always 'dampen a person's general intellect and limit his or her emotional and perceptual range', according to Dr Kay Jamison. Eccentrics deemed to have gone too far find themselves smothered in a worsted blanket of apathy, which can be especially bad if they're artists or poets and they rely on these things for their livelihood. When offered a course of treatment to take the edge off his manic ups and downs Edvard Munch refused, saying, 'I want to keep those sufferings.' Lowell once described life without lithium as living 'with one skin-layer missing'.

At this moment, in the months before his treatment began and before he was institutionalised, Lowell was an eccentric bursting with creativity. So was the grandson of Sir John Betjeman before he was taken off the street and given the first of many psychiatric drugs. Since that moment in his late teens, Dave Lycett Green has been sectioned almost fifty times. His body has withstood a Somme-like barrage of sedatives, tranquillisers and anti-psychotic drugs that have begun to change the shape of his body, affect his mental processes and sap his will to escape. Over the years these drugs have led him to a place where he might, from time to time, like Lowell, feel shrivelled, stale and small.

'All poets are mad,' Robert Burton wrote in *The Anatomy of Melancholy*. Sir John Betjeman, Poet Laureate from 1972 to 1984, was not. Regularly described as an eccentric, when he died he was mourned on a Queen Mum-like scale. He had become a teddy bear: a 'national treasure' whose face made you think immediately of buttered toast, cream teas, branch-line trains and donkey rides on windswept English beaches.

Dave Lycett Green, his grandson, is in his early thirties and when I came to write this chapter was living in a mental health facility. Instead of interviewing Dave I spoke to his brother, John, who gave me an account of Dave's experiences over the previous twelve years.

Although this man's encounter with the UK mental health system is not necessarily generic, so I can't be sure whether his story is typical or atypical, it seemed important to try and flesh out in some way the other side of the process described by Jen: to get beyond statistics about UK citizens who were deemed to be mentally incapacitated and consequently sectioned, though this was not easy. Dave's story is hard to relate. There were different ideas from those around him about how Dave came to be where he was, and the exact nuances of when and why. So it is important to state clearly that what follows is an account based on an interview with John, his loving younger brother. The text has been read by Dave himself, he is happy with its content and has given his oral and written consent to its publication.

Since 1995 Dave Lycett Green has been locked in a cycle. A self-perpetuating, vicious, Catch-22 circuit of events that has had him sectioned forty-seven times. While in care he has been beaten up, locked in seclusion and forced or persuaded to take a cumulatively gigantic quantity of psychiatric drugs. Some of these drugs are injected. The rest come as pills that his brother described as being the size of golf balls. For most of the last eight years Dave has been on the maximum daily dose of sodium valproate, a drug that has made him put on weight (four stone), lose hair, show early signs of diabetes and start to suffer from high blood pressure and sudden sweats. Above all, this drug has corroded his will – his will to escape from the mental health facilities in which he is kept. Although you could argue that this is less of a side-effect and more of a goal. Sodium valproate is a slow-release tranquilliser that coats your serotonin gland so that when you feel, you do so as if through a glove. Dave was also, at the time of writing, receiving quantities of haloperidol and lorazepam when he became noisy or boisterous.

As long ago as 1792 Dr William Pargeter condemned the use of chemicals or narcotics to sedate psychiatric patients. He argued that it was infinitely preferable to subdue patients using reason, personality or what his contemporary, the inimitable Rev. Dr Willis, physician to King George III, called 'catching them by the eye', which meant giving the patient a terrifying, primal glare that would turn any human being to mush. This was at a time when English doctors were at the forefront of psychiatry. While there has been a shift in recent decades within institutional psychiatry towards cognitive therapy and away from drugs designed to sedate the patient, in British state-run mental health institutions tranquillisers and sedatives remain the tool of choice for most doctors and nurses.

Before the drugs had taken their long-term toll, usually during the summer, Dave would escape from whichever institution he was being held in and travel to London. There he'd live rough for anything between a week and three months. Sometimes John would help to break him out. Usually he'd lose him after that. With no cash Dave would live out of dustbins and sleep in squats or abandoned attics. During the day he'd get on a skateboard in a fluorescent pink shell-suit and wind his way through London with a ghetto-blaster on his shoulder blaring out Public Enemy. He called himself the 'Lord of Kensington'. He made people laugh, and it was this that drove him.

For six months during 1998 he experienced some of the best months of his life. He was living in the City of London and became fixated with magic and freemasonry; he'd see dragons everywhere, talk to ghosts and tramp around with one or two imaginary Cherokee Indians just behind him giving him a running commentary on it all. Each morning he'd get up at six, put on a pair of white gloves, and dance outside tube stations as City workers streamed past on their way to work. Either that or he'd run around with a toy mobile phone that he'd painted gold and make pretend drug deals, ordering in Ks of coke, tons of speed, now! He had worked out that by making people laugh, here, in the financial nerve-centre of the nation, he'd have a positive effect on the world economy – something to do with the conversion of masonic energy, John explained.

Each of these playful, inquisitive and magical sojourns would come to an end when someone called the police. Not because he'd committed a crime (with the exception of one incident involving a toy gun) but because a member of the public became concerned. The police would get hold of Dave, look at his history of being sectioned and return him to the nearest mental health unit. Boom. The key turns and he's back to Bedlam, so to speak, bathed in the Spartan light of its regimented halogen strips and surrounded by chairs screwed to the floor and a solitary table-tennis table which no one ever uses.

In the last nine years Dave Lycett Green has spent no more than eight months beyond the jurisdiction of a state-run mental health facility.

When life in one of these units gets him down Dave will talk to his *alter ego*: Dee, from Manhattan. Dee is always upbeat. Dee can't be touched by the drugs. Dee stands for hope and for escape and is someone who never loses the will to fight. When he turned thirty and his parents asked what he'd like for his birthday, Dave asked for an American accent. Repeatedly during our conversation his brother told me not only that Dave was a fantastic artist, that his paintings were like nothing else he had ever seen, also that he was the most pure and honest person you could ever meet. He took immense pride in never speaking about people behind their backs, he never lied and never cheated, and that the longer he spent in different psychiatric institutions the more important this moral honesty has become.

I asked John what did he think his brother's eccentricity, his bipolarity – I did not know what to call it – was rooted in? John felt that you could trace some of it to the experience of growing up in a household that, when he was younger, could be reasonably described as bohemian, or eccentric in the lightest sense of the word. John called the atmosphere 'halfway between posh and artistic'. When

Dave returned from a gap year in India and began to smoke marijuana and talk about returning to India in order to become a sadhu
his parents became worried – as any parents would – that something had changed while he'd been away.

Dave's behaviour in a man of sixty might be dismissed as harm-
lessly eccentric; in a nineteen-year-old it was different. On account
of his age it was not implicit that Dave understood the norm from
which he was deviating, however lightly, which helps explain why
it is so rare to read about a twenty-year-old eccentric. A degree of
old age implies you understand the mores of your society and that
you inhabit the margins consciously.

You can trace this association between eccentricity and relative
old age back to one of the earliest references to an eccentric personality in a 1779 edition of a periodical called the *Mirror*, in which an
anonymous article describes a certain Mr Umphraville, a man who
had 'retired from the world' and was full of 'little singularities of
sentiment and manner' (including having a room in his house where
he could shoot a gun at whatever he liked). The author suggested
that just as the houses with the most character are the ones old
enough to be surrounded by mature yews, so 'the most eccentric of
them all [people] have something venerable about them'. From its
inception the eccentric has been associated with this same senes-
cence. Old age implies an understanding of your society's cultural
norms.

Perhaps more significant for his state of mind than his upbringing
were the varying amounts of LSD, speed and ecstasy Dave had
consumed while at school. Combined with whatever he took in India,
by the time he reached nineteen you could say that he was dancing
to a different drum. On his return from India he went to live in a
tomb on top of the Ridgeway, an ancient track between Stonehenge
and Reading, and took to snorting Ariel washing-up powder because
he believed it was cocaine. He heard and continues to hear voices and
sees things that the rest of us do not, as his brother was the first to
admit, and in defence of the people who treated him John stressed
that most of them really wanted him to get better and that there were
periods of two or sometimes three weeks when he agreed that
Dave should not be out on the streets. But what John could not

understand was how the processes and practices of psychiatry remained so rooted in a series of discrete tags – tags that regularly failed to describe a patient satisfactorily. Dave has been variously labelled as manic–depressive, bipolar and schizophrenic, and accordingly dosed up with the drugs that match these disorders.

Much has been written by heavyweights like Deleuze and Guattari, Foucault or Goffman about the unnatural power of psychiatric institutions and the stigma induced by the labels they dole out. This fits loosely into the anti-psychiatry movement, a series of arguments based on the idea that contemporary psychiatry is overly dependent on labels and that this dependence increases the possibility of mis-diagnosis, which in turn can lead to iatrogenesis – illness brought on by mistaken diagnosis.

As a result of the different chemicals he's been given over the years Dave's life expectancy is shorter than average. The irony is that if he can outlive his uncle, he will inherit a large sum of money as well as a baronetcy. He will become Sir Dave Lycett Green.

I did not envy him trying to explain this to the doctors and nurses.

As John put it, Dave would then be able to leave the mental health facility, become independent from it, and perhaps he would no longer be thought of as mentally disordered. He'd be called an eccentric instead. Unlike so many of the people I had met on my journey, the prospect of being labelled eccentric filled him with joy. Not trepidation.

Though the number of people detained in UK mental health facilities in 2004 was as little as 14,000, having peaked in 1954 at around 148,000, over the last fifty years there's been an efflorescence of new psychiatric syndromes in Western medicine. The guide to recognised psychiatric disorders, the *Diagnostic and Statistical Manual of Mental Disorders*, now contains three times as many mental disorders as it did in 1952 when first published.

There is also, in this country at least, a disturbing new emphasis on trying to diagnose children with mental disorders. In 2004, the Office for National Statistics claimed that one in ten children in Great Britain aged five to sixteen had a clinically recognisable mental disorder, a figure that is ominously out of sync with any previous understanding of how many of us require psychiatric help. Our definition of what constitutes mental illness is broadening and this reduces the possibility of eccentricity. Insidiously.

So from one flank the internet is normalising the margins of English society – as I had seen in the world of BDSM – while on the other, pharmaceutical-company-sponsored psychiatry continues to widen the parameters of what constitutes mental disorder. Eccentricity, the buffer between normality and insanity, is thinning.

J. S. Mill argued that in any given society there should be a clear distinction between when members of the group dislike something or someone, let's say they feel uncertain about it, and the point at which they legislate against it. Fear narrows the gap between the two, and within early-twenty-first-century England the distance between not being sure about a certain lifestyle and designing laws to prohibit it – particularly in the realm of mental health – has become perilously slight. In his autobiography Mill stressed that perhaps the most significant theme of *On Liberty* was to underline 'the importance, to man and society, of a large variety in types of character, and of giving full freedom to human nature to expand itself in innumerable and conflicting directions'. Had he been alive today, surely, he would have spluttered and raged coherently against the shift in England away from the possibility of a society rich with this 'large variety in types of character'. What's more he would have argued that the chief danger of our time was not that so few dare to be eccentric, but that so few are legally able.

'For me, people like my brother pose nothing *like* the risk to society that you read about in the papers,' John told me. 'And I know it's boring to say this because it'll sound like I'm going all conspiracy-theory on you, but I don't know how else to put it. The thing is, there are a lot of people who profit from there being more people with mental disorders, more of us who need pills and more of us to be looked after.' He paused for a moment, allowing his tone to soften. 'I mean yes, my brother hears voices, and yes, he sees stuff that the rest of us don't. But that's gone on since the beginning of time. Think about it. There will always be people like that, people who hear voices and see stuff, but most of the time society will realise they don't pose a threat and let them get on with it. In some places, you know, they become holy men and everyone gives them food.' He looked wistful for a moment. 'Sometimes I dream about getting out of here. Taking Dave somewhere else where he wouldn't get such a hard time.' He glanced down. 'Though I guess that wouldn't work.'

∼

Blessed are the cracked,
For they shall let in the light.

An anonymous subject when interviewed by Dr Weeks for his investigation into eccentricity

14

ONCE WERE WITCHES

'Well, there's no way I could have done this a hundred years ago. Out here by myself? No, they'd have called me insane. Someone would have had me committed, I'm sure of it. Few hundred years before that and I would have been called a witch,' she said, partly to herself as she gazed out at the day.

Framed by the stone armature of the window was Pendle Hill, where in 1612 ten witches were executed following the Pendle Witch Trials. The hill rose out of the Yorkshire Dales like a submarine surfacing. Cloud was coming in low making it hard to pick out details on its flank. The Perspex window was gummed up with dirt and dust and the patina of storms and snow that had left static explosions of white scum across its surface. They made the light in the room directional and white, so the objects around me looked as if they had been set up for a photo shoot. There were boxes of books, paintings hammered roughly into the wall, balls of wool, yellowed newspapers, a medieval-looking loom, several sheepdogs and a wood-stove that gurgled and hummed as it burned through a heap of kindling. The unplastered walls were as thick as 200-year-old oaks and they made the room snug, dousing it with an unnatural silence.

'When I was a little girl my grandfather told me I had a very odd kick to my gallop,' said Sue, in a voice that was both friendly and gruff. 'I suppose he was right, in that I live by my own rules. I have no morals, you see. I have personal principles, but not morals. They're generally things other people impose on you.' Her shoulders were workmanlike and her eyes bright, though she hid them by keeping her head low. 'Which was rich coming from him. He was as mad as a box of frogs.' Her hair was grey and short and falling away in clumps around the back of her head. She got out a pre-rolled cigarette and lit it, her hands trembling slightly.

'So I don't mind when people call me eccentric. England needs its eccentrics. We've always been an island. We've always done our own thing and are terribly proud of our own identity. As long as you don't hurt anyone else, I think it's fine to be eccentric. I forgot to ask. Do you want a cup of tea?'

'Yes, that would be great, thanks.'

Sue left to boil water on a dilapidated Rayburn in the kitchen next door. In the few minutes she was gone I felt my entire being decelerate, like a freewater diver slowing his pulse before entering the ocean. Everything beyond the room became muffled. I had not felt this calm in months. I felt dislocated too. At the point of crossing the threshold a few minutes earlier I'd been transported back to a cave in a Turkish hamlet where I had slept five years before. A widow had put me up before a policeman kicked me out several days later. It was immoral for me to stay there, he had said. A local taboo had been broken. Smell – of all senses the thug, the Neanderthal, the creatine-slurping gym bunny – had taken me back to this cave as I inhaled an identical fug of dog and cat laced with dust. The walls added an earthen bass note to it all. They smelt of rain and rock.

Like Jen in York, Sue Woodcock had once been a policewoman. She was now retired and since 2004 had lived alone in a former sheep-pen high in the Yorkshire Dales. When she first arrived, Mire House was an uninhabitable heap of stones. A skeleton. She had got to work and fixed it up using tarpaulin and scraps of wood and installed a generator that ran on cheap farmers' diesel. Gradually she turned her outpost into a nest, yet at the same time she was forced to fight a battle with the Yorkshire Dales Park Authority. They said she had no right to be there, and that her home was a ruined sheep-pen and not a dwelling and should remain in a state of decay so as to preserve the character of the dales.

Plate III b

H. Hemming   J. Woodcock

The Female Hermit

I had come to see Sue because I needed a female eccentric for my collection, someone other than Ann Atkin or the elusive mad cat lady, a woman whose lifestyle would not have been possible a hundred years ago because of her womanness. In the press coverage of her fight with the Park Authority Sue Woodcock was frequently referred to as an eccentric. It was not just the fact that she was living out in the dales by herself as a woman that warranted this tag, but her mild quirkiness as well.

Next door the water boiled and to my left I heard a squeak. Hidden by the foot of my rocking chair were five terrier pups in a cardboard box. I hadn't seen them as I walked in. Each one was as large as two tennis balls sewn together and as I watched, grinning like someone who's never had a dog and barely knows what to do when he picks up a puppy, they mewed at each other, woke up, fell asleep, their eyes barely open, crawled over each other or peed at will in a winning display of puppyness. One was more adventurous than the others and kept trying to escape from the box. He couldn't work out how to do it. Not yet anyway.

Sue returned and set down a mug of sugary tea next to me and we talked about her dogs and the weather before moving on to her battle with the Park Authority. I asked if it was strange for her, as a former policewoman, to be called a criminal.

She cocked her head to one side. 'In some ways, yes. That was a job I was really passionate about, being a local bobby,' she said in her laddish yet sexless way. 'But I don't see what I'm doing now as a fight against the law. Quite the reverse. It's because I believe in the law that I'm fighting,' she added with force, for that moment transporting me back to Parliament Square with Brian Haw squatting next to me. 'I believe in fair play, and I'll comply immediately with any legal warrant they get to kick me out as long as the people who come have the correct court orders and so on. Otherwise, the only way they'll get me out is in a box. But it seems the thing they're most worried about is me putting my washing out to dry.' Sue scoffed. A puppy squeaked agreement by my feet. 'I wrote them a letter saying, "Anyone who gets slightly turned on by the sight of my nether garments at my age has to be slightly sick." But they didn't see the funny side of that, unfortunately.'

In November 2006 an eviction notice was posted on her door giving her twenty-eight days to leave. After an initial panic she decided to fight the ruling. The twenty-eight days passed, and in April 2007 she won her appeal and was given permission to continue to live there, though for the moment she cannot change the appearance of her nest.

'I don't think the Park Authority realised quite how obstinate I would be,' she explained. 'We're as stubborn as each other you see. And they won't give up. Even now they're still at me. It's like when you tell a puppy off, they always have to have the last yap.'

The media coverage has been kind to Sue. The *Yorkshire Post* liked her and her story so much that they asked her to write a regular column about her life as a female hermit in the Yorkshire Dales.

'Yes, you see, I've a slightly warped sense of humour,' she said, cackling at the thought. 'So I write for them about knitting and staring at shadows for hours and not being quite right in the head, or about the cat dying, the puppies. That kind of thing.' There was something conspiratorial about the way she said it. Her voice was becoming warmer.

Not only was Sue described by the local media as eccentric, she was also the victim of *political correctness gone mad*. Streams of people wrote in after each story about Sue Woodcock's plight saying she had *every right* to restore the house, and anyway, what's wrong with her being eccentric? As long as she's not harming anyone *she should be allowed to do her own thing*. These letters and the articles that triggered them were a neat exposition of an English belief in one's right to do one's own thing, a kind of *On-Liberty*-lite, but with a twist. Sue was a woman, and up until the Second World War, while it was socially fine for men in England to dance to their own drum like this, it was much less acceptable for a woman to do the same.

Sue's three dogs came bounding in from the fields. The largest and wheeziest was part Burmese Mountain, part Welsh Border collie. The youngest and prettiest came up to my chair, laid her snout on my leg and gazed up at me, her eyes bulging so I could see the collar of white around each iris. One by one Sue took the puppies out of their box and let them crawl about on the floor.

'Come on, little ones,' she cooed. 'Here we are.' One of them picked up the corner of a piece of newspaper and began to drag it over a rival pup, who couldn't work out where the newspaper was coming from and became disorientated. Another clambered on top of both puppy and newspaper and started to pee, while the more adventurous one, the one I liked to watch most, set off to explore the rest of the room. It went straight for the elderly collie dog snoozing in the corner and as it climbed up and over his paw – a paw that must have looked like a great wall – the collie growled. Curiosity drove the puppy on. By the time he was clambering up on to the collie's snout the dog began to bark. The puppy retreated amiably.

'I've found that animals have been a great deal more faithful than people,' said Sue, picking up one of the puppies and setting it down on her stomach.

At school she was badly bullied. That was the first time she felt like the odd one out. 'I was the fat, red-haired girl with freckles and no parents,' she said without anger. 'My grandmother brought me up, you see, because my parents decided they didn't want me. They emigrated to Australia when I was five months old. Which certainly added to it.'

'Five months old?'

'Yup. I never saw my father again. I saw my mother in Tasmania shortly before she died and we were able to lay our ghosts to rest, although by then I didn't feel anything towards her. What could I do about it? At the time, growing up, it hurt a lot. I had a terrible chip on my shoulder, especially because it contributed so much to the bullying.' She remembers the names of the two girls who bullied her most. One is now a doctor, the other a housewife. She knows where they live.

'So you could say I've always been the odd one out. When everyone else was mad about the Beatles, and I mean *everyone*' – she dropped her voice to a whisper, in case the bullies overheard – 'I liked Frank Ifield! He could really *sing*. I'd go and buy Schubert's "The Trout", Edith Piaf. Stuff they'd never heard of.'

Following an abortive career as an opera-singer Sue joined the Hampshire police force, even though her grandmother didn't approve, and spent the next thirty years as a motorcycling policewoman specialising in cases of flashing. She was decorated for bravery. As retirement neared she began to pine after a life as a crofter in the Yorkshire Dales; and in preparation began to keep sheep in the back-garden of the police station.

'And do you like living by yourself?'

'Oh yes, I love it. It means I can burp, fart and belch as I like. I can wander round in my pyjamas, make as much mess as I like, go to bed whenever I want and there are no arguments to deal with. On the other hand, it can be lonely sometimes, but,' she sounded upbeat, 'there's always something to do. Something to keep me busy. I've got my writing, the detective novels I do, I've written eight of them, you see, and I think they'll make the perfect replacement for *Midsomer Murders* because those can't go on for ever. Soon everyone in that village will be dead. What else? I spin wool, make socks and jumpers and hats. No one bothers me and I'm reasonably healthy apart from my hair falling out, that is. I mean I have a cold once a year, but that's it.'

'Has living up here been as good as you hoped?'

'Yes, it's marvellous. Oh believe me, when it's bitterly cold and the snow's coming in, and I've got my heating on, there's nothing better than being up here all by myself.' She turned to the window once again with Pendle Hill looming in the distance. 'And you've got bats, owls, plenty of animals, so you're never alone.' Her tone changed, becoming more serious. 'Maybe I'm going back to nature by doing this. There are rhythms of nature that you understand only when you're close to it. Perhaps I'm becoming a wild woman.' She laughed at herself. 'A modern-day witch!'

While use of the word has always been in flux, being called 'insane' does not necessarily mean you are, as the word might imply, out of your mind. Just like 'eccentric' the term is not definite in its meaning, unlike, say, the word 'watertight' – if you look at a bucket of water it is usually quite easy to tell whether or not it is successfully retaining liquid whether you were to do so in the sixteenth century or the twenty-first. Instead the word 'insane' is a cultural construct used to articulate, bolster and enforce the morality of a given authority. It empowers its dispenser and lends weight to its authority.

Within any group of humans a similar kind of power accrues with the character or force doling out labels, calling names or in any other way telling the rest of the group who's normal, who's weird and who's dangerous.

Just as homosexuality in England was classified a mental disorder up until the 1960s, Englishwomen were committed to lunatic asylums as recently as the early twentieth century for transgressions such as having premarital affairs, reading too much, not cleaning their kitchens, taking too many long walks, experiencing post-natal depression, cutting their hair in an unusual way, or living alone just as Sue Woodcock was. Daniel Defoe described his eighteenth-century male contemporaries having their disobedient yet sane wives committed to asylums. The English witch-hunts of the sixteenth and seventeenth centuries with just under 2,500 witch trials and an estimated 750 witches executed continue this depressing and fairly consistent theme of masculine elites not only carving out separate spheres for men and women, but imposing far more conservative codes of conduct on the female sphere.

The early modern witch in her non-conformity, solipsism and mild deviation from the norm should have been a female eccentric. She wasn't, because within the female sphere there was no eccentric buffer between on the one hand 'normal' and on the other 'mad' or 'criminal'. There are a number of reasons why there was no such buffer, most of which can be abbreviated to men wanting their wives to dedicate themselves wholly to the upbringing of their children, or being jealous in a possessive way of their sexuality.

As a result female eccentric biographies never really took off. A review published in 1803 of a new title, *Eccentric Biography: Memoirs of Remarkable Female Characters*, concluded that the book served no useful purpose because it actively encouraged immoral behaviour.

Women were only really called eccentric if they strayed into the male sphere, something they might do by dressing as men. Victorians read about women like Hannah Snell who fought at the Battle of Pondicherry in 1761 under the name 'James Gray' and on her return starred in a musical at Sadler's Wells about her soldiering before having a nervous breakdown in 1792 and being admitted to Bedlam.

Women who wrote under male pseudonyms were also a little eccentric, as were those who moved away from English society altogether and entered the male sphere of abroad.

Lady Hester Stanhope was a famously eccentric female traveller who regularly dressed as a man during her travels. She spent the last few decades of her life in Syria and Lebanon wearing Bedouin robes and was known to her followers as 'Queen Hester'. The niece of William Pitt, Lady Hester crisscrossed the desert with a caravan of camels searching for the new messiah who she planned to make her husband, thus fulfilling her destiny as Queen of the Jews. That was the idea at least. Instead she settled in the hills of southern Lebanon where she established a mini-fiefdom surrounded by Druze villagers who looked to her for arbitration and refuge. She later moved to a monastery near Sidon where she shaved her head, got into debt, hoarded junk and corresponded with Queen Victoria.

Margaret Cavendish was another exception. 'Crack-brained and bird-witted' in the eyes of Virginia Woolf, 'Mad Madge' wrote voluminously during the seventeenth century and did so under her own name in an age when most women used a masculine *nom de plume*. Writing with supreme haughtiness and confidence – a confidence born of privilege – she penned biographies, philosophical treatises, essays, verse, novels, novellas, as well as one of the first works of science fiction in the English language. She also wrote about *herself* in an age when few writers, either male or female, dared. Between 1600 and 1640, forty-two new books were written by women in England. Cavendish produced twenty-three between 1653 and 1673.

By the late nineteenth century, attitudes to women in the mould of Margaret Cavendish had regressed in several respects. Male understanding of women and their womanly ways was now rooted in a version of femininity which emphasised invalidity, physical weakness and hysteria and was reinforced by selective medical research. Even the writings of Darwin were used to help reconstruct women as slaves to their physiology. Madness became an essential part of the female nature and was linked to women's reproductive systems. There were even gynaecological treatments for female psychiatric disorders.

Pre-Raphaelite artists happily fleshed out this strange, almost necrophiliac version of the madness-prone woman at the point of death (where her sexuality was at last tamed), by churning out awful paintings of corpse-like Ophelias or Ladies of Shalott looking equally unwell.

As a result, from the mid-nineteenth century until the mid-twentieth century the majority of inmates in English asylums were female, and, as with any psychiatric overreach, the possibility of eccentricity thinned. With men as the dispensers of both reason and labels, women had become bodies: silent, weak and irrational.

By the dawn of the twenty-first century the boundaries of these separate spheres for men and women had long since blurred. Women were no longer sectioned for reading too much, and there were well-known Englishwomen who might be called eccentric not because they dressed as men but because they represented a tolerated version of female non-conformity: women like Dame Vivienne Westwood, Isabella Blow or Kate Bush.

Still, there is nothing like parity between the sexes when it comes to the way we think about eccentricity today. Psychological surveys continue to suggest that on the whole men find non-conformity in women either confusing or threatening, while women generally find non-conformity in men attractive.

Although the English continue to look for eccentricity mostly in men rather than in women, in much the same way that at a certain level they expect scientific breakthrough, artistic advance and humour predominantly from men (and domestic security and balance from women) – a hangover from the past and like a stone in your shoe a reminder that our gender norms have not changed as much as we'd like to think – a woman who is eccentric in her own right is possible now in the way that she was not a hundred years ago. Sue Woodcock embodied this shift. With every passing year we shuffle closer to some kind of equilibrium, even if it is a balance we may never reach.

Raised by her grandmother, Sue explained that she grew up within a dated and Victorian understanding of femininity. She was taught not to be boisterous, never to mention the black sheep of the family

who had become a suffragette, and was encouraged by her grandmother to loathe men who weren't members of her family; those
who were, she was to worship as gods. Sue was surprised she didn't
turn out gay.

'My grandmother was a very undemonstrative person,' she said
matter-of-factly. 'No cuddles, no outward affection, but I'm immensely
grateful for the way she raised me. I think we share a fighting spirit.
But she could never have done what I'm doing as a woman. Not
in her day.'

She got up from the sofa to feed her puppies, placing a plate of
porridgey gloop in their midst. Once the plate was licked clean
and the puppies' faces covered in food she returned them one by
one to their box. We went outside to inspect her chickens. Sue
also showed me her rare-breed sheep and introduced me to Henry
the turkey. I felt an affinity. Plus we had the same name. He was
a Norfolk Black and would often come into the house to hop on
to her lap and be petted. The scrofulous bobbled skin around his
eye would go red when he was turned on and blue when he was
showing off. It felt a bit like going round a city farm, though
without the fences or signs warning you that the mud may be slippery, the steps hazardous, or that you walked through the farm at
your own risk.

Her house was set in a grassy declivity within a sweep of treeless
moorland, and to the south was a long view down the dale. In the
distance I could make out several cottages with plumes of smoke
funnelling in reverse into the cloud above. The bricks looked like
blackened loaves with the mortar between them the colour of vanilla
custard. Dry-stone walls cast a web over the valley. Hens squawked
and squabbled around our feet as Sue told me about England and
Englishness and how she thought both were being eroded by the
number of immigrants coming into the country. She thought that
as a nation we were bending over backwards to accommodate these
people, which was part of the reason why she's living in Yorkshire.
She wanted to escape 'that England'.

I asked if she had everything she needed in life.

'Everything I need but not everything I want,' she said, thinking
hard. 'I want things like washing machines, proper sewage and mains

water, a degree of comfort. But I also have things that money can't buy.'

'Like what?'

'Like the ability to do my own thing, and to do it my way. That's precious, you know.'

She gave me some eggs, recited a poem and I left her in her honey-, teak- and chocolate-coloured hermitage. Yes, I thought as I reached the nearest village, her mannerisms and patterns of speech were unusual or quirky, she had her own morality, saw herself as apart from society, her lifestyle represented an experiment of sorts, so in many ways she was an eccentric. But the most interesting thing about her was her gender: she was right to say that 400 years earlier she would have been labelled a witch.

As I drove towards London I played over in my mind the sound of kindling spluttering in a wood-stove, the mewing of puppies, and tried to remember the smell of wet stone or the light of a white overcast day coming in through mottled Perspex. Yet before long they faded and I was back in a world of speed bumps, double-yellow lines, Vernon Kay on Radio 1, *Gardeners' Question Time*, service stations, leylandii, flashing lights, flyovers, warning signs, out-of-town shopping centres, Travelodges, Lotto rollovers and people who say 'typical'. The England she had left behind. As the road took me further south and closer to London I thought more about those who choose to take a step back. The ones who break away from it all.

PART THREE

ISLOMANIA

15

MAN AN ISLAND

From time to time someone escapes. The normality and repetition of life in the everyday mainstream become oppressive and in the middle of the night one of us will steal away. Having glimpsed in their mind the possibility of a world where they are lord of all they survey, one where the sun moves around them, the escapee goes to become an island – population: one. In doing this they take to its extreme the English islander mentality.

There is something about people who become castaways like this that the English find fascinating. Perhaps deep down we are all islomaniacs who dream of living in a castle with a moat and a drawbridge.

Lawrence Durrell was the first to coin the term 'islomania', defining it as a 'powerful attraction to islands', having found a reference to 'islomanes' in the notebooks of Gideon; these were the descendants of the Atlanteans, a people forever drawn to a sunken isle.

The fact that we live on an island, a 'scepter'd isle', a 'fortress built by Nature for herself / Against infection and the hand of war' as John of Gaunt's eulogy put it, was and is the first line of almost any attempt to define Englishness, no matter how drunk or highfalutin. From *Treasure Island*, *Gulliver's Travels* or *Robinson Crusoe* through to Radio 4's *Desert Island Discs* you don't have to go far to find mementoes of this islomania. It is an islandness that has changed our outlook and the speed with which intellectual currents from Europe have swept over us, slowing them; it's even affected the shape of our towns. Being an island has more or less removed the need for the kind of defensive urban geographies you might find in mainland Europe because for most of their history the English have lived without the threat of sudden invasion. This island existence has also softened our recourse to hierarchical systems of government, particularly during the Middle Ages, so the moment feudalism began to disintegrate a public sphere emerged in England much faster than it did elsewhere in Europe.

English islomanes, islomaniacs, both by their example and in the way they feed part of the English psyche, present a meandering trail into the heart of English eccentricity.

Towards the end of 1968, with little by dint of ceremony, a nation was born off the coast of Suffolk, 4 miles outside English territorial waters. 'Paddy' Roy Bates, a former British Army major, proclaimed what was once a Second World War Maunsell Sea Fort to be the Principality of Sealand. At little more than 30 feet wide, it was and still is the smallest self-proclaimed independent state anywhere in Europe as well as being one of the most interesting embodiments of English islomania.

Sealand has been going for forty years now and has a strange and chequered history. As well as its own national football team, regardless of the fact that the principality is slightly smaller than a football pitch, Sealand has its own motto and national anthem. Over the years the principality has endured attacks from pirates trying to run radio stations and drug traffickers hoping to use it as a staging post. Passports have been issued as well as stamps and Sealand dollars (each worth $1 US dollar, in case one day you are paid in SD).

Another Englishman, Martin Coles Harman, minted a small number of Puffin coins in the early 1930s soon after declaring himself King of the Island of Lundy 12 miles off the coast of Devon. Unlike Bates and his fellow Sealanders, however, Harman didn't get away with this and was forced to stop producing currency and pay the British government a £5 fine. The coins are now highly prized collectors' items.

Bates went further than Harman in almost every respect. By declaring Sealand to be independent from England he established a micronation. He has also proved in court that English law does not apply in Sealand, which has given him and his mates free rein to fend off invaders using handguns, sawn-off shotguns, Molotov cocktails and an ageing flame-thrower. When not manning the defences,

Prince Roy has tried to run a TV station from Sealand hosted by a Page 3 girl, and at one point thought about turning his kingdom into a holiday island by reclaiming the seabed around its base. It is now used mostly for offshore data storage by a company called Havenco.

I got in touch with the principality to arrange an interview with Prince Roy and over the months that followed received several emails written in a proto-officious tone from the 'Chief of Bureau, Bureau of Internal Affairs, Principality of Sealand', who I later found out was Bates' son, Michael. He calls himself Prince Regent of Sealand. He told me that his dad had retired to Spain and was unavailable for interview.

Although Bates senior and his micronation have been the subject of numerous criminal investigations into murder, fraud and drug trafficking, the British government has generally turned a blind eye to this eccentric outpost. While it does not recognise Sealand as a sovereign principality it has made no attempt to close it down even though Sealand is now within British territorial waters. Clearly it does not pose a threat.

His Royal Highness Prince Roy has given plenty of interviews over the years, and as I trawled through some of them I was struck less by what he described and more by the way he described it. On several occasions Bates referred insouciantly to his *right* not just to claim a former Second World War fort as his own on the grounds that he had kicked out the people squatting there previously, but his right before the law to proclaim Sealand as an independent principality. It reminded me of the way Brian Haw had described his right to pitch a tent outside parliament and shout things at the Prime Minister. For both men this tenet of islomane eccentricity was such an incontestable part of their birthright as Englishmen that to question it was actually a bit odd.

'Nobody took me seriously at first,' HRH Prince Roy thundered in one of these interviews. 'But my lawyer told me I had a legal right to stay on Sealand. From that day I have been determined to prove the point. I never imagined I would have such a devil of a job, but I don't regret a moment of it. We fought for liberty and won. Isn't that everybody's dream?'

We fought for liberty and won. It's what you can imagine French revolutionaries scrawling on walls, shouting to the sky or mumbling into their drink during the Terror that followed the collapse of the Ancien Régime. English eccentricity owes a great deal to the French Revolution. Much more than I realised. Not only did the term 'eccentric' become established as part of a patriotic response to the dark turn of the bloodbath playing out across the Channel in the late eighteenth century, but in many ways the liberty that the French fought for was already alive in England, and it took the event of the French Revolution for commentators on both sides of the Channel to recognise this, articulate it and in a written sense bring it into being. French writers identified *l'exception anglaise* as the modern liberalism that their compatriots had been killing each other to set up. In England, from this period on, eccentric personalities came to be seen as talismans of this same liberalism.

My journey has taken me all over the country. It has shown me different ways of living and drawn me into unusual ways of seeing the country I've lived in all my life. It has also shown me the trajectory of the eccentric through English history, guiding me from the moment he (and sometimes she) first appeared in the late eighteenth century and the way Victorian society developed a fascination for all things eccentric and clamped the term on to our national identity. It has also given me a taste of how Dickens, Spencer and Mill set eccentricity up on high as a goddess of creative non-conformity, and from this point, its zenith, I have followed its slightly depressing slide through the twentieth century as it becomes an anaemic imitation of everything it once was, until the English eccentric arrives in the early twenty-first century out of breath, a little run down and badly in need of its Version 2.0.

Yet perhaps the most important part of this history is something I have not yet explored: why the term emerged in the first place and what political need it served.

Groups of human beings define themselves only in relation to others. They do so either in haste when they feel under attack, or at a more leisurely pace when they are able to combine the way foreigners view them with what they themselves find unusual when they look beyond their borders.

For most of the eighteenth century the English lived with little or no real threat of invasion, so they were not obliged to forge an identity in a crucible of crisis. When they were involved in wars – often against the French – it was Britishness rather than Englishness that mattered, partly because the army fighting the French was polyglot, also because the fighting took place overseas. As Dr Johnson put it, 'In a time of war, the nation is always of one mind.' The nation he was referring to was Britain not England – it was the *British* Empire defended by the *British* Army and the *British* Navy with its mascot *Britannia* that held dominion over the waves.

It's within the second strand of identity-formation, the less defensive one concerned with domestic, cultural or social trends, that Englishness becomes apt. When Rupert Brooke wrote many years later about a corner of a foreign field, even though it was the British Army fighting a British war, the spot he described was forever England, not Britain. 'England' stood for a more emotive understanding of self, it was of the heart, while 'Britain' referred to external political expansion, armies, marching bands and empire.

As the eighteenth century wore on the popular understanding of Englishness matured. Prints and cartoons of Britannia with her trident and shield became less popular after 1785, and in her place came the blundering yet peaceable John Bull, the Georgian everyman, a pin-up for English domestic virtue and the opposite of his arch-rival the effete and immoral Lewis Baboon, a.k.a. Louis Bourbon, that is the French. The fact that Bull was a humble shopkeeper rather than part of a landed elite was testament to the growing importance of the mercantile middle classes within this more everyday English identity. It was proof that Englishness could be less grand than Britishness. It took itself less seriously, with English icons generally more accessible than British ones.

While John Bull embodied a distrust of all things foreign, particularly anything French, it was from a less confrontational encounter with mainland Europe that the English eccentric emerged and in this, the eighteenth century Grand Tour played a starring role.

In many ways the predecessor of the gap year, the Grand Tour allowed wealthy young Englishmen to see for themselves how different they were to Europeans, in the way they dressed, in their manners and in what made them laugh. Compared to their continental neighbours, the English were generally more scruffy, their manners less refined and their humour far more concerned with clowning about and foolery than delivering the finger-kissingly perfect witticism, unlike the Europeans they met.

Having these Grand Tourists unleashed on the continent also allowed European writers to refine their stereotype of the English. In stunned silence they watched as an unlikely army of cultural ambassadors roamed the continent, visiting classical ruins, not understanding local languages and pulling pranks on each other. French observers were struck usually by their characteristic *singularité*. Goethe thought Englishmen had an excess of 'Eigenwüchsigkeit': a mixture of self-assuredness and egotism that you didn't find elsewhere in Europe. Kant suggested the typical Englishman was 'an eccentric not out of vanity but because he concerns himself little about others'. Perhaps the best example of how Europeans saw Englishmen is to be found in a minor German literary genre described by Paul Langford that grew up in the early nineteenth century dealing in tales of opinionated and eccentric young Englishmen travelling abroad and coming into contact with more socially aware Europeans (who were German). In the course of the story the more mature European (still German) ends up showing the lovable English buffoon how to curb his eccentricity. The Englishman is immensely grateful to his (German) mentor.

Europeans also based their opinions of the English on English literature and the island's recent history. In letters the English were the only Europeans to capitalise the personal pronoun 'I', while their recent history of civil war, regicide and the establishment of a republic, followed by a 'Glorious Revolution' heralding a constitutional monarchy, suggested to many Europeans that the English were essentially ungovernable. It's easy to forget that for most of the eighteenth century no other European nation could change its government without a full-scale revolution.

Nikolai Karamzin, touring London in 1790, summed up what most foreign visitors found peculiar about the inhabitants of this island when he concluded that the 'unbounded freedom to live as one wishes, to do whatever one desires on every occasion, provided it is not contrary to the welfare of others, has produced in England a great number of peculiar characters'. He went on: 'Other European countries are like well-laid-out gardens where the trees are all of the same size, the paths straight, and everything uniform. The English, on the other hand, grow up, morally, like wild oaks, according to the will of fate. Though they are of one stock, they are all different.' This last sentence is vital. And brilliant. It encapsulates the inherent difficulties of devising a national identity that was somehow universal but could place at its heart both *difference* and *individuality*.

While their eighteenth-century cultural encounter with mainland Europe prepared the ground for a shift in the way the English saw themselves, it was the French Revolution that provided the push.

By the early 1790s the outcome of the French Revolution looked less rosy than it might have done in 1789, and most of English society was united in its opposition to these upheavals, both within the establishment and without. In towns like Bristol there were popular and spontaneous 'Church and King' riots in support of the status quo.

The French Revolution forced the English, like any group that feels threatened, into a momentary state of introspection. It also provided a political agenda to this navel-gazing. The English needed to think of themselves in such a way that would nullify the rhetoric and explosive idealism powering the French Revolution. The popular English conservatism that emerged as a result found its most eloquent spokesman in Edmund Burke, whose *Reflections on the Revolution in France* (published in 1790) linked liberty, the high priestess of the French Revolution, with both Church and king. This extinguished its revolutionary potential. Burke was one of the most influential writers to make liberty patriotic rather than radical.

As Heinrich Heine put it not long after, for the Frenchman at this time liberty was like a young bride with whom he was infatuated, while for the Englishman she was his lawful wedded wife – even if he didn't always treat her with tenderness, when he thought she was being attacked he would defend her 'like a man'. HRH Roy Bates barking, 'We fought for liberty and won,' is a direct descendant of this sentiment.

As well as inspiring this new patriotic conservatism, the French Revolution cast the English mob in a new light. Powerful and prevalent for much of the eighteenth century, especially in London where it would protest against just about anything – from a tax on cider to the rumoured demolition of cathedral spires – in the wake of the Revolution in France the English mob with its anarchic tendencies needed to be subordinated, something that was done not by repression but by incorporation.

Paul Langford, in *Englishness Identified*, by far the most elegant and thorough exploration of the origins of eccentricity (with fantastic pen illustrations at the start of each chapter), and a book to which my understanding of this subject owes a great deal, has argued that it was at this juncture, when it was unclear how to reconcile the more quixotic whims of the English 'character' or the unruliness of the English mob with a coherent national identity, that the idea of the English eccentric emerged more or less as a *deus ex machina*. The eccentric represented 'engaging diversity without threatening conformity' as Langford puts it, and although the word first appeared in the 1770s it was during the 1790s that it became more widespread, as you can see from the eccentric biographies that began to appear and the first occurrences of the term in legal and journalistic material.

This eccentric figure was fundamentally amiable, not radical. His mild non-conformity and love of liberty were virtuous rather than vicious – not at all the kind of thing to spark a revolution – which helped law-abiding non-conformity become such an intrinsic part of the English national character.

Surely there are English eccentrics earlier than the second half of the eighteenth century? This is something I keep asking myself. Apparently not. An eccentric personality was possible only once the top-down, feudal version of English society made way for a more horizontal plane with a public sphere. For the first time this introduced a political centre-ground, as well as a political right and left. Up until then the resident in-group deviant would have been assigned a role like religious hermit, outcast, scapegoat or natural fool. Not eccentric.

The one factor to which Langford does not give sufficient emphasis when explaining how and why the English eccentric appeared exactly

when he did is the effect of King George III's concomitant oscilla-
tions between eccentricity and apparent insanity. The King's first bout
of illness coincided with the outbreak of the French Revolution.
The overwhelming public affection felt for the King at this time,
itself bolstered by the popular conservatism sweeping the country,
made it that much easier to talk affectionately about the marginal
non-conformist in your midst, the outspoken oddball, the eccentric.
A beloved king provided a clear if unlikely precedent.

As well as inadvertently bringing about a more sympathetic understanding of insanity in England, King George's reign saw a decline in
the monarch's operative power in the daily running of the country.
At the same time there was an increase in the ceremonial attached to
his position. Formal performances of 'God Save the King' doubled in
London theatres after 1786, a new 'Windsor uniform' was introduced
for the royal family, spending on the royal palaces was maintained in
wartime: the role of the monarch was becoming more decorative –
ornamental even. In each definition of eccentricity, and with every
eccentric I had met, there was a similar emphasis on costume and a
degree of exhibitionism. From Ann Atkin and Captain Beany to the
Marquess of Bath, Chris Eubank and Brian Haw, eye-catching outfits
were important. Not only was King George III an eccentric at the
heart of the establishment, dressing up and revelling in the ceremonial, but he was one of the first kings to begin to be less involved
in the day-to-day running of the country, which made him more of
a figurehead than an engine. In turn he became more lovable partly
because he was less culpable when something went wrong. He began
the monarch's transition from team owner to club mascot. And when
you bundle together all of these factors, drives, carrots, sticks, pushes
and pulls something becomes clear: King George III is the godfather
of English eccentricity. One moment labelled mad, the next eccentric, adored by the English public, he was associated with liberty, a
degree of exhibitionism and the kind of unpretentious individuality
that for perhaps the first time in English history was seen as a proud
English trait.

If, as Jeremy Paxman once wrote, 'the most profound influence upon
the English is the fact that they live on an island', and we are indeed

a nation of islomanes, then this explains part of our fascination for hermits. Just as HRH Prince Roy of Sealand was in many ways a man living as an island, like Tom Leppard and Sue Woodcock he was also a hermit of sorts. We are attracted to hermits in exactly the same way that we are drawn to islands.

The nationwide mourning of Josef Stawinoga, also known as Fred, or just the Wolverhampton Ring-Road Tramp, provides a recent reminder of this. In October 2007 he was found dead, aged eighty-seven, in the tent he had pitched on an island in a dual carriageway forty years earlier. During his life local Sikhs revered him as a holy man who had renounced worldly possessions; some would leave food outside his tent and present him with other votive offerings. The effect of the news of his death was fascinating. The residents of Wolverhampton who had become so used to seeing him there missed him desperately, even though they had never met him. A Facebook group was set up in his memory. Wolverhampton residents began to raise money to build a memorial to Fred the hermit, a man who would growl at visitors when they came too close. Others wanted to rename the entire ring-road after him. He was described as 'a brilliantly eccentric icon for Wolverhampton', and a spokesman for the city council admitted that the town 'won't be the same without him'.

Hermits were a mainstay of Victorian eccentric biographies, as well as of later twentieth-century regurgitations of these works, although few were hermits in the traditional, medieval sense of the term – pelicans of the wilderness living as hermits out of religious conviction and therefore dependent on nearby monasteries. Instead they might be aristocratic recluses, like the eccentric fifth Duke of Portland, known as the 'Burrowing Duke' on account of the 15 miles of underground tunnels he built to move around without being seen. Similar to those employed by the brilliant scientist Henry Cavendish, the Burrowing Duke's servants were not allowed to speak to their employer. Messages were delivered through letterboxes. If they weren't aristocratic recluses, these figures might be 'ornamental hermits', part of an unlikely eighteenth-century fad for having artificial wildmen installed on your estate.

Charles Hamilton of Painshill Park in Surrey was one of many wealthy Englishmen who advertised for a hermit to live on his land. He offered £700 in return for seven years of ascetic solitude spent studying the Bible while dressed in a camel-hair robe. Hamilton's hermit would get paid only on completion of his seven years, and on the condition that he did not attack any of the guests, and 'never, under any circumstances, must he cut his hair, beard, or nails, stray beyond the limits of Mr Hamilton's grounds, or exchange one word with the servant'. The only known applicant was sacked when he was spotted down at the local pub three weeks after starting as resident hermit.

Another man who built a grotto for an ornamental hermit was Captain Philip Thicknesse, once described as 'the greatest self-publicist of the eighteenth century' as well as 'buffoon', 'blackmailer' and 'scoundrel'. Upon his death he had his right hand chopped off and sent to his son to remind him quite how displeased with him he was. It was also said of Thicknesse towards the end of his life in 1791, just as the term was coming into vogue, that 'for eccentricity of genius few stand superior to him'.

A contemporary and friend of the artist Gainsborough, Thicknesse left school aged sixteen and travelled to America where he built a hut and lived as a teenage hermit next to a creek, until a vision of his mother came to him while he was out playing the flute one day. She told him to come home. Back in England he married a girl called Maria, having abducted her from an armed escort of soldiers – Maria's mother later committed suicide by jumping on to the railings where Thicknesse had seized her daughter – and following a brief imprisonment in the King's Bench prison after being found guilty of libel, something he would be accused of throughout his life, and by now on his third marriage, Thicknesse set off in 1766 on a low-budget Grand Tour of Europe. Accompanied by his wife, two daughters, a spaniel, parakeet and pet monkey called Jocko (who rode postilion), he drove through France in a two-wheeled cabriolet with a guitar stowed in the trunk to entertain any villagers they met. Thicknesse's account of the journey became a bestseller.

He was also fascinated by hermitages, and tried to buy himself a plot at St Catherine's hermitage in Montserrat before building his own grotto at his home near Bath. Having made many enemies during his life and leaving in his wake an extraordinary trail of scandal and shattered reputations, he claimed to have found a kind of hermit-like peace towards the end of his life. He even wrote a Hermit's Prayer.

Thicknesse was by no means the only Georgian Englishman to have found hermits inspirational or to call them 'abettors of freedom'. Their popularity at this time not only reveals something of the English character, it explains part of the innate sympathy felt for eccentrics when they appeared in the late eighteenth century. As well as being a protester of sorts, by choosing to live within a world of their own, an eccentric is in many ways a hermit.

This same fascination for hermitage runs through the poetry of Wordsworth, Coleridge and Byron, all of whom waxed at considerable length about young men in lonesome, semi-tragic contemplation of nature. Crucially, it was the idea of Romantic hermit-like solipsism as a metaphor for standing alone against conformity that inspired J. S. Mill in *On Liberty* to elevate eccentricity from a charming characteristic to a principle.

In 1816 Byron went one further than his fellow Romantic poets and acted on the centrifugal urge of a hermit, just as Tom Leppard and Paddy Roy Bates would do in the century that followed, or the sixteen-year-old Philip Thicknesse in the century before. Not entirely of his own volition, Byron left England to become what you could call an émigré hermit. It was the event of Byron and others like him living in exile that played a crucial part in allowing the idea of the English eccentric to spread around the world.

Several years ago I sat next to a travel-writer called Tim at dinner. He wore a Nehru suit and told me that he had lived for several decades in Sana'a, the capital of Yemen. He told me was married to his books. I was planning to be in Sana'a the following month, so towards the end of the meal I asked if I could look him up when I got there.

'That's fine,' he said.

'What's your address?' I asked, leaning back in my seat as I pulled some paper from my pocket.

'You don't need it.'

'Oh,' I said, a bit confused, before starting to shove the paper back like wadding down the barrel of a gun.

'Just ask for the Englishman.'

'The Englishman?'

'Sure, the Englishman.'

'And where do I ask for the Englishman?'

'Anywhere in Sana'a Old City. Someone will show you the way,' he explained with a well-meaning shrug.

My plans changed and I never made it to Sana'a so I don't know if these directions would have worked. I like to think they would have done.

There can be few cities around the world that have not, at some point during the chaotic sprawl of the last few hundred years, had an eccentric émigré Englishman in residence, *the Englishman, the Old Englishman, old English, England*: a figure who has chosen to live apart from the repressions or conventions of what for him, or indeed her, was England. This English traveller, or English expat, is as much a stock eccentric character as the bumbling aristocrat.

There is an impressive list of characters who fall into this category of eccentric émigrés, including Charles Waterton during his travels in South America; or the peripatetic autodidact Sir Richard Burton as he snuck into the holy city of Mecca disguised as an Arab merchant; Lady Hester Stanhope touring the Levant as Queen of the Jews; Lord Byron on a one-man mission to spread syphilis throughout southern Europe; James Holman the blind traveller who circumnavigated the world alone; the racist adventurer Colonel Fawcett who disappeared trying to find an imaginary city in the Amazon; the Kurtz-like Sir James Brooke who was made Rajah of Sarawak by the Sultan of Brunei; the orchid enthusiast and surrealist patron Edward James who spent forty years building an Eden out of coloured concrete in the Mexican rainforest; John Wilkes in Parisian exile; the English gentry who had fallen on hard times and were living in Brussels at the time of Waterloo to escape the bailiffs; the homosexual misfits who drifted towards Tangier in the 1940s and 1950s; or any number of colonial administrators or entrepreneurs, usually Englishmen with moustaches, who were once products of Paxman's Game and had left England to be free from the restraints of English society. Many of these were characters with whom you could have had a similar conversation about how to find them in their adopted home: *Just ask for the Englishman.*

Once established in their foreign hermitage most of these expats develop a romantic and selective nostalgia for the place they have left behind, which is frozen at the point they left, or earlier, so their version of England or Britain becomes anachronistic. At the same time, like a belly released from a corset, they turn into exaggerated versions of themselves; they become more natural, more colourful too.

These were the individuals Noël Coward had in mind when he sang about mad dogs and Englishmen going out in the midday sun. English expats who have emigrated around the world over the last 150 years with their larger-than-life characters and nostalgia for an England that has passed, have confirmed to the rest of the world an idea of English eccentricity. In the eyes of others these émigrés would often personify the Victorian identification with the eccentric.

Expats, or émigré hermits as I like to call them, would happily conform to the stereotype of the English eccentric; it gave them an identity in their new setting and in their eyes elevated them. So towards the end of the nineteenth century the idea that the English were famous for being eccentric began to be reflected back on to them by the rest of the world. Foreign writers confirmed this when they came to visit. In 1856, Ralph Waldo Emerson told his mostly American readership that in England 'each man walks, eats, drinks, shaves, dresses, gesticulates, and, in every manner, acts and suffers without reference to the bystanders, in his own fashion, only careful not to interfere with them', concluding that he knew of no other country 'where any personal eccentricity is so freely allowed'. Just under seventy years later the writer George Santayana described England as a 'paradise of individuality, eccentricity, heresy, anomalies, hobbies, and humours'.

This was a very accessible kind of eccentricity that was being described. Eccentricity as a general national characteristic, which is how it had come to be seen from a distance. It was not necessarily the kind of startling or inventive one-off deviation from the norm that confounds those who encounter it, including you, because it is so hard to place. Few if any of these English émigré expats were in the same league as the man I was about to meet.

16

THE KING

When I was eighteen I spent five weeks painting on Dominica with a friend called Al. It's an island in the Caribbean set around a mountainous volcanic heft with a different river for every day of the year. It was the hurricane season when we were there and, though the island was not hit, it rained a great deal during those weeks.

Near Laudat, a village high above the capital, there lived a man called Fixit. He was wild with anger and poetry, and wore his hair in short dreadlocks. With him at all times was a machete.

Fixit squatted in a hut up beyond the other houses in the village and, using white household paint, had covered the place with slogans. Once there was no more space on the hut he had moved on to the road, so in between pot-holes and wild tufts of undergrowth you could make out quotes from the Bible, lines about redemption, come-uppance and all the things that most surely WILL come to those who wait. Most of these slogans were directed against Fixit's nemesis: a Canadian property developer called Robert who would tell you that he had Jesus on his side.

Fixit's favourite slogan, one that he painted a number of times on both his hut and the road, was: 'WHEN COMIN TO SEE THE KING, ONE MUST BRING TIDINGS TO THE KING'.

In his hut he was king. In that sodden patch of elfin rainforest he was a king and in his head he was the King of Kings. I read his slogan about the King so many times that when I saw him I too thought of him as a king and would address him as such. By then he had attained in my mind what Walter Bagehot once described as 'the mystique of monarchy'. Few people can inspire this in those they meet.

★   ★   ★

'You know what, I'm gonna let you in on a secret.' King Arthur put his arm round me and came in close. 'I am, in fact, a wizard.' His voice was raspy and gravelled from his years as a squaddie, biker and protester, sleeping rough in the Great British cold, sheltering in trees, tents and bins or, if he was lucky, tunnels, smoking throughout. 'Now don't worry, I know you're thinking to yourself, "Okay, here we go. Arthur's off on one. He thinks he's a wizard. Whatever." But. I mean,' he spluttered, turning to me, eyes round in disbelief, 'look at what just happened!'

Less than a minute earlier, in full battle-frock and crown with a fistful of druidic rings arranged across his knuckles, Arthur Uther Pendragon had arrived at the security cordon surrounding Stonehenge. It was the night of Summer Solstice and, along with 24,000 pagans, hippies, students, chavs, witches, druids, farmers, tramps, eco-warriors and a handful of journalists, the pair of us were trying to get in.

'Any weapons or sharp or dangerous objects?' asked the security guard, a tanned and short-haired bruiser with a thick West Country accent.

'Er, yes,' replied Arthur evenly. He hitched up his cloak to reveal two weapons strapped to his back. 'One four-foot-long Celtic broadsword.' He gestured at the leather-bound scabbard. 'And a dagger.' He looked up. The security official stared back at him, as did the one on his right. One by one each of the nine officials manning the gate stopped what they were doing to admire the plump bearded man in a tunic with an immense sword attached to his belt. Smiles ran into their cheeks like surgical incisions.

'King Arthur, isn't it?' said the security guard. 'On you go. Have a good night.'

Arthur marched on and I followed, less amazed than I should have been. During the last five hours with him this kind of thing had become normal. As he said much later that night, drunk, and with a glint in his eye, 'For you, all of this is weird, isn't it? All these things that happen to me. But this is my day-to-day! For me this is normal! This', said King Arthur with a lunge of his arm in the direction of Stonehenge, 'is my office.'

★   ★   ★

In 1986, aged thirty-two, John Rothwell died. Having left school aged fifteen and after serving in the army for a few years he joined a different tribe with its own rules, shibboleths and carefully observed uniform: he became a Hell's Angel biker. Known as King John, Rothwell lived out his twenties getting into fights, drinking, biking, working as a labourer and doing odd-jobs. In his early thirties, within a few weeks of each other, his parents died. Something changed in him. For the first time in his life he felt truly adrift, and atomic – a rebel without a cause.

One night in a bare dank squat his mate Kris 'The Whippet' Kirkham told him that he wasn't John Rothwell, but the reincarnation of King Arthur. Following a series of coincidences such as opening a book about the historical King Arthur and reading the words 'King Arthur in Triumph' and interpreting this as a sign because at the time he rode a Triumph motorbike, Johnny Reb as he was also known agreed that he was the modern-day King Arthur. The following week he had his name changed by deed poll.

King John was dead.

Long live the King.

Arthur Uther Pendragon, as he became, was not – and is not – delusional. He knows that until the day he dies and beyond there will be people who think he is, as he put it, 'some wanker who reckons he's King Arthur', and for at least three years following the Whippet's epiphany he would question daily what he had become. They were difficult years, gloomy and full of self-doubt, but with time he would construct a chainmail suit of answers to fend off the doubters and critics, and by the time his story was fully formed these initial doubts had slipped into a semi-permanent state of detumescence.

But what does it mean to be King Arthur? What does one actually do as the modern-day reincarnation of an ancient king of England apart from tell people who you are?

You fight for truth, honour and justice. You bike the length and breadth of the country campaigning to save trees, fields and ancient Saxon burial sites. You successfully pester English Heritage for ten years to have Stonehenge reopened to the public for Summer Solstice. You become an arch-druid. You are run over by a chauffeur-driven Jaguar carrying Lord Hanson. You appear in court more often than you can remember – twenty-six times between 1994 and 1999 – until waking up in a police cell has become entirely familiar. You also earn the legal right to carry your sword Excalibur with you wherever you go, and in the process become adept at manoeuvring your corner of the English legal system. You stand for parliament. An anonymous political backer pays your deposit and you notch up countless appearances in the local and national media before co-authoring a book about your life which is later remaindered. You call yourself a media tart and become a member of Mensa. You sell your house and exist nomadically, sleeping on whichever floor or bed you can blag your way on to or into. You drink a lot of cider and sleep with more women than you care to remember – at least that's what you say you do – you are also granted the legal right to wear an Arthurian crown in your passport photo and take legal oaths on your sword. At the same time, slowly, you become accepted, cherished and in other ways championed within the counter-culture that you call home. You become the point of liaison for the local constabulary, English Heritage or the National Trust when they want to communicate with what to them looks like a chaotic fringe, yet beneath it all you worry that you are being inveigled into the establishment. That's what you do as the modern-day reincarnation of King Arthur.

Throughout – and this is something most people lose sight of amid the lists, hyperbole and sheer atypical individuality of your existence – you have fun. The skin around your eyes is worn with hardship and merriment. Your laugh makes you sound like David Jason playing Pop Larkin in *The Darling Buds of May*: it's a Falstaffian explosion that spreads like an airborne virus so that people on the next-door table find themselves laughing along with you, even if they don't really know why.

'Mine's a Strongbow,' he said, unzipping his leather jacket and unwinding a snow-white kamikaze scarf from around his neck. His accent was south London, with a smattering of somewhere more rustic and local to where we were: Amesbury, a few minutes' drive from Stonehenge, five hours before we would reach the security cordon surrounding the stones.

King Arthur needn't have said a thing. The girl behind the bar was already pouring his pint by the time he opened his mouth. 'Yeah, I've got locals all over the place,' he said, grinning.

'It's always cider, isn't it?'

'Yep. Druid fluid. If I walk into a pub in Avebury they know what I drink. If I walk into a pub in Chiswick they know what I drink. Does that say I drink too much?'

Arthur was shorter than I'd imagined, with a belly and beady eyes that seemed to be designed for living outside. His grey hair was parted roughly down the middle and his beard was trimmed. He looked stupid without a beard, he told me later.

We sat down near the window.

'But where's your real local?' I started. 'You're based locally, right?'

'No,' he said innocently, more high-pitched than before. 'I don't have a home. I live on me motorbike.' He began to size me up, as if he hadn't spotted me before. 'I stay with friends basically. I decided when I started out on this quest that if it was meant to be, the magic would sustain me, which it has. Now that's a very romantic way of putting it. A very practical way of putting it would be to say I've got a lot of mates, and they look after me. But the mad thing is, when I started this quest, I didn't know a single one of them. They've all become mates along the way. So last night I stayed in London. Night before I stayed up in Cumbria. Tonight I'll be at Stonehenge and tomorrow I'll stay at Avebury. And if I end up somewhere I don't have any mates, I'll just walk into town and somebody will put me up. It happens all the time.'

Only then, sitting in front of him and hearing him speak, did I understand how this happened. He had charisma. We'd been chatting for only a few minutes and already I was on the verge of offering him a place to stay next time he was in London. I stopped just short.

'I don't miss not having me own house,' he went on in his blokish, full-bodied voice. 'I mean, I had a house in Basingstoke, I had a mortgage. Now I very rarely wake up two days running in the same bed, or even the same ditch.'

'What's your quest?' I asked. 'What's the holy grail?'

H. Henning   A. Pendragon

King Arthur

He leaned back in his temporary throne. 'Haven't worked that one out yet,' he said, glancing out at the thinly populated pub. 'I view myself as a warrior and I suppose I'm just here to die trying really. To give it my best shot. Part of me thinks, "Right, if this is real, and you are the reincarnation of King Arthur you should be *doing* something about it."' He took a drag on his cigarette as if for emphasis. 'So this is the *doing* something about it. I don't know what I'm doing, I'm just ad-libbing until something becomes clear. But while I'm doing that, I'm encouraging people to fight for truth, honour and justice, protect the environment, and fight for civil liber-ties. I'm doing what I think King Arthur would be doing.' I felt a glow of recognition, and the peculiar sensation that all the traits of English eccentricity I had identified over the last year were coalescing before me in one man. Or was I imagining it? He rearranged himself in the chair. 'As far as I'm concerned there are three Arthurian ages and three Arthurs,' he went on. 'There's pre-Roman, post-Roman and post-Thatcher, and I'm the post-Thatcher. I'm still riding a horse. The only difference is it's a bloody iron horse! But I'm still banging heads together. It might be arch-druids' heads, or a protester and a druid, but I'll be banging their heads together all the same. And isn't that what the ancient Arthur did? He just banged everyone's heads together and said, "Come on, we're on the same side. Let's fight the marauding Irish and Saxons and anyone else who wants to invade."'

Instead of Vikings, Arthur's enemies were town planners in DayGlo bibs and hard hats, townies, builders of roads or those who fenced off sacred sites, aloof politicians, Christians who called pagans heretical, druids who said he was not King Arthur. He had plenty of enemies, which was fine by him because as he said repeatedly that night in his Arthurian growl, 'I'm an old warhorse. I love to fight.'

His phone squawked as a text message came in. He struggled with it for a few seconds, his thumbs too big for the keys, and eventu-ally opened it, looking both relieved and a little disappointed, like someone who has spent thirty seconds tussling with a pistachio nut.

'Wonderful news at Camp Bling,' he read in a loud and detached voice, his eyes in need of glasses. 'The council has backed down and the road scheme has been revised. The Saxon burial ground is saved. We still have trees to fight for, but this is a true Solstice celebration.

Many blessings of the old ones to all our friends and supporters.'
He put the phone down and blinked his eyes back into focus. 'Right.'
His delivery sped up again. 'So what happened, right, I went there,
and for the first time in 1,500 years I laid down a druid curse, a
geis. I laid a curse on anybody who wants to move the burial remains
of this ancient Saxon king.'

'Where is Camp Bling?'

'Southend-on-Sea.'

'And why's it called Camp Bling?'

'Because of all the gold they found there in this Saxon king's
burial chamber.'

'So the druid curse worked?'

'It would appear so,' he said with a grin, sounding like a games-
show presenter telling a contestant they had just won. He looked at
his phone again but it had turned itself off. He started banging it
on the table.

'I read somewhere that you've got an army, what's it called' – I
looked at my notes – 'the Loyal Arthurian Warband?'

'Ah yes.' The phone was back on. 'L, A, W. Law.'

'That's it. Where do you recruit?'

'Well,' he said, as he reached forward and placed his hand on my
head. It was heavy and workmanlike and the weight made me bow
a little. 'Most of the time I just go like this. I say, "Do you swear to
speak the truth?"'

'Right,' I said, waiting for him to go on. But he didn't. The music
in the pub seemed louder all of a sudden, the song was 'Come on
Eileen', and for several seconds I remained on pause in this pub in
Amesbury with a bearded biker king resting his hand on my head
as if it was a crystal ball. No one paid the slightest bit of attention.

'Ah.' I realised what I was meant to do. 'Yes. I swear to speak the
truth.'

'To honour your spoken word.' I repeated it. 'To be just and fair
in all your doings.' I repeated that and he removed his hand. 'There
you go,' said Arthur, lighter now. 'You just swore on my hand, you're
a handmaiden. Ha!'

'A handmaiden?'

'Yeah. I'll make you a proper knight later on.'

'Can't I be a proper knight now?'

'No, I haven't got my sword in here.'

'I thought only girls were handmaidens.'

'Well, you are as well.' I looked glum. 'Now one of your first responsibilities as a member of the warband is to look after the King.' He handed me his phone. 'Tonight, you're in charge of the King's phone. If anyone calls or texts, make sure I know.'

'What else does it mean to be a handmaiden?'

'That you're one of mine now. Not hers.'

'Hers?'

'Her Majesty's. Funny thing is, I mean the weird thought I always used to have when I changed me name to Arthur, is, "Who's going to win here? Me or the Queen?"'

'Wow. Do you still see it like that?'

'No, that's how I used to see it. I used to think, "Would she knight one of mine first, like,"' he paused, 'Sir Swampy? You know? So when I knighted one of hers, an aristocrat I met in Cornwall, David Lord Ogilvy was his name, that was quite a moment.'

'Sir Swampy,' I tried. 'Has a certain ring to it.'

'Swampy's an accountant now. Complete wanker, but whatever. You know why he was called Swampy? Because every single tunnel he dug was crap and went down to the water table. That's why we called him Swampy. But he is one of mine, so he is Sir Swampy. And you're about to be Sir Henry. But I don't have a problem with the Queen.' His voice became reverential. 'I think she does a really good job. I'm not convinced about her kids, but she's great. And you know what?'

'Tell me.'

'Queen Elizabeth is head of state, therefore does not need a passport, correct?'

'Yes.'

'Sooo. I'm the only one in this country who can wear a crown in his passport photo. Look.' He rummaged about in his bag, moistened his lips and thrust a passport towards me. Sure enough, there was a picture of Arthur looking a bit startled with a crown on his head. 'I had a hell of a job getting it,' he chuckled. 'Had to apply to the Home Office and write letters to everybody.'

I thought back to Beany who had also shown me his passport with a photo of him in Captain Beany costume. For both men the passport photo was a critical building block in the construction of their identity; it added a layer of reality to the heroic experiment they had begun.

'Tell me about your tattoos,' I said, noticing a jumble of designs the colour of seawater on his forearms.

He looked nonplussed. 'Not mine,' he shrugged.

'What do you mean?'

'They're John's.'

John Rothwell. The man he once was.

'Does anyone still call you John?'

'Not unless they're trying to wind me up,' he growled. 'The druids who don't believe I am who I say I am, they call me John.'

'So how different are you to John?'

'In some ways very different, in other ways we're the same bloke. Thing is, John was a rebel without a cause. I'm a rebel *with* a cause. When I was John coincidences and magic occurred on a regular basis in his life, but he didn't let it run his life. Much like everyone else, he just thought, "That's weird." But now I just think, "Okay, so that's meant to be."'

'And Arthur doesn't sign on, is that right? I remember reading that.'

'Correct. Can't and won't. Not after what Thatcher did. See, she used the dole as a weapon against us. She talked about the "hippy convoy" and the "mad druids", saying we're all signing on claiming dole. So I thought, "Well, she's not ever going to use that one on me." So I don't sign on. All the same, it doesn't take a mathematician to tell you I'm running at a deficit.'

'How do you get by then?'

'Like this.' He nodded at his empty glass. 'Another pint please, Henry.'

Feeling a bit of a chump, in a good way, I went to the bar to get Arthur his next pint. I liked the way he had just done that. It made me grin as I watched the cider pour out. It also reminded me of the most unusual thing about Arthur. He had a sense of humour. It made him invincible. There's no line of attack you can employ against him that he can't laugh at, and will do so proleptically before you bring it up.

Other Englishmen who believe themselves to be reincarnations of historically significant personages usually don't come fitted with a sense of humour. In 1991 the woefully earnest BBC sports presenter David Icke announced he was 'a channel for the Christ spirit' and that the world was run by a cabal of secretive lizards. He spent the following years wearing turquoise and cassandring about tidal waves and earthquakes he thought were about to strike Britain.

In the summer of 2007 another Dave, the former MI5 employee and whistleblower David Shayler, gave a talk at a crop-circling symposium where he declared himself to be the reincarnation of Jesus Christ, King Arthur and Leonardo da Vinci. At least that's how it was reported in *The Times*. On reading the article Shayler wrote to the paper saying they'd got it wrong. He was not Jesus. 'I was, though, crucified with a crown of thorns and nails when incarnated as Astronges, a Jewish revolutionary put to death by the Romans at around the end of the last century BC.' The paper apologised for its mistake and any embarrassment caused.

Yet perhaps Shayler did have a sense of humour. In an unpublished section of the same letter to *The Times* he made a reference to *The Life of Brian*, assuring the newspaper that 'If you phone my mother I'm sure she'll tell you I'm not the Messiah, I'm a very naughty boy.'

Apart from their humour, or lack of, individuals like David Shayler who swap the name they were given at birth for a more grand, aristocratic or regal moniker – something that has gone on throughout English history from Urbane Metcalfe, an inmate of Bedlam in the early nineteenth century who decided he was heir to the Danish throne, through to Huddersfield's resident eccentric Jake Mangel-Wurzel who recently had his name changed by deed poll to Sir Thomas Henry Erasmus Occupier (T. H. E. Occupier) – allow themselves a clean break with the past. The name-change becomes a starting point. A kind of aggrandising rebirth. It means that whatever experiment in lifestyle follows is unlikely to be half-hearted or whimsical. It will be monumental. It will allow them to become heroic in their apartness. What was so interesting was that just about every person I had met over the course of my journey had described a similarly precise cut-off point with their past.

For Arthur it was that extraordinary night in the squat with the Whippet, and the intensity of his break with the man he once was has made it possible for him to do things that the Hell's Angel John Rothwell would have laughed at, including his decision to stand for parliament.

In the 2005 General Election, as one of the only homeless candidates ever to run for election to parliament, Arthur Uther Pendragon stood in the constituency of Winchester. During the campaign, the Conservative candidate, George Hollingbery, gave Arthur a cheque for £500 – the amount required to stand for parliament. Arthur was stunned. The money was on behalf of Hollingbery and his fellow Conservatives who thought that having Arthur and people like him stand for parliament was an important part of English democracy. He gratefully accepted the cash and promised to use it next time round.

'So the first time I ran I embarrassed the BNP into last place,' he told me once I'd returned with his pint. 'Second time I beat the new leader of the Monster Raving Loonies, Screaming Lord Hope, into last place. Third time I managed to embarrass myself into last place, but I'll tell you what, I still got one per cent. You need five per cent to get your deposit back. One per cent! One per cent of the electorate of bloomin' Winchester wanted me as their MP!'

He sucked on his cigarette like an asthmatic on an inhaler.

'Why do you do it though? I mean, why do you stand for parliament when you know you're going to lose?'

'Because I'm sworn to the sacred and imperial oath,' he said, as if it was blindingly obvious. 'Part of that oath is to fight corruption in high places no matter what the cost. That, I interpret in the twenty-first century, means standing for parliament. The analogy is so simple that it means I *have* to stand basically.' He looked me straight in the eye, at that moment looking a lot like the Marquess of Bath, who won slightly fewer votes than Arthur when he stood for election back in the 1970s. With 581 votes in 2005, Arthur beat Bath's career best of 521.

On that same night in 2005 Captain Beany didn't fare too well in Cardiff Central with only 159 votes. This was better than Lord Sutch who once received 61 votes, or the road safety campaigner Bill Boaks who in a 1982 Glasgow by-election won a miserable 5 votes. In 2005 in Westminster (the seat J. S. Mill won in 1865), Brian Haw finished sixth with only 289 votes, though he finished higher than his predecessor John Wilkes who in 1768 came seventh when standing for election in London.

When you think about these men in relation to each other, there's a clear link between the kind of individualism often referred to as eccentric and the self-belief and exhibitionism required to stand as a one-man party for election to parliament.

One of Arthur's high priestesses turned up: Susanna Lafond, a grandmother, priestess, eco-protester and sometime film extra who wore tinted glasses. There was an engaging intensity to the way she spoke. The conversation moved on from Arthur's recent exploits and what I was writing about to the night ahead, whether it would go according to plan, how much media coverage there'd be and who in the pagan community was going to be there. By the sound of it, all of them. After a few pints Susanna left to go and get changed into her robes, saying she'd meet us there.

By the time Arthur had put away his sixth pint and after three hours chatting in the George, we set off for the stones.

Although there was barely a mile separating the two, it took us more than two hours to get from the carpark at Stonehenge to the site itself. Every twenty yards we were stopped by members of King Arthur's public: people who recognised him from other pagan shindigs, protest sites or perhaps television. To each group Arthur was his matey self. He'd make them laugh, ask where they were from, mention a friend in common and engage with them. It was like being with a gregarious royal as he opened a hospital. Instead of being presented with bouquets of flowers Arthur was handed cans of beer or flyers. I took whatever he couldn't carry and like a dutiful equerry stood a little back from him and informed him of any messages that came through.

As well as modern-day ornamental monarch, King Arthur did a fine impersonation of a feudal problem-solving king. Many of his subjects petitioned him with grievances. There were protests that weren't running smoothly, could he come and sort them out? Or spats between pagans that only he could arbitrate. No problem was beyond him, and he'd tell each of them that he would do everything he could, and you knew he meant it.

It was a great spectacle. From an anonymous distance I watched face after face light up like a Christmas tree as it came into his presence. I could imagine for each of them the flush of meeting a minor royal or celebrity: that pang of familiarity born of voyeurism laced with the frotteur-like thrill of being this close to an icon. There, in front of you, was a human being who in your mind was to be looked at, revered, but what's this? It moves! It speaks, you can affect what it says and it is actually showing an interest in you, not the girl behind you, but you.

In this sense Arthur was exactly what he claimed. He was a king. The people he ruled were not 'the English' in their mainstream national-newspaper-reading, Radio-2-listening, going-to-church-once-a-year-on-Christmas-Day wholesomeness, but pagans or hippies or eco-warriors who made up a particular subset of the English fringe.

At the end of each meet-and-greet Arthur would usually bring the whole thing down to earth by asking the star-struck dreadlockee for a can of whatever they were drinking, preferably cider. As he pointed out a little later, Queen Elizabeth's subjects were better than his lot at pre-empting their monarch's thirst.

On our way to the stones Arthur knighted three people. He began by instructing them in his biker's bark to 'Kneel. I ask you to kneel before the sword of Britain, and take an oath to the sword. Not to the sword-bearer, which is me, because I'm a wanker, but to the sword.' They'd laugh, but inside they were on fire. You'd have to have a stony and quite joyless heart to say no to a bearded druid king who is attempting to knight you. Once they were on their knees he would unsheathe Excalibur with a satisfying ping and get them to repeat his pledge of allegiance. Arthur would declare them to be a knight of the Loyal Arthurian Warband before giving them a bear-hug and a kiss on each cheek. In the past he has knighted Sex Pistol John Lydon as well as Ken Kesey, author of *One Flew Over the Cuckoo's Nest*, who apparently referred to himself as 'Sir Ken' on his deathbed.

'Blessed be,' he'd say as we walked away, before turning to me. 'You see,' he'd hiss, 'I don't even know who those guys were, but to them I'm King Arthur. To me I'm King Arthur! So I reckon that makes me King Arthur.'

He was also canny in who he chose to knight.

'You've got to pick the one who looks the most difficult,' he explained. 'The one that's least likely to succumb to your hierarchy.' Within every group he had a knack for spotting the silent dissenter. 'Of course I'm good at it,' he told me. 'That's what I do. Bang heads together. So when I get out my sword they've got the option. They can say, "Fuck off, you wanker, I don't believe in your reality." Or they end up as one of my knights, and then they go off into the world and tell everybody, "Actually, King Arthur isn't a wanker. He is who he says he is."'

'He's a king,' I said.

'Yeah!'

He gave me another hug and we staggered over the stubble towards the stones, leaving behind us a trail of bewilderment and joy, Don Quixote and Sancho out for an evening stroll.

The Battle of the Beanfield took place in 1985, when a small army of policemen and policewomen ambushed and attacked a convoy of travellers on their way to Stonehenge to celebrate Summer Solstice, the same nomadic column described by Margaret Thatcher as 'a band of medieval brigands'. In the wake of the Battle of the Beanfield, Stonehenge was declared out of bounds for Summer Solstice.

The following year John Rothwell became King Arthur and the first group to take him at all seriously were the druids. Their first challenge for their new battle chieftain? Free the stones.

He set about it in what would become typical Arthurian fashion – at times belligerent and stubborn, yet clever when he needed to be, and charismatic. He performed a Herculean five-month vigil at the entrance to Stonehenge in full Arthurian get-up, and for every solstice from 1990 to 2000 was arrested trying to break into the site. He spent each of these nights in a cell and on one occasion got one of his warband to chain up the doors to the English Heritage office in London. He nagged and harried Wiltshire Constabulary as well as the National Trust, he took the British government to the European Court of Human Rights, protesting his right to worship in Stonehenge as a druid, he petitioned, he campaigned and he campaigned some more, until in 2000 he won. Full and free access to Stonehenge was granted for the night of Summer Solstice. The event would also be more or less self-policing, something Arthur insisted on. So far this has worked. The 24,000 revellers at Stonehenge that night were supremely well behaved and the night passed without incident.

Freeing up Stonehenge was, as he put it, his greatest success and his worst failure. You see, King Arthur loves the fight but not the peace-keeping. Since 2000 he has had to attend monthly meetings to ensure that the night runs smoothly and knows that if anything goes wrong he'll get the blame.

The fact that he's taken at all seriously by what he calls 'the establishment' is significant, especially in light of the egregious antipathy he faced back in the early days.

'You see, twenty years ago, the authorities would say, "Arthur's a wanker. Ignore him." Ten years ago Clews Everard, director of Stonehenge, was famous for saying, "As Arthur says, it will be organic."' His laugh was like a gurgle. 'Now, you know what they say? They just say, "Ask Arthur." That's what's happened. Twenty-one years ago I laid down a mythology. I said, "Arthur's back, handle it." Now I'm reaping the results of that.' It reminded me of the ostension John Lundberg had described. 'Am I the real King Arthur? Or am I just an eccentric?' he said, not for the last time that night.

I didn't feel it was an either–or.

'So you're the person English Heritage and the police talk to throughout the year?'

'Right. I'm their point of contact. They've brought me in. And in some ways that's something that annoys me because what I've worked out, and this is a philosophical point' – I held the Dictaphone closer – 'is that what English society does, is it embraces the people on the margins. And I think this is relevant to the book you're writing. Society'll say, "Okay, we accept you." And that, in their eyes, makes you part of them, part of the establishment. You then have to live up to their customs and expectations. So the English establishment's biggest defence against the margins, and it's a great defence, is to embrace them. And once they embrace them, that person is deemed to have sold out and no longer has the same kind of power in their own community.'

'Has that happened to you do you think?'

'Yes! There are people who think I've sold out because I now sit down twelve times a year and talk to English Heritage. But I don't want to be their pet druid.' His nostrils flared. 'I'm a rebel!'

Finally, we arrived at Stonehenge, where I left Arthur chatting to some young druids to go and have a look at the stones. I had never seen them before. They were taller than I imagined, and in the diaphanous half-light given off by the floodlights, the glowsticks and the occasional spot of a torch their colour seemed strangely ethereal, or sylvan. People around me danced to the music in their heads, blew whistles or bumped into this icon of Englishness. Stonehenge looked entirely unmonumental just then, more like the backdrop for a squat party than a wonder of the world. I liked it for that. It made it English rather than British. A gang of wealthy-looking hippies with dreadlocks drummed bongos unrhythmically in the centre of the circle as I continued to peer reverentially at the stones, sober, feeling like a loser, and fingering the Dictaphone in my pocket to remind myself why I was there. Several hours passed.

I am standing at the edge of the circle on grass knotted with weed that I guess was mowed a few weeks ago. Beyond where I am the grass is taller and is about waist-high.

It's now three in the morning and I've lost Arthur, although I've got his phone so I need to find him. Messages for the king continue to flood in, mostly impersonal good wishes for the night ahead that the person has sent to everyone on their phone.

The stones remain packed. They reverberate to the drumming in their centre and as the night gets colder people move around less and there are fewer bursts of spontaneous and ecstatic cheering that start in the centre and radiate out like tremors until they reach the edge of the gathering where they evaporate, as if embarrassed.

Summer Solstice at Stonehenge feels like a club with its own idiosyncratic language, dress and hierarchy. I'm in the margins here, as I am constantly reminded whenever I start a conversation with a Solstice-goer and it drops dead the moment they realise I'm neither a witch nor a wizard, have no 'shrooms to sell and for some reason find the smell of pagan incense annoying. I've got to stop saying that.

Just before I lost him, Arthur had slurred at me, 'I've told you everything about me, but who the fuck are you?' I told him. He concluded that I came from straight-land, vanilla world, that I was a citizen of the mainstream, and in one of these speeches he told me that in this setting I was the eccentric.

It reminded me that while it was easy to label someone like Krentoma as an eccentric because he spent most of his life within a single group, his tribe, it's slightly harder to call someone eccentric in England today because so many of us move from group to group on a daily basis. In one place you might be the group mascot, joker or lovable eccentric, in another you are a trunk of normality. It's much easier to apply these labels when people exist predominantly in one group.

Although Arthur had disappeared his name was everywhere. 'Oh, you should have seen King Arthur . . .' 'Arthur just couldn't help himself . . .' 'He was all over the place . . .' Like Bilbo Baggins at his farewell party, Arthur had vanished. It was colder now so I went to my car to get a jumper and returned to the stones at about four, only to realise that Arthur's phone had turned itself off in my pocket. I turned it on and it rang immediately. It was Arthur's other half, Kay, whom I had not yet met. She was furious.

'What the hell have you done with him?' a voice thundered down the line in a broad Lancastrian accent. 'You were meant to be looking after him!'

'Sorry,' I said.

'I'm here at the stones and everyone's saying he was in a right state.'

'I'm really sorry—'

'Apparently he's sleeping in a ditch somewhere.'

'In a ditch? Really? I wonder—'

'Yes,' she snapped. 'Really. No one can find him.'

I told her I'd find him. My stomach churned. Hairs greyed. Not only was I meant to have told him when people called, that was one of my duties, that and buying him drinks, but from what Kay had said it sounded as though I was in charge of making sure he didn't get too drunk. A straitjacket couldn't have kept him from his drink, let alone a skinny writer person who didn't think he was that drunk in the first place.

It was lighter now and as the crowd shifted towards the southeast station stone I performed Hajj-like circuits of Stonehenge, until at last I found him. He was with Kay.

'Here he is,' said Arthur.

'Ah right,' said Kay, gruffly. 'That's the one, is it? Well, you're fired from looking after him ever again,' she said by way of introduction.

Arthur had sobered up a little and was now entertaining a crowd of several hundred pagans. The dawn sky was brightening, though a stubborn crust of cloud was asleep on the horizon so there would be no explosive sunrise.

He began with a pagan naming ceremony, the equivalent of a christening. Arthur's muscular voice boomed out over the crowd: 'By the power invested in me as Arthur Druid. I name you Oliver Asterix. Come.' He kissed a baby. 'Oliver Asterix.' He turned to the crowd. 'You won't thank your parents for that, let me tell you.' The timing was perfect. The crowd roared with laughter. I remembered that John Rothwell had been a stand-up comedian.

'Don't know why he said that,' muttered the woman next to me, gazing ahead. 'I've just named one of mine Jedi Crystal.'

There were a few other faces in the crowd looking equally miffed at that point. Most of the pre-Glastonbury revellers had moved on and this lot were mainly witches and wizards from such-and-such a coven, all into different kinds of magic and very friendly. There were some interesting stag headdresses going on, plenty of robes, trinkets everywhere, Celtic rings, sticks – in fact most of the pagans there had sticks with magic mushrooms or animals carved into the head. All eyes were on the King.

Having finished with the baby, Arthur moved on to a pagan wedding, known as a hand-fasting. A serious young couple came forward covered in pagan tat. 'Ah, they look in love, don't they?' he crooned at the crowd, who murmured back. 'Oh! Young love!' he went on. 'Do you remember it?'

King Arthur offered them the choice of being bound for a year, a lifetime or eternity, addressing pretty much the entire ceremony to the bride. She looked doe-eyed and willing. She agreed with Arthur that a year-long union would be best.

Following the wedding, Arthur finished with a scattering of ashes.

'And as we bring in the new,' he bellowed, 'we send out the old, and it is part of the cycle. Ashes to ashes. Dust to dust. If the Lord don't get you, the devil must!'

Everyone laughed again.

'Well met, well met, well met,' he said, sounding like George III going, 'What, what, what.' The ashes were scattered.

During all of this he seemed to have grown several inches. His delivery throughout was compelling, and not only free from the lassitude that should have followed a night in a ditch but devoid of cant or anything in the way of religious sententiousness. He compèred the ceremony like a mechanic telling you what was wrong with your car. It was brisk, demotic and firm.

The sun had risen and I went to a café in Amesbury for a fry-up with Arthur, Susanna and Kay. I drank instant coffee, got through everything on the oval plate set before me and drove back to London. I was delirious with fatigue and coffee that tasted of polystyrene and collapsed in my bed when I got home. Having dreamed well I woke that afternoon to try and separate the bizarre reality of Midsummer's Night from the dream that had followed. Fortunately I had four hours of Dictaphone tapes to help out.

'Five hundred years' time from now, historians are going to say, "Yes, Arthur did come back in the late twentieth century. This is what happened."'

Arthur had been on pint number five, but was every bit as lucid as Arthur on pint number two and more persuasive than most of us on no pints at all.

'I mean, he might have been a complete wanker and not have achieved anything, or whatever, however history sees it. But history will say, "Arthur came back."' He lowered his voice and again narrowed his eyes at me. 'If you look at the legends, right, and you look at the misconceptions. Look at Camelot. Everywhere claims to be Camelot, right? Now in a similar sense, I've been quoted on TV as being "King Arthur from Tintagel". But I'm not from Tintagel. The report implied I was. I've been quoted as being from Basingstoke, from Aldershot, I've been Arthur from Yorkshire, because that's where I was born. I've been Arthur from Cumbria because that's where I spend some time. Arthur from South Wales. Arthur from Cardiff. And they've all got a modicum of truth in them. So where's Camelot? It's exactly the same! The ancient Arthur went around and used local troops, local *kings* as they've become known historically. And he'd say, "Right, we've won the battle for you, but now that we're off, build the fucking hill-fort there, right?" So it would become locally known as Arthur's Fort because he told them to build it. Later, five hundred years later when they're writing it up, it's Camelot.'

'Where should historians say you're from?'

'I'm mongrel English. Me old man's a scouse, me old girl's a cockney, and I was born in Yorkshire, raised in Hampshire.' He chuckled to himself. 'It's going to be real fun for the historians looking back at this Arthur, because they're going to make the same fundamental mistakes they're making now.'

'So are you consciously leaving a paper trail for future historians?'

'Yes! Yes I am. I can see them arguing, "It says here he's from this place." "No, but it says here he's from another place." "It says here . . ." Is it any wonder that the previous Arthur was so confusing?'

We had both paused. I remember glancing out of the half-timbered window through a pane of glass coated with a film of car-exhaust.

'Where will you go when you die?' I asked, turning back.

'My body or spirit?'

'Both.'

'Well, my body will be buried somewhere secret, somewhere no one can get at it, and my sword will be divided up into five constituent parts and thrown into five lakes throughout the land.' His voice was matter-of-fact. 'And my spirit? Hopefully if I've done enough I'll be able to rest. Otherwise I'll have to come back and do it all again.' I nodded. 'It's harder than it looks,' he said, looking up at me once more. 'This is the third time I've been back.'

~

Am I alone in thrilling to the sight of this noble throwback to the age of Celtic Romance? Our Prime Minister is a grinning, charmless twerp, our Archbishop of Canterbury has as much spiritual charisma as a raw potato, and the House of Windsor is Dullsville. I'd dump the whole pack of them tomorrow and replace them with a single, Royal, Spiritual and Political Leader – King Arthur.

A. N. Wilson in praise of Arthur Uther Pendragon, né John Rothwell
Evening Standard, *1997*

PART FOUR

THE ROOT OF CHANGE

17

CREATIVITY

In 1964 the English Opera Group commissioned a piece inspired by Edith Sitwell's *The English Eccentrics*. I ordered up the score at the British Library. Each page had been colour-photocopied on to paper as thick as card and for several minutes I stared impotently at a tube-map of squiggles, notes and notations, before realising that even with my grade 3 at piano I had no idea what it should sound like. The words were easier. The libretto involved different eccentric personalities – all dead – wandering on and off stage and interacting loosely with each other or singing about their amusing habits. It was a sort of eccentric hell set to music, and in the background one word was sung repeatedly, each syllable a passaggiato of notes that spanned six or seven bars – 'eccccc-ceeeeeeent-riiiiiiiic, eccccc-ceeeeeeent-riiiiiiiic'.

In my head the words became a monotone wail, sonorous and low like a foghorn. Moving back and forth between the library and my flat, day after day, this word had begun to sound in my mind like the chorus in a Greek tragedy, *eccccc-ceeeeeeent-riiiiiiiic*, every bit as ominous as it was absurd.

I was at saturation point. This obsessive quest to understand a single word and what it might mean was beginning, at times, to feel irrelevant or, worse, indulgent, and the earnest young man in me hated that. Whenever I had this thought I'd try and remember what had drawn me to the subject in the first place, the section of the journey I was looking forward to most and as a result had left to the end: finding eccentric artists, scientists and inventors. In my mind as much as my formulation of what I hoped to be true these were the ones helping to turn the crankhandle of English cultural advance.

Having pinned to the wall of an imaginary cabinet several part-time eccentrics, an eccentric collector, leopard-man hermit, trickster figure, exhibitionist, two toffs, a celebrity, dominatrix, political protester, female hermit and a reincarnated king of England, I would finish my journey by meeting a painter, a musician and a fashion designer, as well as a deviant scientist and an inventor: all people who made unusual connections and had the conviction to defend them. It was only after I understood their relationship to the broader scheme of English eccentricity that I'd know who my updated eccentric was.

Doubting the journey and trying to remind myself why I was on it also revealed something of what it had become. Beyond the thrill of finding people whose lives represented a *sotto voce* protest against conformity, or tracing the peregrinations of a word as it pinballed through English history, eccentricity, as a facet of Englishness, had opened up the country I had lived in for the last twenty-seven years, in the way that a grain of grit can shatter a windscreen when aimed at the right spot. It was as if I was seeing England with cataracts removed – cataracts I didn't know I had. The scenery was no longer familiar. It was brighter too. The people had unusual ticks, habits, mores, and every conversation I had or book I read now informed this new understanding. Home had become away.

All the creative personalities I hoped to meet shared a dependence on their creativity. They used it to make a living. In the last decade or so in England creativity has become big business. Not only has it been turned into an academic discipline in its own right but its processes have been broken down, commodified and translated into systems of thought that can be taught, and it was through these that I began to understand the role of eccentric thinking in business today, particularly within creative industries.

In 1997 the Prime Minister Tony Blair set up the Creative Industries Task Force. Its remit? To gauge the growth and future success of businesses specialising in advertising, music, art and antiques, archi-tecture, design, performing arts, crafts, designer fashion, software, film and video, publishing, television and computer games. Their report concluded that the UK's creative industries in 1998 contributed £60 billion to the British economy, up tenfold from £6 billion in 1988. Over that same ten-year period employment in the creative industries shot up by 34 per cent, and by 2000 creative industries accounted for 7.9 per cent of the national GDP.

The task force generated plenty of other statistics that you could turn into three-dimensional pie charts or power-point presentations. All led unambiguously to the same basic conclusion: the English economy was increasingly dependent on 'creativity', whatever that was. One of the problems they did not pick apart, though other studies have, is the way the national curriculum remains out of date with this development and continues to siphon off creativity into marginal subjects with fewer resources like art, fashion studies, music or Design and Technology.

Once a nation of manufacturers, we are becoming a nation of intellectual labourers. With English agricultural and manufacturing industries struggling to keep up with cheaper global competition, this trend is set to continue.

Creativity has become so important to English businesses that it cannot be expected just to *happen*. Instead creative consultants are hired by businesses to teach their creatively challenged employees how to think outside the box. These consultants argue with proselytising zeal that creativity is not a gift you are born with, like perfect pitch, and that actively trying to be creative should not sound oxymoronic. Ideas do not have to come from dreamlike fits of inspiration, long baths or drunken chats. Most creative consultants disagree with Freud's dichotomy between primary- and secondary-process thought that posits creativity as the result of entering an irrational, feverish and essentially primitive state of mind, an idea that goes right back to Ancient Greece where to be in-spired was to have ideas *breathed into* you by an external force. You, the artist, became an unwitting vessel for this god-like creative inflation. Creativity was supernatural, metaphysical, in every way superior to human beings who were at times barely worthy of its receipt, and as a result when it came to them they might go a bit loopy. 'No great genius was ever without some mixture of madness,' as Aristotle suggested, via Seneca.

Romantic artists and poets reinforced this link between creative genius and madness to imply that rational thought was something that got in the way of creativity. As Schiller wrote: 'In a creative brain reason has withdrawn her watch at the doors.'

Successive psychological and psychiatric studies have blown apart this age-old causal link between madness and creativity. In terms of raw statistical data there is nothing to suggest that if you are creative you are more likely to suffer from, say, bipolar disorder. It would be just as wrong to imagine that those suffering from mental disorders are more likely to become artists. While you can, just about, sketch a correlation between bipolar behaviour and creativity, it is a solecism right up there with trying to be eccentric to claim a causal relationship between the two.

Our understanding of creativity is midway through a J-curve. Rather than see it as the result of emotional irrationality or some kind of feverish regression, creative consultants now teach rational systems of thought that encourage free associations and the kind of original connections that J. S. Mill once eulogised. They urge you to turn the object of your head-scratching upside down and place it in an unusual setting in order to see it in a new light.

As I went through various different studies of creativity and became familiar with the techniques used by creative consultants, the witch doctors of the modern business world, the expressions they used began to sound uncannily familiar. The further I went, the more it became clear that in many ways creative consultants were doing no more than teach eccentric thought. Instead of creativity born of madness they were advocating seeing your environment as an eccentric might. I read repeatedly about the need to see the world differently, to invert it, be childlike and curious, to make original connections and have sufficient faith in your ideas to be able to defend them, all of which was a precise breakdown of how an eccentric apparently thinks.

There's a neat parallel here between the English being famous for eccentricity, and the English economy becoming increasingly dependent on creativity. So it makes sense that both eccentricity and creativity should come to us naturally.

At the heart of any creative consultant's manifesto is the importance of childlike curiosity. They won't try to teach this because they can't – no one can; all they can do is encourage you to rediscover the curiosity you once had. As well as being one of the defining features of eccentricity, curiosity is also the first quality to be realigned in a child during his or her formative years. You could read Kafka's child being induced into the Lie as a synecdoche for curiosity being tamed. Much of what a creative consultant is trying to do is address that suppression and remind you what it was to see the world as a child. They teach you to think eccentric.

As a child you're taught that there are times to restrain your curiosity so as not to sound stupid or cause offence to the people around you – *children say the funniest things!* But what if the child is quite happy to come across as ignorant and doesn't mind causing offence? Perhaps, like Sebastian Horsley, they enjoy saying the unsayable and continue to do so throughout their adult life until there comes a point when there is almost nothing unsayable left to say.

18

THE CULT OF THE ARTIST

Dear Henry,
    I suggest tea at 4.00. Horsley Towers.
    Heterosexual tea, kinky tea, G& T, or notoriety?
    Although of course you know my favourite?
    Insincerity.
    Sx

~

I was shown in by a former Page 3 model called Rachel wearing
thick heels and a dress that gave on to a deep, lace-edged cleavage.
Her lipstick was the colour of claret and her bottom so perfectly
formed that it had a website dedicated to it. By her feet was a white
bichon frise dog that hopped up on its hind legs and pawed the air
to celebrate my arrival. The door shut behind me. The room smelt
of oil paint, turpentine and Rachel's perfume. The fittings were dark,
the colour of a Bedouin tent, the walls cream, and the upholstery
was made from red velvet. Above the mantelpiece was a grid-shaped
wooden cabinet with a skull in each of its thirty-six pigeonholes.
Several had entry and exit wounds from when the previous owner
had been shot. Before them on the floorboards, in a similarly grid-
like pattern, were piles of magazines and newspapers each containing
a photo of the man I was about to meet. Most also had a review
of his autobiography that had just come out, *Dandy in the Underworld*.
In all there must have been about thirty of these votive offerings to
notoriety laid out on the floorboards and they cordoned off half the
room like Malraux's *Museum of the Mind*, though with each pile
democratised by the floor like this I had no idea which were the

rave reviews saying the English soul (if there was such a thing) needed characters like Sebastian Horsley, or which were the ones calling him 'an attention-seeking tosser'. This was it. An unwitting Moses before a sea of public affection, the man I was about to meet could not help but divide his audience. As he told me later, the idea delivered in pure Sebastian-speak — all word-perfect aphorisms layered around a nugget of meaning: 'I think it was Wilde that said, "When the critics are divided, the artist is at one." Was that Wilde or was that Shaw? I'm not wild about Wilde and I'm not sure about Shaw, so I never know. What they mean is that for something to be good, opinion has to be divided, and if the right people hate you, then you get the people who like you to love you. I wrote that book to get me out of hell. And in a way it's taken me to heaven, which is confusing.' This was said with a delicious purr.

Outside, Soho was being rained on. Rachel went through to make some tea, calling over her shoulder to say that Sebastian would be out in a moment.

Not only was it a little strange to meet Rachel, someone whom I'd pictured only the day before wearing not very much as I read about her performing threesomes with Horsley and a prostitute called Claudia, or having heroin speedballs injected into her forearm, I was also a bit daunted by the man about to enter the room.

Sometime writer, escort, artist and above all Dandy with a capital D, Sebastian Horsley started as he meant to go on. The survivor of a failed abortion, he was a heroic failure. When his mother found out she was pregnant she took an overdose — he once wrote that had she known he was going to turn out the way he did she would have taken cyanide. A manic–depressive and alcoholic, she tried repeatedly to kill herself. On one occasion when her car-keys were confiscated she drove a lawnmower to the nearest off-licence; on another she ate her father's ashes for breakfast. Horsley's grand-mother succeeded in killing herself after spending half her life in an asylum, while his father was a crippled industrialist billionaire who contrived to ignore Sebastian from the moment he was born, something that, as he makes clear, you don't have to be Freud — Sigmund or Clement — to realise has had a considerable bearing on who he has become.

As a young man Horsley tried to kill himself by jumping into a quarry. He failed. Having also failed to become a rock star he began a ten-year affair with Jimmy Boyle, a convicted murderer and former Glaswegian gangster once described as 'Scotland's most violent man'. Horsley met him on his release from prison wearing a Nazi outfit. In the 1980s Sebastian made a million on the stock market, most of which he spent on Class A drugs, prostitutes and bespoke three-piece velvet suits in a sybaritic explosion of different lurid colours, each one lined with holsters for heroin-bearing syringes; the rest, he says, he squandered. He has slept with transsexuals, transvestites, amputees, old women, old men, over a thousand prostitutes, and believes a 'whore fuck' to be the purest form of sex. He has been hooked on heroin, crack and smack, and at one of several nadirs described covering himself in his own shit and festering like this for three days while listening to Beethoven. In the name of art he has swum with sharks and been crucified in the Philippines – though this was no sham crucifixion. It was nails through hands, more pain than he can remember, the film-maker fainting at the sight of it, near-death poetry in the name of trying to resurrect his artistic career. Like Jesus in his much vaunted attempt to save mankind, Horsley didn't think it really worked. Several years after this cruci-fixion he was described on Radio 2 as 'a pervert who stands for everything that is wrong with British society today'. Apparently he quite liked this. He was an artist. That was why I had come to see him. An eccentric artist.

The door flew open and Sebastian Horsley entered the room, at which point it became full. He was wearing a top hat the size of a wheelie bin, a red double-breasted velvet waistcoat, a frock-coat and a puffed up tie of his own design that came in beneath an elegantly sharp jaw. His buttons were covered – he has always found the sight of a naked button offensive – he was at least 6 foot tall, well proportioned and good looking in a chiselled yet moderately run-down way. Rachel stood to attention and said goodbye.

'We'll see you later, darling,' he said. 'And don't be late.'

'I won't,' she promised.

Plate VIII^b

H. Hemming   S. Hordly

The Dandy

'Some people are always late,' he mused, as Rachel bent down to put a lead on the dog. Sebastian gazed at her miraculous bottom. 'Like the late King Henry VIII.' He turned back to me. His face was expressive. It made everything he said feel loaded. 'And why is it that all hot-water bottles look like King Henry VIII?'

Rachel and dog scampered out.

'I used to hate that dog,' he said, reaching for one of the cuttings on the floor. 'The little tampon. Until this.' He thrust a magazine towards me open at a page showing the dog, Rachel and him dressed in shimmering red sequins outside a Soho strip club. They looked unbelievably sexy. 'It's the perpetual boast of an Englishman that he never boasts,' he snorted, getting into his stride. 'But I'm having none of that. We look fucking fantastic. Including that dog. Now.' He began to look around for a place to sit. 'Do you want me to leave my hat on?'

With regal comportment he lowered himself into a chair in the corner.

'The last few weeks have been non-stop,' he sighed once settled. 'What with my book coming out. You see, I'm used to sitting round here watching afternoon telly,' he said, sounding both debonair and debauched. 'Which is quite difficult really, given that I don't have a telly.'

'So have you been happy with the reviews of your book?'

'Oh yes.' His face lit up.

'Even the bad ones – do you mind them?'

'Of course I mind! Always have done. The first time I got a bad review for my art I went bazonkas!' His eyebrows came together in a Mount Fuji shape. 'I got a Tiffany's box, defecated in it, and sent it to the critic in question. She phoned the police,' he crooned, sounding hurt. His eyes at this moment were unexpectedly sad.

'And how about people who appear in the book, people like Jimmy Boyle, how have they reacted?'

He laughed at the mention of the ex-gangster's name.

'I wrote Jimmy a letter,' he said, stretching out his right leg and laying it gently on his left knee, as if it was asleep and he didn't want to wake it. 'His wife responded. Publicly. She wrote something in the *Scotsman*. That thing there.' He pointed at a pile of news-papers. 'She says' – he went shrill – '"My husband has been accused of many things, of murder and so on, but never of being a homo-sexual." Which I thought was hilarious. Murder, okay. Buggery, forget it.'

'So he himself hasn't said anything?'

'Nooo,' he said, sounding a bit camp. 'But if I disappear in some strange gardening accident, given that I don't have a garden, you'll know something's up. The way I look at it, insulting other people is a kind of recreation. I mean just *think* how many boring, blame-less lives have been brightened by the blazing indiscretions of me. I think it's funny. Anyway I'm a comic writer. Try to say some-thing nice about someone and make me laugh. Come on. I bet you can't.'

I couldn't.

'So if we were talking about Rachel, and I said she's a lovely girl and she's got a nice dog.' He paused to let the words settle. 'Actually that is quite funny. No. If I'm trying to make people laugh, of course I have to be rude. What do I say about Rachel in the book? That she's a life-support machine for an enormous pair of mammaries? The point is you need a bit of ill nature in a sentence because it's the barb that makes it stick. So in answer to your question, what does Jimmy Boyle think? I don't really care. Now we've established something,' he said, clapping his hands together. The way he spoke was hypnotic. It was a magical blend of sincerity and irony, so with each sentence you were never quite sure which way it was going to go until the very last word.

'Do you ever get hatemail?'

'Oh yes. Often. They email me and say' – he put on a block-head voice – '"I'm going to come down and kill you," and I always do the same, I write back and say, "Dear So-and-so. Would you like an appointment? Yours sincerely, Sebastian Horsley."' He looked out of the window wearily. 'My experience of gangsters is that they don't phone you beforehand to tell you they're going to kill you.'

'And do you now think of yourself as a writer or an artist?'

'Oh, dandy. Dandy covers everything. Anyway I'm not a writer, and I've got a book to prove it. I'm not an artist either, and I've got a retrospective on at the moment to prove that.'

I went to see it the following day, and for someone who has the courage to be crucified his paintings were surprisingly timid. I'll almost certainly get a gift-wrapped turd for that, but it seemed as though the best work there was Sebastian himself, and I think whoever was putting on the show had realised this. The most successful parts of the exhibition were dedicated to his personality and its accoutrements, including several silver-encrusted syringes and the 'Horsley shirt', his singular contribution to the world of fashion (a shirt with all its buttons hidden). Sebastian Horsley was a monumental and self-destructive artwork. There was nothing offensive or rude you could say to him that had not been said before, and said by him. His existence was a more intoxicating hit of humanity than any number of his paintings of sunflower fields, in a style somewhere between Francis Bacon and Monet, which is part of the reason why his memoirs were so brilliant. They articulated this mesmerising existence. If his lifestyle was shocking, his art was not. For many twenty-first century artists the opposite was true.

I had wanted to meet Sebastian Horsley because from a distance he seemed to be an eccentric artist, in the sense that he was not in thrall to the artistic sensibilities of his age, nor was he hellbent on becoming an artistic superstar in the mould of Damien Hirst. Nevertheless he was an artist and he spent a lot of his time painting in his studio, where we were now. It is a famous studio. In early 2007 a modelling agency sent round a lackey to try and secure it as a location in which to photograph one of their models, Kate Moss. Sebastian asked how much they were planning to pay. Er, nothing. Sebastian exploded. They offered a few hundred pounds on top of the chance to say that Kate Moss had once been in his studio. 'I don't want fucking Kate Moss in my studio, thank you very much,' he responded publicly in the *Evening Standard*. 'Does Kate Moss want Sebastian Horsley in her lavatory? I don't give a toss for Miss Moss. I'm not remotely interested in her or her world . . . To me her looks and her greed are both ugly. Tell her this pretty boy will do it for £10,000 and I'll throw in a "Good morning" for that price. I won't, however, get out of bed.' When he breezed into the Groucho Club the next day he got a standing ovation.

While I couldn't really tell if Sebastian had the talent to be as successful as a Hirst, he certainly lacked the appetite. Heroic failure was at the core of the dandyism he preached. In his eyes, even having his memoirs published was a kind of betrayal of his beliefs because it resembled success. Sebastian was far more concerned with the expression of his take on the world than with how it was received. Numbers weren't important. He believed in a romantic nihilism that most of his contemporaries had either set aside or never known.

His entire being is subsumed within a single word – dandyism – which he explained with the zeal of a prelate, giving me a detailed catechism of exactly what a dandy did and did not do.

Number one: he does not breed. This was where Oscar Wilde had gone wrong. The whole point of dandyism, he growled, like a teacher who's gone through this a hundred times before, is to deny the body as a useful tool.

'The only place a dandy would push a pram is into the Thames.'

Nor does the dandy sue.

'Not only did Wilde breed,' he said, with a trace of his Hull roots coming through as he lengthened the word 'breed', 'he also brought a lawsuit against the Marquess of Queensberry! I mean . . .' He made a disapproving hacking sounding with the back of his throat. 'How did he expect to invoke the laws of the society he professed to despise? Wilde was a complete scoundrel.'

If the dandy goes to prison, as Sebastian reckoned he might on account of the .38 Colt revolver he kept on a velvet doily next to his bed – I saw it, it was loaded, it looked very real – the dandy must on no account be shattered by his experiences there. Wilde was, which suggested he cared too much about how society saw him.

'A real dandy would have been prepared,' he said, sounding a bit pissed off. 'I mean, I know I am. All it takes is for you or some other tosspot – sorry, darling, I don't mean you're a tosspot – but all it takes is for someone to make a phone call to the police about my illegal firearm. I'll turn up at the gates of prison, and I'll say, "Well, I'm going to prison. What've you got?" Porridge. Buggery. Class A drugs. I'm amazed there isn't a five-year waiting list.' He flung his head back. 'I'd waltz in, and I'd waltz out, with an aphorism in one hand and my hat in the other.'

He went on, explaining that dandyism was quintessentially English. It was an inevitable eruption of caprice from a country loaded with guilt, repression and tension. Dandyism was more than just a fancy costume, he added, it was a way of performing your life, and at its root was a nihilistic playfulness made possible by the realisation that life was one big metaphysical joke. A joke that the dandy is in on. In many ways it was like Buddhism, 'only without those *awful* clothes'.

After fifteen minutes of disquisition on the art of dandyism it dawned on me that there were remarkably few, if any, 'dandies' who lived up to Sebastian's exacting standards. Beau Brummell was too much of a snob, Oscar Wilde a wimp, and litigious, Russell Brand was just starting out – leaving Quentin Crisp, who was the only dandy Sebastian seemed truly to admire.

'So why don't you just say you're following in the footsteps of Quentin Crisp? Why bother with dandyism?'

'Ah, because the dandy I have in mind is a composite figure. There are parts of Wilde I love. Parts of Byron. I think Byron had a foot – a club foot – in dandyism. Johnny Rotten was a great Irish dandy in those years . . .'

'Or why not just talk about Horsleyism? It seems to me with dandyism you're trying to create something slightly larger than yourself to follow. As if dandyism is a kind of religion where you make the rules?'

'Yes,' he purred, as if to say he hadn't thought of that. 'I suppose it is a religion,' he said, before shifting up a gear. 'Of course it's a religion! But I couldn't do Horsleyism. That would be too arrogant, even for me. The truth is I've put it all together. I have stolen from so many different sources, I mean we've all borrowed and stolen, but I do so deliberately. I acknowledge to the world that I know what it is they're laughing at. Horsleyism wouldn't work because I don't consider myself to be great. I'm mediocrity on stilts,' he said with his eyebrows dancing up and down like two slugs doing the Charleston. 'My heroes are people who have brought new meaning into the world and I just haven't done that.' His voice was forceful, urging you into the mettle of what he was saying. 'I've done the odd amazing thing. I think the crucifixion thing was good. I think the book's good. But it's not great. It's not fucking genius. Francis Bacon was a genius, Shakespeare was a genius, perhaps Warhol was a genius? I read the other day that Morrissey was a genius. What does that make Mozart?' He was animated now. 'A double genius with chips?' He stopped suddenly. 'Sorry. I'm talking rather a lot. Do you want me to shut up?'

'No, no, carry on.'

'Now, you're here to talk about eccentrics. You see I don't mind if someone calls me an eccentric artist,' he went on, twirling his fingers in the air. The cherry red of his nail varnish glittered in the half-light. 'They're not going to get a lawsuit. But I suppose part of the reason I don't call myself an eccentric is it would diminish my power. The word "eccentric" is a shotgun, whereas I see myself as a sniper. You see, I've got something to do and I'm utterly clear about how to do it.'

'Can't you be a sniper as an eccentric?'

'I don't know. What do you think?' he said, meaning it. 'What does the dictionary say?'

'Well, it's a bit vague. It talks about an eccentric as an unusual character, a deviation from the norm, someone who's whimsical, peculiar. There's also an astronomical meaning to do with planets that have irregular orbits.'

'Irregular orbits. I like that. The problem with eccentricity for me is that it suggests something's been domesticated or neutralised.'

'Sure. It's a label that confirms something or someone does not pose a threat. Only what I'm finding is that it's no longer being used only as a label, it's become a historical term as much as a label because it hasn't been updated for so long. It's got stuck. Like madness, it should keep shifting, in the way that homosexuality was called a mental disorder in England as recently as 1967.'

'Was it really?'

'Yes.'

'What fun.' He rearranged himself in his chair. 'The point is, I think, with me if you strip away the drink and the drugs I'd have been a policeman. There's a discipline to what I do. Everything is considered. Stirling Moss once said, when asked why he was a racing car driver, "Because every decision matters."' He said these last four words slowly, so they sat before me in the silence that followed, semi-attractive, like congealed puddings on a dessert trolley.

'Then why do you spend your life saying nothing matters very much? Clearly it does!'

'I know. Well, there you go. For everything you say about me you can also say the opposite. The best way to contradict me is to let me speak.' He launched into a knowing smile.

'What I also don't understand is while you don't want to be called an eccentric, you don't mind if I call you an *eccentric artist*.'

'Absolutely. They're separate. Anyway I'm not an eccentric. To employ the labour-saving device of self-quotation, the eccentric is to an individual what "a character" is to a person of real character. Eccentricity is willed. Worse, it is a mask for nonentity.' He was talking about the artificial eccentric here. The impostor. 'And anyway the English indulge their eccentrics only on the basis that they are rich.'

'Nooo,' I cried. 'They don't.' I told him about King Arthur, Tom Leppard, Anne Atkin, Brian Haw, Captain Beany.

'This King Arthur person, did you ask him why all the people who believe in reincarnation are always King Arthurs, or Tutankhamens. They're never thirteenth-century shoeshine boys. Why is that, I wonder?' He let the question settle. 'I'll tell you. There are two universal truths about human beings. The first is that we're all pretty much the same, the second is that we all say we're different. Now it seems to me that one's entire character is a flight from the terror of existence. Kierkegaard writes about this, that we manufacture our character because we're terrified of death, of the abyss. So our character is a neurotic defence against despair. I don't know whether you're with me on this?'

'I am, yes. And I know those moments when you lose sight of that, of your character, and words come out all wrong, you don't make sense, even to yourself, and you can see it in the people around you.'

'Panic. It's a kind of panic. And you then see a pure essence of yourself.' He rearranged his enormous collar. 'Kierkegaard argued that our entire personality is also about becoming heroic. That's why people are reincarnated as King Arthur or what have you. That's also why I'm sitting here talking to you wearing a top hat and perhaps why you're writing your book. It seems to me that the central calling to human beings on this planet is the urge to heroism. We all have fantasies of fame and greatness, and life for most of us is a process of being gradually disabused of those. The urge to be heroic is natural and, to admit it, honest. Much as we're sitting here in a flat in Soho talking about dandyism or eccentricity, all of that – it's nothing more than us enclosing our wilderness in a wall of words. That's all we're doing. Running after the wind. The ultimate thing is that—' He started. 'Is— Oh I don't know what the ultimate thing is,' he sighed. 'I'm a romantic nihilist. That's all. I'm only interested in the words of the shipwrecked. The rest is rhetorical. It's posturing. Farce. I know that's rich coming from me who is a posturer if there ever was one, or if there's such a word. But it's the people who can see through the construct of character that I'm interested in.'

He once wrote:

Life is a tragedy. We get washed up on some random shore and spend our lives building shelters and waving at ships. Then the tide turns. The waves crash inwards and sweep the lot away. We are left with a desert. We end up weeping alone in an empty church. Remember me, whispers the dust.

It is a passage of staggering clarity and beauty. In this, and in what he said about our fantasies of greatness, Sebastian revealed an absolutely essential quality of the people I had met on my journey. He made me understand something of their longing for a kind of heroic apartness. Often their reinvented lifestyle was no more than a trussed up expression of this urge.

'Do you see yourself as particularly English?'

'I've got a mixed relationship with England,' he said quietly. 'I think English people have withered hearts, full of envy and spite and bitterness. I say that because I'm English and my heart is certainly withered. In England success breeds envy. In America it breeds hope. But that same withered English heart can produce an Oscar Wilde, a Samuel Beckett, Quentin Crisp, Francis Bacon.' The names came out as a rhythmic chant, and as with everything he said there was a musicality to it. 'Those kinds of people don't come out of America, they don't come out of France. They're all people trying to put themselves back together or make up for some lack, and it's out of that disequilibrium that you get dynamism. The other thing I like about England is the language.' He sat up in his chair. 'I've just had a thought. Do you think English eccentricity is to do with the English language?'

'Go on.'

'You see, the English language is deeper, broader, richer than any other language in the world. That's got to be worth something. With the English language and the way we use it there's almost no situation you can't defuse with your tongue, and of course the tongue is the only weapon that sharpens with use. And because the English language is so rich, I wonder if it isn't related to our eccentricity? Right now people are trying to translate my book. This is patently absurd. Reading my book in translation must be like trying to fuck through a blanket. I mean I'm not against fucking through blankets, but you've got your work cut out. The English language lends itself to play, to inversion, and inversion appears to be at the heart of eccentricity. You don't get that everyday inversion elsewhere. I was in America recently when a friend of mine died. He committed suicide.' His words were for once flat. 'The person I was staying with asked if I was going to go to his funeral, and I said, "Of course I'm going to his funeral. After all, I want him to come to mine."' He paused. 'The American turned to me and said, "But he's dead."'

He looked at me blankly. We both laughed.

'I hadn't thought of that, about language and eccentricity. Though I don't for a moment think that a national character stems from its language. It's the other way round, surely.'

'Yes. But it's interesting, isn't it? Having said that, the one thing that really confuses me about England is the occasional inability to play. I've seen it in some of the reviews of my book. That one in the *Telegraph* for example.'

He reached for the offending article and held it out before him.

'Listen to his prose. Really. If you can't make a sentence sing, just get off the stage and leave it to people that can,' he spat. 'Yeah, listen to this, "He comes across as an attention-seeking tosser."' He looked up. 'Yeah, and you're not. Honestly. Rachel Googled him. He's short, ugly and fat. I would feel sorry for him if he didn't write so badly.' He put the review away. 'I represent, and he resents, the life beautiful. Which is part of the reason why I'm not a better artist. I'm too handsome,' he said, deadpan. 'Take a look at the great artists, they're all fucking ugly. Toulouse Lautrec, Van Gogh, Francis Bacon, Warhol, Picasso, Damien Hirst. It's all produced from a lack! Having said that, I can see his point. If I didn't know myself, I would think, "Who the fuck is that prat?" But we need people like him.' He jabbed a finger at the newspaper where it had landed on the floor. Just as he needs people like you, I wanted to say, but didn't. 'Individuality, eccentricity, dandyism, none of these can exist without their opposite. I mean it's just not possible. If everyone was like me, I'd have to become an accountant. We can't all be stars. Someone has to sit on the pavement and either clap as we go by or throw cabbages.'

It was pure Horsley. Vicious, self-aware, contradictory, shambolic, funny, penetrating and utterly lovable. Somehow he had coined his own brand of adorable abrasiveness. It was inimitable.

We left his flat and walked through Soho to Mayfair where his friend Sarah Lucas was about to perform several poems. On the way we passed Chris Eubank's Peterbilt truck. I remembered riding in it. Sebastian posed in front of it while his friend Roberto tried to take a photo. He couldn't get his camera to work. A little beyond the truck I spotted a fashion boutique with the words 'Vivienne Westwood' in hurried handwriting above its window; the neon lines fizzed blue in the evening drizzle: I began to think about the next person I was planning to meet.

Sebastian's top hat made him about seven feet tall. He was an extraordinary and wonderful sight. The people we passed either stopped, smiled or snarled, though most smiled.

'Would you say you do this to be loved?' I asked as we approached the gallery.

'I want love,' he said, facing ahead. 'But I'll settle for a slap in the face.' He turned to me. 'All I really want', he said with the faintest of sighs, 'is to join the world without bevelling down my individuality.'

We walked into the gallery and the crowd of people turned towards him like sunflowers to the morning sun. The room was now full.

On Sebastian's wall to the left of the window was a collection of cuttings, much like Captain Beany's shrine to himself, only smaller and less kitsch. It was there to remind him of who he had become. In the middle of it was the front page of the *News of the World* from the Sunday following his crucifixion in 2000. The headline read: 'ART FREAK CRUCIFIES HIMSELF'.

This idea of the Art Freak plays an interesting part in the story of English eccentricity. A minor part, but a part nonetheless.

The original Art Freak was Michelangelo. Thought by Vasari, one of his biographers, to have 'been sent from heaven to bring perfection to the arts', Michelangelo was the first modern artist. Ever since 'Il Divino' the Western artist has been made out to be something more than the workaday artisan he previously was. The way we think about artists is not at all timeless. Plato, for example, saw making pictures as a low and uninspired profession, but the event of Michelangelo's genius allowed later artists to be seen in the mould of this messianic creator–hero thought by his peers to be blessed with unique and special vision, someone who was also prone to strange decisions or odd behaviour.

In England it was not until the nineteenth century that the artist-as-god delusion really gained currency. Once Romanticism and everything it stood for had taken root, the emotional ups and downs of an artist might warrant paintings in their own right. The typical Romantic artist was narcissistic and introspective: he saw himself as not only apart from society but also *above* the mollycoddled panopticon of non-artists he'd see when looking out from his garret.

By the end of the nineteenth century this incarnation of the artist as a tragic loner who saw rational thought as an impediment to creativity had seeped into mainstream literature. In Somerset Maugham's *The Moon and Sixpence*, Henry James's *The Private Life* or more famously James Joyce's *The Portrait of the Artist as a Young Man* you can see an identical artist figure. He (and it is still a he) imagines himself to be an icon of resistance against industrialised society and its bourgeois tastes. He is the Promethean risk-taker, a rebel, a heroic martyr for his artistic cause, yet it was not enough for him to express this in his avant-garde paintings or sculptures. His sense of apartness had to be channelled into his behaviour too.

Yet in nineteenth-century figures like William Blake, Samuel Palmer or Lord Leighton you see the beginning of the more amiably eccentric version of the artist that would follow.

By the early- to mid-twentieth century the caricature of the artist ceased to be quite so dangerous. Though he continued to be seen by society as frivolous or spiritualistic, childlike, solipsistic, sensitive, curious, semi-wild and randy, the artist was no longer made out to pose the threat he once did. It is at this point that the artist began to be seen as typically eccentric, rather than degenerate.

Although the twenty-first-century contemporary artist has little in common with the Romantic artist – he or she is more of a lay interventionist rather than a mystical recluse – the earlier caricature of the artist that persists in mainstream depictions of artists. It's as if English society needs its artists to be semi-wild, marginal and eccentric. They want their Sebastian Horsleys to be Art Freaks.

Not only does the existence of an Art Freak remind them what's normal and what's not, but it allows them to transgress vicariously. By caricaturing the artist as everything that they are not (untamed by authority, semi-wild, morally loose) but still within the bounds of moral sympathy – something the artist is happy to go along with – when reading about these artists or buying their art the rest of society assuages a lack. When following the misadventures of an eccentric artist like Sebastian Horsley as he sleeps with a thousand prostitutes or walks down a street in a pink suit, a baboon in a velvet cocoon, you remind yourself that this is abnormal while simultaneously performing these transgressions in the back of your mind.

More importantly, the way that artists are portrayed as eccentric means that there is less occasion to use the e-word. By using the term 'artist' you now imply a degree of eccentricity.

Helen David runs a fashion boutique called English Eccentrics. I went to meet her and she told me about how she'd come to call her company by that name. Just after she'd left fashion college she wanted to set up her own fashion label, only she did not know what to call it. At about the same time she was reading Sitwell's *The English Eccentrics*, a book she enjoyed, even if she found the style a bit trying and the author too snooty at times. Still, it prompted her to look up 'eccentric' in the dictionary. She liked the astronomical meaning especially and it was because of this that she decided to call her fashion label English Eccentrics. She thought it was especially apt because her clothes were about combining things that didn't really go.

'Have you yourself ever been called an eccentric?' I asked.

'When I was younger, yes,' she said, her lipstick the colour of a satsuma. 'But it's hard to combine being eccentric with a normal life. It doesn't really work to be eccentric when you're married with children, I don't think.'

The world's first fashion label was set up by an Englishman, Charles Worth. He had the idea of stitching labels bearing his name into his clothes, something he began to do in 1858, the same year that John Ruskin gasped in Victorian indignation at the sight of Turner's erotic nudes and Charles Darwin began to wonder how the world would react to his interesting new theory.

Dame Vivienne Westwood is a fashion designer too. Married, and with several children, and thought to have been the fashion world's leading innovator during the 1980s and 1990s, Vivienne Westwood is the undisputed queen of British fashion. She is also often referred to as an 'eccentric fashion designer', or just 'an eccentric'.

It began in the 1970s when she was married to Malcolm McLaren, the manager of the Sex Pistols. Committed anarchists, these two were the founders of punk. Together they ran the boutique on the King's Road that sold the first punk outfits – McLaren once described the Sex Pistols as little more than coat-hangers for their designs. Less than thirty years after Vivienne put safety-pins through the Queen's nose on T-shirts worn by the Sex Pistols, the Queen appointed her Dame Vivienne Westwood. Vivienne was thrilled. By that stage of her life she had become very fond of her monarch and no longer felt that she embodied English hypocrisy. Westwood's son, Joe, turned down an MBE in 2007 in protest at Tony Blair's foreign policy. Vivienne was proud of this, and saw no contradiction between this and her acquiescence. As she put it when we met, she was still attacking the establishment as Dame Vivienne, only she was doing so from a position of authority. She saw the establishment as a car going at 100 mph, and you can't stop that car; the only way to alter its course is to travel faster than it, at 200 mph.

Vivienne Westwood is rare. Not only is she a phenomenally successful woman in an industry dominated by men, but she started late, in her mid-thirties, and did not go to fashion college. She is self-taught and supremely talented with a creativity that no team of creative consultants could imitate or anticipate. She has the enviable knack of being able to spot a fashion trend long before anyone else, even if she hates the idea of trends in the sense that she won't follow them.

The Vivienne Westwood look is rooted in her study of historical costume, something that sets her apart from other designers, though she has often said she'd prefer it if it wasn't that way, and that we should all spend more time studying history and getting to grips with 'culture', something she sets up on high. Her clothes are both historical and contemporary, and that's not a trite paradox in the vein of *where east meets west, old meets new, familiar and foreign,* the kind of thing you get in half-hearted art-gallery press releases. Take the eighteenth-century corset: by reducing the boning, adding elastic side panels and inserting a zip down the front that rendered the laces at the back purely decorative, Vivienne turned this symbol of constraint into a triumph of feminine sexuality. There is a freedom to her clothes, a high romance as well as an unlikely mixture of sexiness and Britishness.

She has been called irreverent and iconoclastic. She has a reputation for being prickly, variable, undiplomatic and lacking in all but the most basic notion of business acumen. As well as being forthright she really does not care what people think of her, and for many years, as one of the key players in the world of fashion, she was renowned for refusing to use taxis or put her money in a bank, preferring instead to get about by bike and hoard her cash under her bed.

Vivienne Westwood is all of these things, perhaps, but it was the way she has been labelled eccentric that drew me in. Of course it did. In the same BBC poll that crowned Chris Eubank the most eccentric British celebrity she came eighth equal alongside Sir Jimmy Savile. But was she an eccentric, or just an eccentric fashion designer?

Over the last 150 years the fashion designer has claimed for itself a slice of English eccentricity, as has the artist and inventor. This meant that as a typical fashion designer you are not only allowed a greater degree of eccentricity in terms of society's expectations of you, but as an up-and-coming English fashion designer you might in some way be required to display a degree of eccentricity in order to look, sound and taste more like an authentic fashion designer. This was not the case in the days of Charles Worth.

Like a national railway network being broken up and privatised, over the last century certain parts of English eccentricity have been broken off and incorporated into various creative industries. We now expect artists to be Art Freaks, or fashion designers to be eccentrically flamboyant. This is why in newspaper obituaries over the last twenty years the majority of the people described as eccentric are artists, scientists, musicians or fashion designers.

The staff of Vivienne Westwood's Battersea workshop are gathered before me. There's about sixty or seventy of them and they know each other well enough to do instinctive double-takes at the sight of me, the stranger in their midst. We are waiting for the performance to begin but it can't right now because we're missing our fulcrum. Nothing moves without it. No one knows where she is. At the far end of the room are several bright, scribbled designs set up behind the spot where the action will take place, and above them a microphone hangs down from a series of intersecting cords over a semi-circle of chairs. In the middle of this amphitheatre is an ivory-coloured chair with embroidered back and arms. It's larger than the other seats and more ornate. It looks like a throne. It is central and empty. The room smells of cheap red wine being drunk from plastic cups.

The inaugural performance of *Active Resistance to Propaganda*, Dame Vivienne Westwood's cultural manifesto, is about to begin. It has twenty-four speaking parts including Pirate Progress, Diogenes, Talking Cricket, Aristotle, Alice (of Wonderland), Beautiful Slavegirl and Pinocchio, and is Vivienne's delicious and at times delirious attack on consumerism and the way we perceive culture in today's society – we're getting it wrong, she says. Her manifesto will help put it right. According to the notes above the title her text 'penetrates to the root of the human predicament'. Several months ago she read it out at the Hay Festival. It didn't go down well. The audience found it hard to follow and didactic in a hectoring way. Several people shuffled out of the tent when Dame Vivienne announced that the problem with people today was that they didn't read enough. This was, after all, a literary festival.

The employees who have been given parts to read look nervous and chat vacantly to each other while we wait. They are dressed well. Not in the sense that their outfits are expensive but they're bold and well assembled – there's a giant orange cowboy hat, several striped pirate t-shirts, handkerchiefs round necks, waistcoats and a rainbow of unusual colours and cuts. Collectively they ooze cool and make a great spectacle, sitting there, waiting.

Then she arrives.

The first thing you notice is the way her flame of hennaed hair sits next to the alabaster of her skin. There is an electricity where they meet that makes me think of the angry, choppy water you get when two rivers come together. She's wearing a navy-blue silk smock with a kangaroo pouch of a pocket on one side. Lines sweep diagonally across her body, the cut of the dress is askew and there are several brooches on its lapels. Then you come to her eyes which, even from where I am, 20 yards away, fizz.

Plate III a

H. Hennig   V. Westwood D.B.E.

The Fashion Designer

The performance begins. After one line it stops.

'Now I don't want to explain everything in this,' she says peremptorily, her Derbyshire accent humourless yet affectionate. 'Because it would take too long a time. But I think I should explain this one bit . . .' She explains the first sentence, the performance continues, we stop for the third sentence, she apologises and we carry on. We stop again, and it thuds on like this with regular breaks for Vivienne's exegesis. Few of the players are native English speakers so they read deliberately and slowly, as does Vivienne, though she does so for emphasis.

It's unbearably tense. There is no laughter, and with the performers static there's no spectacle. For an hour everyone in the room follows the script and we turn the pages in unison; each time this happens it makes a fluttering sound like a flock of birds taking off.

Centre-stage the grand dame of British fashion is bent forward, deep in concentration, mouthing the lines as they are read. She's wearing glasses with oval white frames and looks thrilled. This is her castle, her hive. Here she is queen bee. Queen V. And her eyes, throughout, are alive with a mesmerising intensity. They are super-charged: the eyes of someone who is a ball of such will that it makes you want to run out of the building and *do* something, start something, make some THING happen. It does not, however, make you want to roll outside and howl with laughter at the ridiculousness of it all, unlike an afternoon with Sebastian Horsley – but that doesn't matter just now. Perhaps this is what it means to be inspired by the force of someone's personality. I was not sure. I had not felt it until then.

Before the performance began we spoke for three hours in her office tucked away at the back of the building with her dog asleep beneath a rail of clothes. She smoked regularly, and for the first half-hour apologised every few minutes for her words not coming out quite right. She was tired and had spent the first part of the day with her mother who had not been well, she explained in between slugs of tea.

Once we got going, the thing she wanted to talk about more than anything else was her manifesto, as well as her fear that too many people these days saw themselves as eccentric.

The setting for her manifesto is the fact that she likes to read –

not just fiction or fashion, but history. Great history doorstops that
dads are given for Christmas. This is important. Her conversation
was full of references to European history and she talked about it
with the familiarity of a seasoned time-traveller. She didn't like
Romanticism, Beethoven; the Hanoverians were 'such a stale bunch';
fin de siècle Paris was one of the most exciting times to be alive;
and the artists of the twentieth century will be seen by our great-
grandchildren as members of 'the lost generation'.

So she fits her frustration with contemporary England into a
much broader European historical framework, even if her worldview seemed to have a few chronological and geographical gaps.
What Dame Vivienne really disliked, the thing that had inspired
her manifesto more than anything else, was the modern-day cult
of the individual. She loathed the idea that, say, everyone has a
novel in them, or that art is to be judged by 'Do I like it?' and
that 'I am perfect because *I feel*.' She rejects subjectivity and thought
that what we really needed in the way we talked about art was
objectivity. It was because too many people believed in the idea
of artistic progress that there was no longer any vital art being
made in England, she added, before moving on to eccentricity.

'Everyone wants to be eccentric nowadays,' she groaned – though
for her eccentricity was about self-obsession. It was a sense of 'Me me
me. I'm special. Nobody's better than me.' She put on a whiny voice
for effect. 'You know? If you take that as your idea, then it means that
as a person you cannot develop. If we're all equal, then in ten years'
time I won't be any better than I am now. I'll still be running around
in my own head. That's my general thing, regarding your subject. So
I don't wish to be eccentric. I think that these days to be against
eccentricity is to be radical,' she said, before blowing her nose.

Other things that inspired the manifesto included her idea that
children shouldn't be dumped in front of televisions, that it was
better to study biology than fashion, that we should watch less television, and as a society we've surfeited on consumerism. In other
words, her reasons for writing *Active Resistance* were conservative
and quite sensible, but from the way she described them she wanted
them to sound radical.

The tendency of her text to dismiss great swathes of European cultural output in a tone of naive infallibility often made it hard to know what to do with *Active Resistance*. All the same, her manifesto was being read. Not because of its critical nous or philosophical acuity, but because of who she is. Perhaps the bewilderment people feel when they engage with it will make her heroic. In the patois of an intellectual martyr she told me she didn't mind what people thought of her manifesto, and that they could call her a snob, but so what? In her mind she was right and nothing else really mattered. It reminded me of Chris Eubank or Brian Haw and their unconscious recourse to the heroic.

Her voice throughout was both energetic and exasperated – exasperated at how many of us were getting it wrong – yet beneath this was a warmth that made you want to agree with her even if there were times when I found this difficult.

Her patterns of speech were interesting too. In between different points she would leave no more than the tiniest gap, so it was hard to alter the direction of what she said, and although she dealt in tangents each digression returned to more or less the exact point from which it departed, so we moved forward in a succession of loops.

Once beyond the manifesto she relaxed a little. She told me that the story of her life was 'When I finish this pair of trousers I can read this book.' I asked her when she was happiest. She said it was probably that morning. Every morning when she wakes up in her husband's bed she'll look out of the window, and because of the angle of the bed she can see only part of the window. But that's enough. It allows her to see the sky.

'And that is just . . . It just makes me so glad to be alive,' she beamed. 'I woke up to the fact recently that every day is *special*. It's just a thing that I recommend to people, to look at the sky when you wake up. It's usually quite dull. But for me it stands for continuity and makes me really happy to be alive.' She lit another cigarette. The way she said this reminded me immediately of the ageless Serpentine swimmers, and of Dr Weeks' idea that eccentrics live longer because they don't worry as much as the rest of us.

Andreas, her German bisexual husband, twenty-five years her junior, walked into the room carrying a Tupperware pot. It contained a salad that Vivienne had made that morning, the happiest morning.

He removed the lid with the application of a clock-maker and began to eat. Vivienne urged him to put the salad on a plate in order to mix up the different layers – it would taste better that way, she suggested. There was an unexpected tenderness in her voice. He said he quite liked it unmixed and continued to eat it like that, before turning to inspect me and ask in a gentle baritone what we had been talking about. I explained. He listened carefully.

'I think', he began, 'eccentricity is about seeing things the other way round. Also that it is involuntary.'

He returned to his salad, chomping on the leaves in monkish silence and gazing intently at the pot as if there was a television hidden in there or a couple of ants performing a tango. In a couple of sentences he had more or less summarised what I had spent the last year working out, which would have been annoying if he hadn't done it with such polite economy.

Soon after the performance I left. Artist and fashion designer were accounted for. Next, I needed a musician.

Pete Doherty is sitting next to me in the backseat of a minicab, glued to his computer screen, a bit like Andreas with his salad. I'm wondering whether to interrupt. It's midnight and a blur of London has begun to rush past the window in a river of purplish greys and yellows. We're accelerating away from the cameras and the fans outside the arena who were hoping to catch a glimpse of their idol. It smells fresh in here after the fug of beery sweat and hot dogs in Wembley Arena, where he's just played his biggest and perhaps best gig with Babyshambles, his band.

The seat is covered by a dark-brown material that has the feel of a hug-hardened teddy bear. Pete winds the window up a little so the cab fills with a thudding noise like a flag fluttering in a gale. His skin is pale, sepulchral almost, with a concentration of spots and scratches round the back of his jaw. His eyes, when I glimpse them, are round like lollipops, and hopeful. He's taller than I'd imagined, loose-limbed and rangy, so when he moves around a room he lurches and sways like a spinning top – you never know where it's going to end up. He's still now and as the cab speeds up he closes the window completely. Everything becomes quiet.

Plate IX b

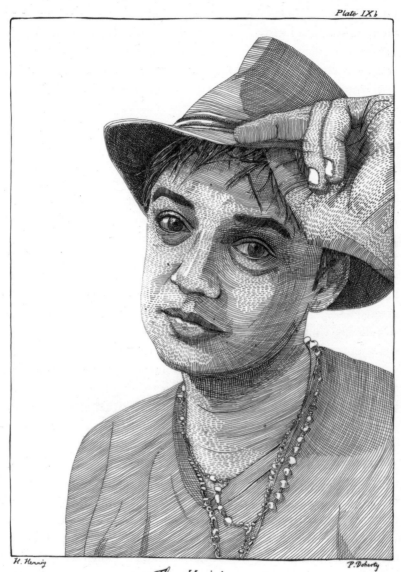

H. Hennig

P. Doherty

The Musician

This, here, now, is rare. When Pete's manager Andy called earlier to say he could get me backstage that night I'd imagined five minutes in the dressing room. I didn't expect this, nor any of what followed: my twenty-seven hours in and out of the company of the most written-about musician of his generation, Pete Doherty, ex-lead singer of the Libertines, one of the most exciting British bands in recent years, ex-boyfriend of Kate Moss, (sort of) ex-heroin junkie, convict, poet, painter of blood paintings, cat-lover, figure of un-relenting tabloid scrutiny, follower of Byron and of libertinism, Emily Dickinson's number-one fan, but more than any of this, I was in the company of Pete Doherty, unique musician.

He's notorious for being exceptionally hard to pin down for an interview; I'd been trying for the previous two and a half months and at the end of the following night his manager would tell me that I had spent light years longer with him than any other writer or journalist over the past two years.

But why him? How does he fit into this book?

Just as for some Sebastian Horsley is an eccentric artist, or Vivienne Westwood an eccentric fashion designer, I saw Pete Doherty as an eccentric musician. He slotted into my vision of modern-day eccentricity as someone at the edge of mainstream morality, an Englishman who saw the world differently and whose life seemed to be an experiment in living, a kind of protest. His existence was at times inspiring or fascinating, just as it could be childlike and irreverent. He's not like other musicians. There's more to him. He also seemed to be very English, and this was some-thing I had come to crave in the icons of creative non-conformity I was tracking down. In his songs and poetry he writes repeat-edly about Albion, while the stage design for the concert I'd just seen was a collage of VE-day bunting, standard lamps, 1950s pack-aging, Churchilliana and a bouncing ball with a St George's cross on it.

'Where's Albion, Pete?' I ask.

'It's the earth under my feet,' he says in his instantly recognis-able breathy gasp. It has a gentle rasp to it, as if he's coming to the end of a sore throat. 'And all around me and all inside me, it's my heart and soul. It's in the past, it's on the TV screen, it's in the water.' He turns to watch the city as it floods past. 'It's somewhere over the railings,' he says, as if they are the last words on earth.

I am hooked.

The road is wide, empty and mostly quiet. A car pulls up along-side. Out of its windows hangs a broadside of grinning faces and hands waving Babyshambles memorabilia. We're going at about 45 mph on a dual carriageway; their car is two feet away.

'Pete,' they howl. 'Pete, will you sign this for us, will you sign this, Pete!'

'Hello, fellas,' he says, stretching an arm out of the window to sign one of the programmes.

'Omigod,' a girl is screaming from somewhere inside the car.

'Pete, I love you!' says one of the boys.

'Omigod,' the girl screams again.

'Check out my band,' one of boys shouts. 'They're on Myspace, they're called—'

Our minicab pulls away.

'So how do you think the gig went?' I ask.

'I liked it,' he says, upbeat. 'I've always been into mobs and crowds.' His pitch is dreamy and melodic, though the delivery is quick. The gaps in his speech are in between sentences, never in the middle of one. 'I've always liked seeing bodies writhing around. But yeah, I can't believe we've done it.' He smiles sheepishly. 'They said QPR or Babyshambles would never get to play Wembley. Well. They were half right.'

He described going to his first gig eleven years ago when he was seventeen. Morrissey was playing and he managed to get on stage and touch the great man's leg.

'I risked life and limb to touch that leg. I also got the shit kicked out of me by the bouncers. But it was worth it.' He sighs, turning to me. 'Never seen anything like it.' He rearranges his legs behind the passenger seat and shifts about a bit.

On the cover of his latest album, *Shotter's Nation*, is a pen-and-ink version of the iconic mid-nineteenth-century painting, *The Death of Chatterton* by Henry Wallis. It shows a young poet dead on his bed with dawn rising over London and unpublished poems scattered across the floor. To a Victorian audience Chatterton stood for the idea of the tragic Romantic artist, a young man who believed so much in his work that he'd die for it, and for whom rejection was an open wound. I ask Pete if he sees himself as Chatterton.

'No,' he says, turning to me. 'Not really. People often make assumptions about me. They assume certain songs are about certain things, or certain images mean things. They sort of tar me, if you like, with a certain ideology, yet I don't see it like that. I just like the picture.' He drifts off.

That brings me to the other reason I'm here. I want to explore beyond the cartoon character bearing his name that appears so often in tabloid newspapers. I hope to get beyond the *Sun's* 'Potty Pete', a caricature drug-addled wildman in the mould of the Sex Pistols' Sid Vicious or Johnny Rotten. This figure is shambolic, strange, sometimes immoral or amoral; yet throughout he remains within the bounds of sympathy in the sense that he's someone you're asked to root for in his battle against heroin addiction. Ageing rock stars who were once wild and have since become old, cuddly and eccentric – men like Ozzy Osbourne and Keef Richards, famous respectively for biting the head off a bat on stage or claiming to have snorted his father's ashes – are asked to comment on the state of Doherty. They say they hope young Doherty gets through it all right. You sense that the natural order of things is for Pete to end up doing this kind of thing thirty years from now, doling out the same advice to the same cartoon figure he was once made out to be. I ask him about this.

'Yeah,' he says, sounding interested. 'But this character they've created for me, he's quite doom-laden. He doesn't seem to have much luck really.' His tone is light. 'Like today it was in the papers saying how Babyshambles were having trouble selling tickets, leaving fans cold, and venues were half full. And it's just not true. I don't know why they persist really.'

'Do you think at some point it's going to turn – when you get older, that is?'

'Well, I can't really afford to care about that character, because he's so far removed from the truth and it's tabloid and there are enough people who are interested in the music.' He trails off once more. I worry that I've said the wrong thing. He suggests that we carry on tomorrow, gives me his number and tells me to call the next morning.

'We'll go to that place that sells trinkets on Chiswick High Road,' he says. 'Can't remember the name. They do screenings too. We'll have a proper writer's lunch. Go sit in the park and everything.'

It sounds great. I get out at a traffic light and take the tube home. The following day at about eleven I give him a call but his phone is off. I leave a message. Several hours later, having heard nothing back, I realise that there's no way he'll have time to see me as he's playing in Birmingham that evening. I begin to write up our conversation from the night before.

At this point my phone rings. It's Pete Doherty. He says I should come over to Chiswick and call him when I get there. I do so, and call him eight times over the course of an hour as I pace up and down Chiswick High Road trying to find this shop. I get no more than a few words out of him. He sounds distracted and he's mumbling. Each time he hangs up after about ten seconds.

I mutter to myself a middle-aged 'I told you so' before trudging to the nearest tube station in order to head home and write up the events of last night.

Again, he calls just as I think all is lost. He's much sharper now.

'All right, Henry, where are you now?'

'Er, Chiswick, where we were going to meet.'

'Oh yeah, okay, well.' He draws out the word for some time. 'How do you fancy coming to a gig tonight?'

'I thought you were playing in Birmingham?'

It was four o'clock now.

'Tell you what, get in a black cab, right, I'll pay for it when you get here, come to Kentish Town, to the—' – I could hear him calling over to his manager – 'to the Lord Stanley pub, and we can go to the gig from there. But you've got to come now. No time to lose.'

I get into a taxi, the driver tells me his life story, we get to the pub in Kentish Town but Pete and his manager have moved on. I don't have enough money for the cab. My body is a barrel of adrenaline, heart vibrato, legs sprung, and somehow I persuade the taxi driver to let me run away ten pounds short of what I owe him. I sprint down the road to the antiques shop where I find them, Andy and Pete, looking at records, coat stands and old wood-turning instruments as they meander through a cavern of Victorian bric-à-brac. I catch my breath and try to look as though nothing's happened; they both say hello and carry on with their browsing, eyebrows raised.

Andy Boyd has managed Pete Doherty for several years now. Not much older than him, he's skilful around his client. He seems to know when to back off and let Pete do his own thing, as well as understanding how to get him to do something. He's also a die-hard fan of Pete and his music. He truly believes in both. There'd be moments during the night that followed when their relationship resembled that of a father in his late thirties with a teenage son: one moment Andy would be a figure of censure, the next he's a mate sharing a joke, then he's his number-one fan telling him how talented he his, and at other times he's there to provide unconditional and almost parental support for Pete when he's laid low. As Andy told me several times that night, managing Pete Doherty is not like managing anyone else. There's no template.

Pete finds a rickety pump organ and begins to play. A Turkish girl who's been loitering outside for a few minutes finally plucks up the courage to ask for an autograph. Several minutes later the man thought to be the epitome of everything that was wrong with England by the writers and readers of some of the more grumpy columns in right-wing newspapers buys two art-nouveau ashtrays, an antique tailor's dummy and a pair of tiny silver salt spoons. I ask if these are things he's grown up around. They're not. His parents were always scrimping and saving and because his dad was in the army he was often on the move. In some ways he's developed a taste for these things as mementoes of someone else's childhood, he says as we cross the road.

The three of us get into Andy's Jaguar and for the next two and a half hours we drive to Birmingham. The conversation ranges far and wide: from the Star of David that Pete's grandfather left him, via *Monty Python* sketches, stories about dosshouses Pete has scored in, how the band came together through to which is the best audio-book of Joyce's *Ulysses*. Pete's good at telling stories.

He can impersonate just about anyone, and an interesting thing happens when he's relating a story in which he appears. When he's describing what he once said, his voice goes right up in pitch, making him sound like a caricature thirteen-year-old urchin, a Dickensian scruff you can imagine being held by the ear as he pleads, *It wasn't me what done it. Aw go on matey, let us off.* There was a part of him that identified with this Artful Dodger scamp. I ask him which dead English people he looks up to.

'In the early days it was always characters from fiction,' he says. 'People like Billy Liar. Brigsby. Pinkie. Or Gulliver. The way he carried himself! He was almost perfect, wasn't he? Even when he landed in Lilliput he was too frightened to take a dump because he didn't want to ruin everyone's day. There's just, there's so much of Swift in that. He was so moral, and although he was a Christian man he was open-minded and keen to learn other religions and languages. He's like a lost Englishman he is,' adds Pete wistfully, slowing himself and letting the sound of the road return. 'You don't really see them any more. People with . . . fuck it, people with moral fibre basically. Moral backbone. People who really stand by their principles.' A police car wails by. 'People who would rather die than go against their word.'

'Would you like to be a martyr for something?' I ask.

'Doesn't that involve sacrifice at some stage?'

'I think it involves death,' Andy chips in.

'Ah.'

There is a silence, which I break by talking about islomania and the way the English seem to like reading about people who live on islands, or those that are washed up on them, especially where their hidden heroism comes to the fore.

'Right,' Pete gasps – I'm not sure if he really gasped, but from the way he speaks it often sounds as though he's gasping; his voice has a breathless quality. 'Because every community Gulliver lands in,' he goes on, 'every new tribe he meets, they've all got that in common. They're isolated. They don't know anything about the rest of the world that exists, and they think he's mad when he tells them about the political system in England. But it's all satire,' he whispers. Andy takes a call. In the background I can hear Pete carrying on to himself. 'He always manages to get the odd swipe in, does Swift.'

Andy talks about the venue we're heading to, reminding me that the gig starts in a few hours. I ask Pete if he gets stage fright.

'I suppose so, yeah. I don't want to beat round the bush here, you could call it that. It's more like climbing the fucking walls, to be honest. It's a weird kind of terror.'

'Did you have it last night at Wembley?'

'No, it subsided a bit. Back in the day it used to result in me going about fly-kicking moving buses or just not turning up. But', he collects himself, 'I just had to get it into my head that yes, people are there because they want to hear the music and not because they want to assassinate me or whatever. You can get some weird ideas, believe me.'

'Is it different when you're sober? Stage fright, that is.'

'No, drugs never really helped with that kind of feeling. In fact they probably make it worse. When you're sober you're more confident that you can perform to the best of your ability.'

Andy starts to talk more about Birmingham.

'Of course!' Pete exclaims. 'We're going to Birmingham. That's where Tony Hancock was born.' This is the most animated he's been all night. Along with his dad, Pete used to be a member of the Tony Hancock Appreciation Society.

'What do you like about him?'

'Hancock?'

'Yeah.'

He thinks for a moment.

'When I was younger what was fact and what was fiction was often a bit blurred. And I've always liked that, people who adopt characters. In the end it destroyed him – Hancock, that is. It suffocated him. But the character becoming real in everyone's eyes, you know? That's what I like. It's death by association for some people. Wilfred Bramble. He was a very talented actor but completely unknown until he did Steptoe. After that he couldn't walk down the street without everyone going, "Haroooold!" "Do yer funny face!" And he revelled in it, because it made him rich and it made him famous. But, actually, he's someone who didn't give a toss. He had a fantastic old career. Spent most his time down the bogs at Tottenham Court Road, mind you. But you see Hancock despised the character he became, the character everybody loved. Hated the gimmick of it.'

'Do you think everyone in some way has an *alter ego* that they bring out from time to time? I mean, do you ever feel that?'

'I feel like an actor sometimes, singing certain lines if I'm not in that particular mood. But it always comes back round again and I'll end up feeling that way.'

Andy puts on a Rolling Stones CD and the three of us sing along to 'Gimme Shelter'. When Andy and I shut up, it's Mick Jagger duetting with the person behind me, and I keep thinking to myself how much it sounds like Pete Doherty singing with Mick Jagger. Then I remember where I am and what's going on.

'Rape! Murder! It's just a shot away, it's just a shot away . . .'

This song has never sounded so good.

Andy gets on to Leonard Cohen, and the times his song-writing becomes too obvious.

'Well, that's the danger of honesty, it can be clichéd,' Pete adds, with 'Sympathy for the Devil' pounding away in the background. 'That's almost the definition of honesty really. All that cliché is, is something that's predictable, something that's ready-made.' He fires his lighter and it makes a crackling sound. 'Honesty doesn't rely upon originality, but cliché relies upon unoriginality.'

'Like the line about kites in "Music When the Lights Go Out",' Andy says. 'I remember, Pete, you were saying that at one point you weren't sure about that line,' as if to say, 'Go on, tell that story.'

'Yeah,' he purrs, as we glide further north.

'So how did the line come about?' he tries again.

'Okay. I don't know if I'm making this up, and I don't think I am, but me and the girl I was knocking about with when I wrote that song, we either planned to go kite-flying on Hampstead Heath, or we did. So we didn't actually fly any kites together but we tried to make one out of a plastic bag. Either that or I just wanted something to rhyme with nights and fights and lights,' he says with a questioning lilt. 'There was a time when I thought that line was a bit papple. But taken with the rest of the song, it seems to work.'

He sings it.

'. . . *the fights and the nights and the blue lights, all the kites we flew together. Thought they'd fly for ever. But all the highs and the lows, and the to's and the fro's, they left me dizzy. Won't you forgive me? I no longer hear the music . . . Oh-no.*'

We arrive at the stadium, Pete gets out and he's off, body swaying this way and that, head up like a hound trying to pick up a scent, hat perched a little precariously towards the back of his head, and his knees bent as they bob his body up and down. All eyes are on him as he ambles through the backstage area into the dressing room. I meet the band, the tension builds and an hour later I'm in the Babyshambles dressing room with the four members of the band and the tour manager who's had her head in a collection of Chekhov short stories up until then; now she's got a walkie-talkie in her hand. She's waiting for the signal. The band is in a circle, bubbling with anticipation, yelping occasionally, holding their hands out to see how much they wobble. Pete is the tallest and the most busy. The walkie-talkie crackles.

'Right!' she cries. 'Let's go.'

She marches out of the room and they follow in single file, fast, each man's tight-jeaned legs and pointy shoes exaggerating his gait. I follow behind them as if the fifth member. Through one corridor, down another, the roar of the crowd gets louder, a set of double doors is whooshed open and it's louder still as we enter a vast space that is the back of the arena. It's dark, all polished concrete and lorry trailers. The sound of the crowd echoes around it. A path is lit by a sporadic avenue of security guards with torches that look like truncheons. Still the sound grows and the band are walking fast, one behind the other. I'm jogging to keep up. Closer and closer, louder and larger, until we reach a black curtain held apart by another official. One by one they file through and climb a slim set of stairs before reaching the stage. They come into view and with the force of a thousand realisations the crowd erupts. The lights go up and there, before them, is a sea of hands and eyes drinking them in, expectant, giddy, revved up and sweaty. The four men place guitar straps over their necks, pick up drumsticks, exchange glances, and with a nod it begins. Birmingham roars.

Bobbing, weaving, dodging pints of beer that are thrown on stage, smoking one of the many fags thrown at him – for which he may later be fined – adjusting his hat in between songs, chatting to the crowd and making them laugh: as well as being very good at making songs, Pete Doherty is a great front man. He soon has the crowd eating out of the crack-stained palm of his hand. At one point he hops down from the stage and launches himself head first into a sea of Lynx-flavoured Brummie flesh. The security guards flap. The crowd cheers.

Babyshambles play a great gig, though there's little by way of an after party, so an hour after the concert Andy suggests we head back to London. We'll go first to Pete's house in Wiltshire and then he and I can carry on to London.

The three of us leave the stadium and head towards the car. Pete spots four bald men waiting behind a grille of iron. They want him to sign their programmes. He goes over and chats to them; one of them says he doesn't have anywhere to sleep that night because he's missed his train. Pete stuffs £200 through the fence and tells him to find a nice hotel. We get into the car and at the gates a gang of teenagers who have come down from Liverpool rush over to the window. Omigod. Omigod. Pete. We love you Pete. Omigod. One of them has Pete's lyrics from a song he wrote with the Libertines tattooed down his arm: 'If you've lost your faith in love and music, the end won't be long.'

'Does that feel at all weird, seeing those tattoos?' I ask a little later.

'No,' he says emphatically. 'I fucking kissed his arm. I enjoy it. Doesn't feel weird, feels beautiful. *If you've lost your faith in love and music, the end won't be long,*' he sings. 'You can't argue with that.'

It's one in the morning now and we're flying. The motorway is empty. Pete's been rummaging about as usual in the back seat, singing lines from songs, chatting to himself, doing impressions and saying 'Blood clot' a lot in a Rastafarian accent. From time to time he'll get out his baby wipes and give the backseat a clean. In between he'll talk about anything I ask him, like his blood paintings. He said I could commission him to make one. He'd do an Albion special. In return I could write an essay in my own blood. Or he'd talk about how as a teenager he used to get on the tube and pretend to be a foreigner, talking on his phone in a foreign accent and reading French newspapers upside down. This is how I imagined the conversation would carry on until we got to his house, but with almost an hour to go everything changed, quite suddenly.

In the space of about thirty seconds the interview died of a sudden heart attack.

The car we were in was sleek and modern and I was in the passenger seat directly in front of Pete. He began to talk about how much he was looking forward to getting home and just as he said this I felt my seat jerk backwards. It felt as though someone had given it a little tug from behind, only the seat continued to move back electronically after the initial jerk.

'Push the seat forward,' he says.

'How do I? Where's the switch?'

'There!' He points at the dashboard. I reach forward to try and find it. There's no lever where he's pointed. I start scrabbling around by my feet. Still the seat is going backwards very slowly.

'Move the fucking seat forward!' he shouts, and at this point, somehow, hooks his right leg round and starts to kick me in the back with the heel of his boot, stabbing down as hard as his leg would allow with a rapid jabbing motion. I've never before been kicked so hard, and for several seconds, like a rabbit caught in the headlights, I can't move for the shock of what has just begun.

'Push the fucking seat forward, you fucking cunt!' he shouts, as he continues to drive down into my back with his heel. Still the seat is moving backwards.

I generally work faster when not being bludgeoned by someone's boot, and in my panic start to pull on any part of the seat I can find. At this point he starts to throw fruit juice at me.

'Andy, where the fuck is the switch!?' I shout.

'I'm about to crash!' He's going at about 80 mph. Still a heel jams into my back like a bassline, thud, thud, thud.

'Where's the FUCKING SWITCH!' I try again as I rummage more beneath the seat. There follow ten seconds that stretch out for an age as the seat continues to glide backwards at the speed of an electric gate and the kicks rain down on my back like hail from hell and the drink sprays in bursts against the back of my head and Pete Doherty is just behind me reminding me that I'm 'a fucking cunt!' while Andy Boyd is shouting at the pair of us that he's about to crash, and for those ten seconds everything feels miraculously still in my head. At last I find the switch, over on the left of the seat, nowhere near where Pete had pointed, and hold it down. The seat whines forward with the smug efficiency of a machine that has no idea of the mayhem it's just caused.

Silence. I wring some of the fruit juice out of my hair. My back is sore.

Pete starts to mutter to himself about how he saw me doing it, and that I was grinning while I did it and I was trying to injure him, that was it, I was trying to prove a point, he says, asking if I feel vindicated now. I turn round and tell him he's being ridiculous, that I had no idea where the switch was and there's no way I'd try to hurt him. I get upset.

'I'm not talking to you,' he says petulantly. I repeat what I have just said. 'Not talking to you,' he says again and starts to fiddle with something in his lap.

We continue in silence. Five minutes later he hands me a baby wipe to clean up some of the drink that's been sprayed over the car's fawn-coloured upholstery. Half an hour later he offers a hand and says softly, 'Are we all right, fella?'

I want us to be all right but clearly we are not. Deep down he thinks I am out to get him and there's nothing I can do to talk him out of this, so I give up.

Pete Doherty is often associated with drugs. Usually when you read about him in the mainstream press the news is drug-related rather than musical. I haven't mentioned any drug-taking during the time I was with him, not out of some unwritten *omertà* but because up until this point in the encounter it doesn't seem relevant. Perhaps there were plenty of drugs consumed during the course of that night, perhaps none at all, perhaps I was involved too and even ended up paying one of his dealers, so there can be no hint of implied judgement on my part. All the same, here, at the close, Pete's accumulated drug-use over the last eight years becomes a part of the story in the way that it can exaggerate anyone's highs or lows, turning valleys into canyons, hillocks into Himalayan peaks and generally make you more paranoid than you might otherwise be.

I'm not overly attached to my back – emotionally, that is. We don't see a lot of each other. So I don't have a real problem with it being kicked once in a while, and in a strange way there was something enviably real about waking up the following morning and inspecting the bruises in the bathroom mirror. They seemed to be proof that this journey was actually happening. That I was alive. That humans are animals, and they crunch into balls when under attack presenting their backs as targets; or they lash out when they feel trapped.

Andy called the following evening to ask if I was okay and if there'd been any bruising or bleeding. It was good of him. I said I was fine. He hoped the kicking had not left a bad taste in my mouth, adding that he thought I'd handled it well, which I think meant I didn't do anything. I agreed that I was great at doing nothing.

I'm glad I met Pete Doherty when I did. In the way he moved, his peripatetic dreamy detachment, learning and wit, as well as his creativity, he was what I imagined a Thomas De Quincey figure to be. At other times he had the raffish rebelliousness of a Rimbaud or Byron, as well as their need to be seen. I'm referring to these people only because they're figures he has been compared to at some point in his life. Beyond any historical comparisons, Pete Doherty is a fascinating and utterly original human being. He exudes an inimitable, magnetic charisma: a quixotic flightiness and help-lessness underscored by this very real threat of violence, as I found out, which perhaps helps explain why supermodels fall for him and he has so many fans around the world. Especially in France. They love him there.

'How's your French, Pete?'

'Yeah, it's all right,' he says, as if to say 'Thanks for asking'. 'Can't speak the language though.'

I guess he'll follow a similar trajectory to other great English creative spirits who are, at first, the subject of society's tough love, but, if they survive this, are winched up on high, asked to appear on *Desert Island Discs*, given titles and talked about in reverential terms, a lot like Dame Vivienne Westwood. At this point they might also be described as eccentric. In this sense I think I met Pete Doherty about twenty years too early.

19

THE INVENTOR

If English artists, musicians and fashion designers are now among the best in the world, this is a recent development. Not so in the world of invention. The English have been extremely good at inventing things for at least 200 years. Invention comes to us naturally. It appeals to a very English set of virtues. Not only does it involve a creativity that rarely gets bogged down by the need to be beautiful, it is the embodiment of utilitarianism, bloody-mindedness, making do, individuality, and a certain kind of everyday humour that routinely combines things that don't ordinarily go. Research in the mid-1980s from the journal *Cornelius* suggested that 'more than half of the new ideas adopted by manufacturers worldwide originate in this country'. Yet like so many parts of the contemporary English character, this genius for invention is by no means timeless. It begins only in the second half of the eighteenth century, yet, as Sir James Dyson (of Dyson vacuum-cleaners fame) explained to me, it may soon be in danger of disappearing.

Though the first English patent was issued by Henry VI in 1449 (to a man who made stained glass), it was not until the Regency that the English ceased to rely on European ingenuity. Holding them back beforehand was a religious belief in Providence that would reveal new ideas in His or Her own good time. The moment technological invention was seen as a celebrated act of genius, and mechanisation an opportunity rather than a threat, the cult of the English inventor could begin.

From its inception this figure has been eccentric. Invention and scientific advance are predicated on taking intellectual risks, seeing the world differently, mining the realm of the wildly improbable and generally making the kind of original connections that eccentrics are famous for. It's because of this emphasis on imagining the unimaginable that even the greatest scientists will often get it spectacularly wrong. This is at the heart of what they do.

As well as being the visionary who transformed our understanding of gravity, light and calculus, Sir Isaac Newton spent a large chunk of his life grappling with the arcane and mystical intricacies of alchemy, natural magic and the meaning of apocalyptic prophecies of early Christian texts. Described by John Maynard Keynes as a 'strange spirit, who was tempted by the Devil to believe he could reach all the secrets of God and Nature by the pure power of the mind – Copernicus and Faustus in one', Newton believed the mathematical formulae he presented in *Principia Mathematica* to be part of a series of sacred truths bestowed by God upon an elite group of mystical philosophers at the dawn of time, a group to which he belonged. A man who could go for weeks removed from the world, Newton was secretive, neurotic, egotistical and eccentric. He is now revered as one of the world's great scientists.

Since 1991 there has been a light-hearted awards ceremony held once a year to celebrate eccentric scientific achievement. It's called the Ig Nobel Prize. The criteria for inclusion are inventions that 'first make you laugh and then make you think'. Past winners include the scientist who claimed to have worked out the geographical location of hell.

This prize is more important than it might at first sound. In many ways it is an essential corollary of the more heavyweight Nobel Prize. It is a reminder that in the house of scientific advance the ridiculous and the sublime have always drunk from the same cup.

Just as scientists will fire duds in the name of advancing human knowledge, they can also lose sight of morality. In the early twentieth century Aleister Crowley conducted a series of scientific experiments to try and work out whether cats really had nine lives. As he explained in his autobiography: 'I caught a cat and having administered a large dose of arsenic, I chloroformed it, hanged it above the gas jet, stabbed it, cut its throat, smashed its skull, and when it had been pretty thoroughly burnt, drowned it and threw it out of the window that the fall might remove the ninth life. The operation was successful. I was genuinely sorry for the animal; I simply forced myself to carry out the experiment in the interests of pure science.'

Though Crowley was more Satanist than scientist, it's interesting to see how the words 'pure science' can evoke a world where anything goes. By the nature of what they do, all scientists and inventors will, at some point, come up with ideas that may perhaps make schoolchildren titter 200 years from now. Only with some of these unusual theories or inventions the children will be laughing not at it, but at us, for laughing at those who came up with the idea in the first place, people like Chrissie de Rivaz, whom I was about to meet.

What's more, Chrissie would probably be there herself in 200 years' time leading the laughter. There'd be tears streaming down her face. 'We' would have become the ubiquitous 'they' who throughout history have laughed at people like Christopher Columbus when he said the world was round, amongst others.

'So,' I began, 'let's say I want to live for ever.'

She looked at me encouragingly.

'And that I wanted to sign up to your cryogenics—'

'Cryonics,' Chrissie corrected me. 'Cryogenics is different.'

'Sorry, cryonics. Still, how do I go about it?'

'Well,' she said, moistening her lips. We were in an uncomfortably wide room on either side of a battlefield of green carpet. 'First of all you'd have your temperature taken down to minus 197 degrees,' Chrissie began with the measured delivery of a sales pitch, though without any of the push.

'Minus 197?'

'That's just beyond the boiling point of liquid nitrogen,' she went on. 'Where all biological activity ceases.' I nodded as fast as my head would allow. 'As we see it there's no reason why the body shouldn't be preserved like that until technology has advanced sufficiently to repair what caused you to die in the first place, patch up the cell damage caused by freezing, and recreate the cells in a viable state. So in other words my ageing body won't come back looking like this.' She gestured at the loose flesh traffic-jammed around her midriff. 'The idea is I'll come back fit, healthy and at an age when my body doesn't have bits of fat where it shouldn't.' Her face broke into a jolly smile that said, 'Next question please.'

I was sitting opposite Chrissie de Rivaz in her bungalow on the north coast of Cornwall. The sky that day was grey and full of bluster. During the gaps in our conversation you could hear wind whistling through cracks in the house. Chrissie had a hearty, convivial face: the kind of person you could imagine running a gymkhana in Hertfordshire or selling homemade jam at a summer fête. Her cheeks were the colour of ketchup, she wore loose-fitting clothes and over her forehead came bangs of fine grey hair. As well as being the author of more than twenty-five romantic novels – she writes as Chrissie Loveday and her books have titles like *Lovers Don't Lie, Conflict of Love, A Love that Grows, The Path to Love, First Love, Last Love, Food for Love* – Chrissie is the chairman and media manager of Cryonics Europe, an organisation that freezes its members when they die so they can be reanimated at an unspecified date in the future. The group has about forty members in England. As media manager, Chrissie is the one who's interviewed on television when cryonics gets into the news, something she enjoys, particularly when it's Richard and Judy asking the questions (she mentioned her interview with them four times during our conversation), otherwise she'll give talks at specialist societies, or perhaps cryonics will come up when she's out walking the dogs. Some people are quite interested, she said moderately, others hate talking about death.

From the amount of cryonics jargon she had used in her introductory spiel, as well as the group solidarity I could sense already, the shared semi-sacred texts and crypto-religious justification for doing it, I realised quite early on that Chrissie was part of what Erving Goffman would call a 'deviant community', one that adheres to an informal creed. Eccentrics generally aren't so good at following strict rules and being part of a chorus.

Though she was not a full-blooded English eccentric, Chrissie was certainly an ambassador of eccentric science.

She told me about how much she was looking forward to returning in a few hundred years and seeing what had changed in the world – she hoped that by then someone would have got round to inventing a time-travel machine like the one they have in *Star Trek*. Then we moved on to fees.

The cost of joining her group, having your body frozen and transported to a storage facility in America, as well as the paperwork involved and the running costs thereafter comes to about £20,000. That was if you went for the deluxe option that involved having all of your body frozen. Some cryonics companies only take your head. It's cheaper that way. Chrissie tutted at the thought. For non-members the price of full-body preservation is closer to £50,000.

Although a growing number of people concede that cryonics may one day be possible, and acknowledge that test-tube babies owe their existence to the ability of certain human cells to withstand being frozen, most agree that the technology is not nearly advanced enough to freeze and then unfreeze a human corpse. With the exception of the British spy Austin Powers, who was frozen in the late 1960s before being reanimated in 1997 (to save the planet), no man or woman has successfully entered a state of cryonic vitrification and been brought back to life.

'So,' I continued, reeling a little from the costs she'd just run through, 'what would happen if I realised I was going to die in the next five minutes and I paid you £50,000? Right now. What's the procedure?'

'Yes, well, it's a lot easier if you know when you're going to die,' said Chrissie reassuringly. 'So first of all, once you were legally dead we'd replace your bodily fluids with a kind of human antifreeze. This is called perfusion and it gives the body cells as much protection as possible. Then there is the protectant.'

As well as protectant, there was a glycerol-based perfusate, to be used in advance of the cyroprotectant solution, which helped the process of perfusion and vitrification.

Each word was a building block. They made the structure sound more solid.

'So at the moment,' Chrissie continued, perching forward,

'although we know how to preserve the body and store it, we still haven't worked out how to reanimate it.' Her husband, John, who had wonky teeth and was smaller than Chrissie, was about to say something – I imagine about how technology was bound to advance sufficiently in the coming years – but Chrissie cut him off. 'The other problem is that you need the consent of the families of the deceased for everything to run smoothly, and some people are a bit against it. But we're fortunate because we both agree this is what we want to do. So whoever dies first will be fine.'

There followed an exquisite silence. It was a noiseless implosion, quiet as stone, that must have lasted four or five seconds as both husband and wife pondered which one of them was going to die first. Their eyes remained glued to the carpet.

'So it begins with a legal pronouncement,' John began in a nasal, trainspotterish voice. 'Once that happens, then Cool Down Process can commence.'

'Great. And how does the Cool Down Process work?' I began to picture machines with flashing lights, computer screens and teams of scientists to ensure that deanimation, vitrification and perfusion all ran smoothly.

'Well,' said Chrissie, 'cold water is a good start. And ice. Yes, we've got quite a lot of ice cubes in our freezer.' She smiled politely. 'Frozen vegetables, you know, anything like that.'

'Frozen vegetables?'

'Yes, that kind of thing. They usually help.'

I gulped. 'And have you actually seen this happen yet, the er, the perfusion process?'

'No, no, I haven't.' Chrissie shook her head, her body wobbling with it. 'There haven't actually been very many from England.'

'How many have there been?'

'Two actually. Just two.'

'Most take place in America,' John chipped in.

'But we do wear a medallion,' Chrissie added, reaching for a brooch that hung round her neck. That's all right then, I thought. With the medallion and the frozen vegetables there'd be no stopping them. I padded across the room to get a better look at the dog-tag round Chrissie's neck. She'd disguised it as a necklace. Engraved on the back were several numbers that were to be called if Chrissie died while out shopping and if the medics stopped to have a look at her jewellery as they whisked her into the ambulance.

At this point, apropos of not very much, John began to talk about Jesus.

'What did Jesus do?' he barked from his side of the sofa, crunched up slightly. 'He went around healing the sick and raising the dead, saying, "If you follow me, you will live for ever." So far nobody who has followed him has lived for ever. They have all died. So if you think about it like that, that Jesus told his followers to follow him, and he went around healing the sick and raising the dead, you could argue that cryonics is actually entirely in keeping with the Christian faith.' His voice went right up to give this last line the feel of a conclusive punchline.

I suggested that Jesus was talking about an incorporeal life after death. Heaven. John did not respond.

On their cryonics website Chrissie and John had posted a series of arguments similar to the one John had just run through. Beneath the main body of text as you navigated the site were quotations from a dead Russian philosopher called Fyodorov. They ranged from the faintly obvious – 'Memory of one's dead kin is not the same as the real person' – which even I could tell you and I'm neither dead nor a Russian philosopher, to the more apocalyptic: 'the choice is not between cryonics and continuing to live your normal life, the choice is between cryonics and annihilation'.

In the background I heard Chrissie's dogs yapping at each other.

'And do people ever take their pets with them?'

Chrissie's face creased with embarrassment.

'Er, yes. It does happen.' She glanced nervously at her husband. 'I know of one creature that's been frozen. It's cheaper than preserving a human. I mean I wouldn't do it.' She sighed sympathetically at the implied silliness of doing such a thing. 'And I have dogs, I adore my dogs, but the ones I've got now are my sixth or seventh, and I wouldn't be able to freeze all of them. Although they're a big part of my life and I spoil them rotten, when they're gone I'm afraid that's it. They'll be replaced.'

Which is what I imagined happened to human beings, more or

less. They are replaced by their offspring. Soon afterwards I left, and drove back to London.

Between Sir Isaac Newton and Chrissie de Rivaz there is a dizzying array of English inventors and scientists ranging from the professional to the visionary to the amateur. All are blessed with a fearlessness born of eccentricity – or eccentricity born of fearlessness, take your pick, they exist in a loop – that has helped them in their particular breakthrough. From Jonas Hanway, the eighteenth-century philanthropist who invented the umbrella and was mocked by the Hackney coachmen whose livelihoods his invention would eventually ruin, through to the lovable Professor Colin Pillinger with his bushy sideburns who led the unsuccessful Beagle 2 Mars Space Project, there are a surprisingly large number of tragic figures in the canon of English inventors. Most were decades ahead of their time and as a result marginalised by their contemporaries.

Oliver Heaviside was one such eccentric scientist, shortlisted for the Nobel Prize in 1912, who once wrote: 'If it is love that makes the world go round, it is self-induction that makes electromagnetic waves go round the world.' He devised a way to eliminate distortion on long-distance telephone calls, came up with a series of breakthroughs in the field of electromagnetics and was a pioneer in the use of mathematical notation. Yet he never received any formal training, so he'd present his work in such a way that almost no one understood what he was talking about, which meant that most of his papers were excluded from technical journals. He was also highly secretive and lived alone and in the dark. He suffered from thermophilia which meant he would work in rooms that visitors described as 'hotter than hell'. Towards the end of his life he was said to have replaced his furniture with replicas made of granite. Heaviside also liked to paint his nails cherry red, like Sebastian Horsley.

Heaviside, Hanway and Monboddo are massively important within the history of English eccentricity. They represent creative eccentricity at its most practical, and by their example underline the extent to which the English depend on their creative fringe to move forward. Sometimes we lose sight of this.

Perhaps one of the most telling differences between the First and Second World Wars, in terms of how they were led, was the openness of Churchill and his generals in the latter to the ideas of eccentric inventors and scientists like Barnes Wallis or Geoffrey Pyke. D-Day, with its floating harbours, pipeline under the ocean and mine-sweeping tanks, was an exhibition of the English genius for invention as well as the ability of the army to harness this potential. The British Army during the First World War, by contrast, was led by blimps brought up on the Game: individuals who did not understand the value of eccentric thought and imagined they could break the stalemate using loyalty, teamwork and courage alone.

How about English invention today – what is its future? James Dyson was not sure. He worried that inventors and engineers in this country had an image problem, and that this was putting students off the idea of working in these fields. Not only was engineering thought to be geeky, dirty or just plain unsexy, too few people understood the degree of creativity involved. As he told me: 'We have to stem the gravitation of our young people towards philosophy, sociology and media studies. As interesting as these subjects may be, they're not going to provide us with a workforce that can create practical solutions to our twenty-first-century challenges of energy, housing and an ageing population. Engineering can.'

As a nation, he felt we were losing both the confidence and propensity for invention that we might have had 200 years ago. In typical inventor fashion, having perceived the problem, Dyson has set about fixing it. As well as trying to reform the British patent system, he has put in motion plans for his very own School of Design Innovation, in Bath, which, among many other things, will reposition design as exciting, risky and creatively challenging.

It's tempting to describe more eccentric English inventors who were ahead of their time, because they are absolutely central to any examination of English eccentricity. But it might end up looking like a list written horizontally. I prefer lists when they are vertical. So for the next few pages this will become an almanac, like one you might buy in the weeks leading up to Christmas to give to your grandchildren or grandparents, or both, if you and your family have cracked cryonics.

A List of English Inventors
(with the inventions for which they are most famous)

Roger Bacon (1214–94) – magnifying glass
William Oughtred (1575–1660) – slide-rule
Robert Hooke (1635–1703) – Hooke's Law of Elasticity
Sir Isaac Newton (1642–1727) – calculus, reflecting telescope
Thomas Savery (1650–1715) – steam engine
Edmond Halley (1656–1742) – diving bell
John Shore (1662–1752) – tuning fork
Jethro Tull (1674–1741) – seed drill
John Hadley (1682–1744) – octant, predecessor of sextant
John Harrison (1693–1776) – seaworthy clock, to measure longitude
Humphrey Gainsborough (1718–76) – tide mill, self-ventilating fish carriage
Earl of Sandwich (1718–92) – sandwich
Joseph Priestley (1733–1803) – soda water, rubber
James Hargreaves (1720–78) – Spinning Jenny
John Wilkinson (1728–1808) – cast iron
Henry Cort (1741–1800) – steam-rolling machine
Lionel Lukin (1742–1834) – lifeboat
William Wouldhave (1751–1821) – lifeboat (it was either him or Lukin)
Henry Shrapnel (1761–1842) – shrapnel shell
George Manby (1765–1854) – fire extinguisher
Henry Maudsley (1771–1831) – screw-cutting lathe, machine-tool technology
Richard Trevithick (1771–1833) – railway steam locomotive, Cornish engine
Sir George Cayley (1773–1857) – glider, caterpillar track, seatbelt, small-scale helicopter
Sir Humphry Davy (1778–1829) – Davy lamp

George Stephenson (1781–1848) – national steam-railway network
Samuel Christie (1784–1865) – Wheatstone Bridge
Joseph Aspdin (1788–1855) – Portland cement
Charles Babbage (1791–1871) – programmable computer
Michael Faraday (1791–1867) – rubber balloon, electrical transformer, benzene
John Herschel (1792–1871) – infra-red radiation
Edwin Budding (1795–1846) – lawnmower, adjustable spanner
Sir Roland Hill (1795–1879) – postage stamps
John Stringfellow (1799–1883) – steam-powered aeroplane
William Henry Fox Talbot (1800–77) – calotype photograph
Sir Charles Wheatstone (1802–75) – electric telegraph, concertina, microphone and automatic transmitter
Isambard Brunel (1806–59) – propeller-driven ocean-bound ship, Thames Tunnel
William Armstrong (1810–1900) – hydraulic crane
Alexander Parkes (1813–90) – celluloid
Sir John Lawes (1814–1900) – super-phosphate fertiliser
Sir Francis Galton (1822–1911) – self-ventilating top hat, eugenics
Robert Whitehead (1823–1905) – torpedo
Sir Joseph Swan (1828–1914) – light-bulb
Sir William Perkin (1838–1907) – synthetic dye
Oliver Heaviside (1850–1925) – Kennelly-Heaviside Layer, distortion-free long-distance telephoning
Sir Charles Parsons (1854–1931) – steam turbine
Joseph Day (1855–1946) – two-stroke engine
William Friese-Green (1855–1921) – cinematography
Arthur Wynne (1862–1945) – crossword
Frank Hornby (1863–1936) – Meccano toys, Hornby model railways
Harry Brearley (1871–1948) – stainless steel
Sir Barnes Wallis (1887–1979) – bouncing bomb
Archibald Low (1888–1956) – radio guidance systems
Percy Shaw (1890–1976) – cat's-eye road stud
Geoffrey Pyke (1894–1948) – pykrete
Katharine Blodgett (1898–1979) – non-reflective glass
Sir Donald Bailey (1901–85) – Bailey bridge

Sir Alec Issigonis (1906–88) – Mini
Sir Frank Whittle (1907–96) – jet engine
Christopher Cockerell (1910–99) – hovercraft
Alan Turing (1912–54) – artificial intelligence
Trevor Baylis (1937–) – wind-up radio
Sir Clive Sinclair (1940–) – pocket calculator, folding bicycle
Colin Pillinger (1943–) – Beagle 2, Genesis spacecraft
Sir James Dyson (1947–) – dual-cyclone bagless vacuum cleaner
Sir Tim Berners-Lee (1955–) – internet

Lyndon Yorke (1944–) – Tritania

'And then they said, "The winner is . . ." And suddenly they announced it was me! I thought, "Bloody hell." It really was an incredible surprise,' he said, reflective and sombre for a moment like an actor who had just won an Oscar. 'Because I don't consider myself eccentric.' Lyndon let out a full-stop laugh. His speech was punctuated by laughs like this. They signified either a comma, semi-colon or full stop, depending on how long they lasted; a paragraph break was signalled by a full-blown chuckle. Shortish, with ruddy cheeks that made him look robust, Lyndon Yorke was a well-mannered man. He was also immensely happy, and smiled so much that there were times when his face seemed to be paralysed into a grin.

As well as being an amateur inventor, or *adapter*, as he put it, correcting me, Lyndon Yorke was the winner of the 2001 Best British Eccentric Award, finishing ahead of Captain Beany at number four, and seventh-placed gnome-collector Ann Atkin.

We were in the front room of his cottage in Buckinghamshire near the end of an airstrip from which vintage biplanes took off every few minutes. Behind him on his bookshelf I could see his Dafta figurine. It looked just like Beany's, only Lyndon's had not been spray-painted gold. It was less prominent too and a film of dust had gathered on its shoulders.

Not only did Lyndon find the ceremony a bit of a shock, so too was the experience of driving up to London in his 1928 Model

A Ford Tudor with his favourite invention in a trailer behind him. The Tritania is an amphibious 1922 wicker bathchair welded on to a catamaran the size of a Mini Cooper. As he drove towards Hyde Park with it in tow motorists honked at him and waved, particularly taxi drivers. He must have felt like Chris Eubank in his truck. Lyndon beamed at the memory. He later showed me Tritania, which looked like something Heath Robinson's Professor Brainstawm might have designed. It had been customised with an array of 'wacky bits and bobs', as Lyndon called them, most of which moved and were powered by windscreen-wiper motors. There was a mechanical pigeon that flapped its wings, a rotating umbrella, a wind-up gramophone, a machine that blew bubbles and, stowed next to him in the craft, a pole with a claw that he would use to collect drinks from people who liked his boat. Tritania comes out each year at the Henley Regatta, and in a nation that likes to drink it seemed apt that a glass of Pimm's was equivalent to a thumbs-up.

It is there, at Henley each year, that Lyndon plays the fool. He becomes the resident eccentric, just like Krentoma in the village of Nansepotiti, Tom Leppard in Kyleakin, Sebastian Horsley strutting through Soho, or Captain Beany in Port Talbot. Each man was the in-group deviant who lent a kind of balance to proceedings.

Lyndon's get-up for Henley involved a pith helmet, goggles and safari suit. Sometimes he'd include a top hat. Costume was important as it allowed him to distinguish Lyndon at home in his workshop, tinkering and drinking tea, from Lyndon the Best British Eccentric, glugging champagne and on show. As well as ensuring that people look in his direction, the costume will always remind him that he is *on*.

As he explained, it's because of this costume that he doesn't mind being called an eccentric. Anyone who calls him eccentric is referring only to the part of his character that comes out when he's dressed up.

'So if I'm honest,' he went on, 'I think someone like Sir Patrick Moore should have won that award, as his entire character is eccentric. With me it's just one part.'

There is a club in Henley called Phyllis Court. Lyndon explained that it was very prestigious. During the regatta this is where the best-connected Henley grandees will go to get respectfully drunk.

'And when I'm approaching Phyllis Court – you know, there's all these people on the balcony dressed in their finery – and I can hear odd bits of conversation wafting down the water before I get in sight of it,' he enthused in a wholesome, home-counties kind of way. 'And you can hear people saying, "Where is he? I wonder where he is?"' His voice went from speculative to exuberant. '"There he is!"' And then they're all cheering as I go past, which gives me such a thrill, it really does.'

It was the same thrill that drove Captain Beany, or Dave Lycett Green as he limbered up outside a London tube station in the early morning with City workers streaming past, grim-faced and teutonic. Eccentrics will often feel this urge to entertain and bring some kind of joy to an occasion.

Yet, as Sebastian Horsley pointed out, from time to time the English can forget how to play. Lyndon told me about passers-by who would respond with a kind of militant grumpiness to the sight of him in his bathchair. They were a minority, he explained, and would tell him his boat was pointless, or that he was point-less. The sight of him irked them beyond their habitual indifference.

Lyndon used to live in Marlow until he was forced out. Next to his house was a garage with a flat roof, and one day he got his hands on a gun turret from a Second World War aircraft which he duly bolted on to the roof of his garage. He added some flashing lights and a dummy. His neighbours seemed to like it. Word spread and soon people were travelling from nearby villages to see this strange gun turret. After a few weeks he received an anonymous note from a neighbour who demanded that the turret come down. Lyndon ignored it. Five days later he returned from a party to find the gun had been ripped from the roof, thrown to the ground and smashed.

'How strange,' I said. 'Why do you think they did that?'

'I don't know,' he replied hospitably.

'Or what kind of a person would do it?'

His eyebrows moved up beyond the rim of his glasses.

'It was one of these people that lived in a very pretty, organised house and environment, and I had something a little bit different. They took exception to it.'

He moved house. Surrounding the garden of his new home was a wooden fence that made the place feel like a Charles Waterton walled paradise. He had stuffed it with his favourite follies and curiosities – he called himself a 'follyologist', a word he hopes to get into the dictionary one day. Almost all of his adaptions involve giving a defunct mechanism a new use, one that was in some way entertaining. As well as the wicker car, wicker boat and many other creations made from obsolete machines, he showed me the antique car he had used to tow Tritania into London for the awards ceremony. He had found it in New Zealand abandoned in a field and had patched it up before driving it overland to England. I asked him how people had responded during that trip to the sight of him in his 1920s Ford. He said that funnily enough, because there were so many other Englishmen going round the world in taxi-cabs, bicycles, tricycles, doing it in eighty days, eight years, for charity, or following in a forebear's footsteps, most people in places like Iran or Afghanistan were quite used to the sight of an Englishman on a long journey in an unusual vehicle. They always guessed that he was English, he added. Paragraph-break laugh.

I wondered if in some Iranian villages there was actually a word for an eccentric Englishman on an epic adventure.

After he'd shown me the rest of his creations I left the man once described as Britain's most eccentric and began to drive home. The journey that had begun over a year ago when I saw Zac Monro and his whale-shaped hedge was coming to an end, and for once as I returned from an interview my head was not a jumble of different eccentrics and eccentricities following on from one another in a confusing, apparently infinite Borgesian library of historical themes and traits and personalities. For the first time I felt a sense of resolution – though this was tinged with sadness that the journey was drawing to a close. I had enjoyed meeting Lyndon and people like him. They seemed to cast England in a different light, and that was one of the most surprising parts of this journey. Although in many ways a deviation from the norm, each of the characters I had met represented a concentrated shot of Englishness. When put together they formed a portrait of this country that was far richer than I had expected.

The journey was coming to an end because I was no longer searching. To continue would be sight-seeing. I had found what I was looking for which meant there was only one place left to go. I needed to make a pilgrimage to the hedge where it all began.

On a wintry afternoon in November I went to meet Zac Monro, the architect whose topiary had set me on my journey. He was shorter than I had imagined, though just as friendly, and told me about the day the cameras came to Solon Road in Brixton to film him and his whale-shaped hedge, the one that the council planned to cut down.

Having formed a local residents' association only months before in order to plant more flowers and trees in their front gardens and generally make the street look less squalid, Zac was annoyed when he got the letter from the council. He emailed a reply, copied in his local newspaper, and soon the BBC picked up on the story.

At dawn on Tuesday 15 August 2006, the day it began, the local council ordered in an army of street-cleaners to tidy up Solon Road before the cameras arrived. Soon after, a representative from Lambeth council turned up. At the sight of the BBC camera crew this man apparently became like a thirteen-year-old girl in front of her favourite boyband, dropping his shoulders, batting his eyelids and saying that this particular case was different now that the BBC were involved. The cameras rolled. The council official said that all he wanted from Mr Monro was some kind of concession. Zac produced a pair of scissors and snipped off an inch of topiary. The council official thought for a moment, and said he wanted more of a concession. Inch and a half. At this point he agreed that the hedge was 'no longer a dangerous structure'.

In the months that followed Zac's neighbours congratulated him on taking a stand against the council.

The whale survived. Zac now runs an air-guitar night in his spare time and hasn't really had a chance to give his hedge a trim over the last few months so it was overgrown when I saw it. But it continues to get compliments from passers-by. Lads chewing gum and clutching bottles of water still ring his doorbell at three in the morning to tell him that they think it's beaut-i-ful and they can't believe he made it, and that they'd never before seen a hedge in the shape of a peacock.

20

THE END

In the late eighteenth century, partly in response to the French Revolution, the English indulged in a moment of navel-gazing. For a group so pathologically wary of introspection on this scale – mainly because they couldn't cope with the idea of conforming to a singular identity – it made sense that part of the character to emerge was so non-conformist. The eccentric Englishman stood for freedom and liberty. He didn't care too much about what other people thought of him. He was patriotic, often playful and child-like, and wore clothes that were unusual or at times outdated. Although strange, he was not threatening: the eccentric was fundamentally amiable, which meant you could laugh at him, lightly. Usually his eccentricity came from taking one facet of Englishness to its morally and legally acceptable extreme. He was also older than most which suggested that he understood the norm from which he deviated. Above all, this character was entirely free from pretension. Nothing about him was fake, which was a neat continuation of the medieval Church's antipathy towards the artificial fool, or the much broader dislike of pretence that characterises so much of English literature and thought, from *Hamlet*'s Polonius telling his son Laertes, 'to thine own self be true', all the way through to Jade Goody, star of *Big Brother 3*, talking repeatedly about the importance of 'being true to yourself'.

During the nineteenth century, tales of eccentric English personalities became increasingly popular and as they did, around about the middle of the century, the eccentric became more virtuous. He was linked to the Romantic ideal of singular resistance, and in the writing of men like J. S. Mill or Herbert Spencer he became heroic.

In their eyes, the eccentric was an avatar of resistance against mainstream conformity.

As the nineteenth century wore on, the cult of the English eccentric blossomed and some of this virtuousness was lost. All over the country eccentric biographies and magazines were being snapped up faster than ever before; there were performances based on eccentric characters; merchandising was produced; an Eccentric Club opened (with a clock that went backwards); and in literature, particularly the work of Dickens, there was a newfound thirst for eccentric characters. At the same time, on the back of imperial expansion and consolidation, the idea of the English eccentric spread around the world until it began to be reflected back on to the English, reinforcing it as part of an English autostereotype.

Just as this is the moment when eccentricity appears to reach its zenith, it is the point at which it changes shape ever so slightly. For the first time English people might *try* to be eccentric, in which case they end up playing a part, which of course is anathema to real eccentricity.

Another effect of this commodification was that by the early twentieth century the word was not only being used as a label like 'mad' or 'morally acceptable'. Instead it began to be associated with a particular historical moment: the Victorian age. Along with antimacassars, Pre-Raphaelite paintings, grottoes and gnomes, eccentricity was seen as something the Victorians specialised in, so twentieth-century figures like Edith Sitwell who claimed to be eccentric were often seen as throwbacks to this age. This has continued into the twenty-first century where many continue to think of the English eccentric as a Victorian or perhaps Edwardian character.

In other words, the term has become a little stuck.

Every label within our language, including 'eccentric', naturally gathers rust and dust until it is stripped back, scrubbed down and looked at in a new light. When you do this there's every chance you'll decide the label no longer has any use, in which case you forget about it. More often you try and update it, so like a Japanese Zen garden that is raked afresh each morning the word is resuscitated.

But when you strip back the meaning of the word 'eccentric', as I've tried to do over the last year, and you look at it anew, is there actually any need for it in England today?

I think there is. Setting aside for a moment all references to England or Englishness and turning instead to the use of the word in relation to other, more abstract groups – any herd of humans that's large enough to have rules and margins – an eccentric is important because he acts as a testing ground for unusual ideas or experiments in lifestyle. This is what Krentoma represented. As well as trying to start a one-man architectural revolution Krentoma had reintroduced shamanry to his tribe (after drinking some diesel fuel by mistake and hallucinating).

As a cushion between normality and insanity an eccentric buffer allows the cultural norm to be defined with greater precision. In a totalitarian state where citizens are galvanised by the fear of a shared Other, what you can or cannot do is defined only by what gets you thrown into jail. There is almost no eccentric cushion between right and wrong. This makes it impossible to get a sanctioned idea of what is, say, a little bit strange, marginal, slightly odd, and with that, your understanding of taboo becomes binary. In a more expansive, secure and liberal society where eccentric lifestyles are tolerated, the cultural norm can be defined with greater nuance. It exists in three dimensions. There is room for experimentation and this allows the whole thing to move forward, because within any community that tolerates eccentricity this archetypal in-group deviant and his or her ilk are the ones most likely to chance upon change. The eccentric is expected to make unusual connections. So not only is he the boundary-marker of acceptability but he becomes a source of diversity and fresh ideas.

Moving back to the English, we, or perhaps they, have become especially adept at embracing their eccentrics over the last 200 years. It's hard to know why, or exactly where this stems from beyond some of the ideas I've outlined so far, but it has happened again and again throughout English history and continues to this day. In the trajectory of, say, Dame Vivienne Westwood, Banksy or King Arthur, you can trace an identical pattern. As young adults each was in opposition to what they saw as the establishment. Since then all three have been drawn gradually towards the centre and in different ways – whether it involved being awarded a DBE, rapid transformation from vandal to cultural icon, or elevation from chief protester outside Stonehenge to one of the people running its largest event – with similar effect, all three have been embraced. Their rebelliousness has been used to breathe life into the whole rather than undermine it.

If there is such a thing as the genius of the English, surely this is it.

So there is a case for updating the word 'eccentric'. It's a handy label. It reveals something of the English in terms both of their history and of their future. But what is the reality of trying to insert this word into the present? What is the future of eccentricity in this country?

This brings me back to the point at which I began when unsure whether it was actually possible to be an eccentric in twenty-first-century England.

In English society today the eccentric zone has narrowed, yes, and it continues to thin. It is reduced by the efflorescence of psychiatric syndromes in recent years, as well as by the internet's ordering of our society's margins into groups. Most of these groups have their own jargon and rules and are surprisingly strict and intolerant of eccentricity. On top of this, English society has become increasingly risk-averse and litigious over the last twenty years.

So on three fronts the possibility of eccentricity is reduced, though it has not been extinguished and will not be for some time. There are three reasons why.

The first may sound a bit optimistic, or just naive. It concerns the ability of any relatively free group of human beings to correct themselves once they acknowledge that they are living in an unnatural way – let's say their society has become too uncivilised or perhaps over-civilised. Just as J. S. Mill and other like-minded Victorians sensed in the mid- to late nineteenth century that instinct in their society was being straitjacketed, the group was able to correct this over the years that followed. In a similar sense, what is often referred to as 'the nanny state' in England today represents an identical trammelling of instinct. It runs counter to Mill's absolutely correct belief in the importance of having, within English society, 'a large variety in types of character'. History suggests that in time this will be corrected, which of course improves the possibility of eccentricity.

Two: professions like those of artist, fashion designer, musician, inventor, scientist and perhaps academic or actor have claimed for themselves over the last 150 years something of what was once eccentricity. As has 'creativity'. Any one of these terms, such as artist, now implies a degree of eccentricity. So instead of hearing the words 'English eccentric' you're more likely to read about an 'eccentric artist', 'eccentric inventor' or 'eccentric musician', until each coupling may one day sound tautologous and you'll end up with just 'artist', 'inventor' and 'musician'.

The final thing that I think will keep the English eccentric alive for the foreseeable future involves the Queen. Well, not the Queen *per se*, but the monarchy that she represents.

As the political power of the British monarch diminished throughout the nineteenth century, the level of pageantry, ornamentation and ceremonial attached to the Crown mushroomed. The best example of this is Queen Victoria's Diamond Jubilee in 1897, a ceremony on a scale quite unlike anything that had preceded it. An account in the *Daily Mail* described this event as unparalleled 'in the history of the world'. The role of the English monarch was being redefined. No longer seen as primarily a decision-maker, he or she was becoming an ornamental figurehead. As the British Empire fell away during the twentieth century, so the level of ceremonial attached to the Crown was pruned back, but it remained significant, and as the monarch continued to be sidelined politically this ornamentation became increasingly prominent.

With the Queen now an 'Olympus of decorative, integrative impotence', as David Cannadine put it, it seems the monarchy has fashioned for itself a position within English society that seems to suit both it and us. As well as being sufficiently toothless to be thought of as benign – and therefore lovable – the monarchy is now politically marginal *and* centric. It has little political power, yet legislation is channelled through it. The absurdity of the Queen's Speech – where the government's proposals for the forthcoming session of parliament are delivered via the Queen's mouth, so that she acts as a kind of bejewelled tannoy system – articulates this paradox perfectly. The monarchy is an institution defined by its unusual and eye-catching outfits. Different rules apply to its members, who are all heroic in the individuality of their lifestyles, and as there can only be one monarchy it is in every sense an anomaly. In the words of Rolf Harris: Can you see what it is yet?

Over the last fifty years the English monarchy has metamorphosed into a national mascot – England's resident eccentric. In its visual prominence and colour – Kate Fox once described the Queen as 'the best example of English sartorial eccentricity' – unusual lifestyle, antiquarian feel, and the way this institution is the chosen symbol of the group it represents, the monarchy matches – at times word for word – the role of in-group deviant that Erving Goffman once described.

As resident eccentric the monarchy has found a role that makes sense, it fits, which may help explain why there is so little chance of it being removed, either gradually, or suddenly, like Lyndon Yorke's turret atop his garage. By the logic of what I had learnt over the last year, this role also gave it a kind of function. It provides balance within a polity dominated otherwise by a parliament made up of drab careerist politicians toeing party lines.

In some ways the best illustration of the monarch as national eccentric, or mascot, is yet to come. When, or if, Prince Charles becomes king we will have on the throne a man who not only reveres above all other monarchs the godfather of English eccentricity, King George III, but is regularly and fondly referred to as the 'eccentric prince', a man who likes nothing more than to potter about his garden in an Afghan gown, talking to plants or contemplating the world from beneath an architectural folly, but also someone who has been deeply concerned about the environment long before the rest of us. In this prescience he starts to resemble a far-sighted inventor or Vivienne Westwood figure as she spots a

trend years before anyone else. As well as championing environmental causes for the last thirty years and lecturing anyone who'll
listen about organic farming and carbon footprints, Charles has for
many years advocated greater understanding of Islam and was busy
promoting inter-faith dialogue back when 9–11 was no more than
the number you saw actors dialling in American films when something went wrong.

With the monarchy transformed into national mascot, we have
a highly visible example of what the English eccentric might be.
This suggests that the *idea* of this character will persist for some
time.

Perhaps Prince Charles should be my updated English eccentric?
But I haven't interviewed him, and besides, why have a prince when
you can have a king?

King Arthur Uther Pendragon was a composite of all the qualities I hoped to find in a twenty-first-century English eccentric.
His lifestyle was utterly unique, and while he was happy to laugh
at himself, he was by no means artificial. He not only saw the
world differently to those around him but he believed in his
particular worldview enough to abandon his house and live
nomadically for twenty-one years. He was someone who really
did not care what other people thought of him; yet he also
displayed the kind of exhibitionism that was undoubtedly part of
being an eccentric. What's more, over the years he has become a
mascot figure within a series of different communities. There was
also something solitary, hermetic and heroic about Arthur and his
extraordinary journey. Not only was his life a kind of protest,
and he a political protester, but his existence and what he claimed
to be forced those who encountered him to question the way
they saw the world. King Arthur was a law-abiding experiment in how to live your life, yet for me the most important
part of his story was the way he has been embraced by English
society over the past twenty years and his understanding of
Englishness.

In the carpark round the back of the pub, before the two of us
set off for Stonehenge, King Arthur had unsheathed Excalibur and

with the flat of his blade made me one of his knights. I arose Sir Henry.

I had one more question.

'Go on.'

I asked him about England. I wanted to know what made his England *English*.

His face registered little as he steadied himself before speaking.

'We', he looked me in the eye, 'are a mongrel race.' He looked away for a moment, before turning back. 'England has always embraced its margins, the weird, the wacky, the ones on the outside of things. So as a geographical place we've always been a nation that accepts, that takes in refugees from around the world, and because our nation is built on that we can't say we're insular. That's a myth. We're an island, yes, but not an island race. And if there's anything that's quintessentially English, throughout history, and hopefully from hereon in, it's simple, it's a belief in fair play, and fair play does not involve marginalising minorities.' His face tightened a little. 'Having a separate judiciary is at the heart of our belief in fair play and you can see it in the way people who go on political marches, the Tolpuddle Martyrs and what have you, are tolerated. That, for me, is Englishness. It's the realisation that there are people in the margins with vision who, if given the chance, are able to change the mainstream for the better.'

It was a drunken masterpiece. I had nothing to add. He loaded his gear into the back of my car and we drove towards Stonehenge.

Before us, with cars from all over the country pouring towards this ring of ancient monoliths, the sun began to set. The longest day was drawing to a close. Midsummer's Day was gathering up its robes and making way for Midsummer's Night where the everyday order of things would be turned on its head, the world made topsy-turvy, 'normal' would become 'weird', eccentric made centric, and in the midst of it all a grizzly ex-biker, ex-squaddie from Winchester, Tintagel, Liverpool, London, depending on which day you ask him, a man who believed himself to be the reincarnation of an ancient English monarch, a campaigner who had battled to make this solstice celebration possible, someone who understood England and Englishness better than anyone else I had met and who never tired of telling me that he was no man's fool, would, for that one night in the eyes of the people he met, become king.

NOTE ON THE ILLUSTRATIONS

The twelve illustrations that appear in the text are etchings I made in response to the work of Sydney Parkinson, or, more specifically, to a series of prints based on drawings he made when he accompanied Captain Cook on his voyage to the South Seas. Parkinson was the expedition's artist. The journey lasted from 1768 to 1771, though Parkinson died of dysentery in 1771 just before the party returned to England.

Although he's generally known for his meticulous botanical paintings of the flora and fauna gathered by Joseph Banks during this journey, Sydney Parkinson's portraits of indigenous people, many of whom were seeing Europeans for the first time, are brilliant. As well as being technically superb – each one a microscopic fingerprint of loops and whorls, contours and gradients arranged in a complex system of interlocking lines – they are expressive. Fantastically so. Somehow he achieves a degree of familiarity and intimacy that belies the nature of the encounter between artist and sitter, brought together from opposite ends of the earth within the parameters of a portrait.

There are several reasons why I wanted to depict the individuals I met using the style of the great Sydney Parkinson. First, he was working around about the same time that the word 'eccentric' came into vogue. In the sense that throughout this book I've been trying to update a late-eighteenth-century term, similarly with these etchings I've portrayed early-twenty-first-century characters using a late-eighteenth-century lens. This is part of the reason why I've numbered the different plates in such a way that they fit into the original sequence of Parkinson prints.

Another reason relates to my fascination with the *way* Parkinson portrays his subjects. It would have been easy for him to depict the people he met as freakish, or excessively exotic. But he didn't. Instead each figure has the blithe familiarity of a favourite uncle or aunt at home in front of the fire. Again there was a parallel: I didn't want to portray the people I met as incomprehensibly alien.

There's one other thing to say about these etchings, or rather, what I've done with them, but it takes some time to explain and besides, I've already over-run the brief paragraph I had in mind when setting out to caption these images. So if you'd like to know more about these etchings and what's happened to them (and see images of the Sydney Parkinson originals), please go to www.henryhemming.com.

SELECT BIBLIOGRAPHY

Charles James Apperley, *The Life of John Mytton*, Routledge, London, 1870

Sabine Baring-Gould, *Yorkshire Oddities*, 1877

Sandra Bilington, *The Social History of the Fool*, Harvester Press, Brighton, 1984

Andrew Birkin, *J. M. Barrie and the Lost Boys*, Yale University Press, London, 2003

Julia Blackburn, *Charles Waterton, 1782–1865*, Century, London, 1989

Harriet Bridgeman and Elizabeth Drury, *The British Eccentric*, Michael Joseph, London, 1975

William Brockie, *Sunderland Notables*, Hills & Co., Sunderland, 1894

Edmund Burke, *Reflections on the Revolution in France*, London, 1790

David Cannadine, *Ornamentalism*, Allen Lane, London, 2001

Catherine Caulfield, *The Man who ate Bluebottles and Other Great British Eccentrics*, illus. Peter Till, Icon Books, Thriplow, 1981

Linda Colley, *Britons: Forging the Nation 1707–1837*, Yale University Press, London, 1996

Charles Darwin, *On the Origin of Species*, John Murray, London, 1859

Rainer Emig, 'Eccentricity Begins at Home: Carlyles's centrality in Victorian Thought', *Textual Practice* 17(2), 2003, pp. 379–90

Waltraud Ernst, ed., *Histories of the Normal and the Abnormal: Social and Cultural Histories of Norms and Normativity*, Routledge, London, 2006 (especially James Gregory's chapter, 'Eccentric Lives: Character, Characters and Curiosities in Britain, c. 1760–1900)

F. W. Fairholt, *Remarkable and Eccentric Characters*, Richard Bentley, London, 1849

Michel Foucault, *The History of Sexuality*, vol. 1, trans. R. Hurley, Allen Lane, London, 1979

Kate Fox, *Watching the English*, Hodder & Stoughton, London, 2004

Vic Gattrell, *City of Laughter*, Atlantic, London, 2006

Judy Giles and Tim Middleton, eds, *Writing Englishness 1900–1950*, Routledge, London, 1995

Erving Goffman, *Stigma*, Penguin, London, 1968

James Gregory, 'Local Characters: Eccentricity and the North-East in the Nineteenth Century', *Northern History*, 42(1), March 2005, pp. 163–86

Joseph Hamburger, *John Stuart Mill on Liberty and Control*, Princeton University Press, Princeton, 1999

Heinrich Heine, *English Fragments from the German of Heinrich Heine*, trans. Sarah Norris, R. Grant & Son, Edinburgh, 1880

Sebastian Horsley, *Dandy in the Underworld*, Sceptre, London, 2007

Tamara Hunt, *Defining John Bull: Political Caricature and National Identity in Late Georgian England*, Ashgate Publishing, Aldershot, 2003

Lewis Hyde, *Trickster Makes This World*, Farrar, Straus & Giroux, New York, 1998

Rob Irving and John Lundberg, *The Field Guide: The Art, History and Philosophy of Crop Circle Making*, Strange Attractor Press, London, 2006

Susanna Johnston and Tim Beddow, *Collecting: The Passionate Pastime*, Viking, Harmondsworth, 1986

N. M. Karamzin, *Nikolai Karamzin, Letters of a Russian Traveller*, Voltaire Foundation, Oxford, 2003

John Keay, *Eccentric Travellers*, John Murray, London, 1982

Ian Kelly, *Beau Brummell*, Hodder & Stoughton, London, 2005

Carol Kennedy, *Eccentric Soldiers*, Mowbrays, London, 1975

Raymond Lamont-Brown, *A Book of English Eccentrics*, David & Charles, Newton Abbot, 1984

Paul Langford, *Englishness Identified: Manners and Character 1650–1850*, Oxford University Press, Oxford, 2000

Brian Levack, *The Witch-Hunt in Early Modern Europe*, Longman, London, 1987

Ben Le Vay, *Eccentric Britain*, Bradt Travel Guides, Chalfont St Peter, 2005

Ben Le Vay, *Eccentric London*, Bradt Travel Guides, Chalfont St Peter, 2007

Ida MacAlpine and Richard Hunter, *George III and the Mad-Business*, Pimlico, London, 1969

Alan MacFarlane, *The Origins of English Individualism*, Basil Blackwell, Oxford, 1978

Christine MacLeod, *Inventing the Industrial Revolution: The English Patent System, 1660–1800*, Cambridge University Press, Cambridge, 1988

John Michell, *Eccentric Lives and Peculiar Notions*, Thames & Hudson, London, 1984

John Stuart Mill, *Autobiography*, Longmans, Green, Reader & Dyer, London, 1873

John Stuart Mill, *On Liberty*, Parker, 1859

John Stuart Mill, *The Subjection of Women*, Longmans, Green, Reader & Dyer, London, 1869

Vladimir Nabokov, *Speak, Memory*, Weidenfeld & Nicolson, London, 1967

K. C. O'Rourke, *John Stuart Mill and Freedom of Expression*, Routledge, London, 2001

George Orwell, *The Lion and the Unicorn*, Secker & Warburg, London, 1941

Sydney Parkinson, *A Journal of a Voyage to the South Seas in His Majesty's ship The Endeavour*, London, 1773

Jeremy Paxman, *The English*, Penguin, London, 1998

Arthur Pendragon and Christopher James Stone, *The Trials of Arthur: The Life and Times of a Modern-day King*, Element, London, 2003

Clifford A. Pickover, *Strange Brains and Genius*, Quill, William Morrow, New York, 1998

John R. and Hunter H. Robinson, *The Life of Robert Coates*, Sampson Low & Co., London, 1891

Ken Robinson, *Out of Our Minds*, Capstone Publishing, Oxford, 2001

Julia F. Saville, 'Eccentricity as Englishness in David Copperfield', *Studies in English Literature, 1500–1900*, 42, 2002

Edith Sitwell, *The English Eccentrics*, Faber & Faber, London, 1933

Herbert Spencer, *Essays: Scientific, Political, and Speculative. Library Edition, containing Seven Essays not before republished, and various other Additions*, vol. 3, Williams & Norgate, London, 1891

Andy Thomas, *Vital Signs: A Complete Guide to the CROP CIRCLE Mystery and Why it is NOT a Hoax*, Frog Books, Mumbai, 2002

John Timbs, *English Eccentrics and Eccentricities*, Richard Bentley, London, 1866

John Timpson, *Timpson's English Eccentrics*, Jarrold, Norwich, 1991

Nathaniel Wanley, *Wonders of the Little World*, London, 1678

David J. Weeks and Jamie James, *Eccentrics: A Study of Sanity and Strangeness*, Weidenfeld & Nicolson, London, 1995

David J. Weeks with Kate Ward, *Eccentrics: The Scientific Investigation*, Stirling University Press, London, 1988

Robert W. Weisberg, *Creativity*, John Wiley & Sons, 2006

Gebhardt Friedrich August Wendeborn, *A View of England Towards the Close of the Eighteenth Century*, for P. Wogan and others, Dublin, 1791

Henry Wilson and James Caulfield, *The Book of Wonderful Characters*, London, 1869

X.Y.Z., *The Eccentric Club: being a Short Outline of its Past, Prior to the intended removal of the society to new premises*, Simpkin, Marshall & Co., London, 1880